THIS IS CALLED MOVING

MODERN AND CONTEMPORARY POETICS

THIS IS CALLED MOVING

A Critical Poetics of Film

ABIGAIL CHILD

The University of Alabama Press
Tuscaloosa

Library of Congress Cataloging-in-Publication Data

Child, Abigail.
    This is called moving : a critical poetics of film / Abigail Child.
        p. cm. — (Modern and contemporary poetics)
    Includes bibliographical references and index.
    ISBN 0-8173-1444-X (cloth : alk. paper) — ISBN 0-8173-5160-4 (pbk. : alk. paper)
    1. Experimental films—History and criticism. 2. Motion pictures—Aesthetics.
3. Motion pictures—Philosophy. 4. Child, Abigail. I. Title. II. Series.
    PN1995.9.E96C42 2005
    791.43′611—dc22

                                                           2004015748

for Hannah Weiner
"don't quote"
1928–1997

A composite of frame enlargements from Abigail Child's *Covert Action* (16 mm, b/w, sound, 10 min., 1984).

Contents

Illustrations

Poetry in Motion

TOM GUNNING

Abigail Child's *This Is Called Moving: A Critical Poetics of Film* opens a space of intersection between film and poetry. Words play a strong role in the sound tracks of Child's films (many of which are transcribed in this book). But a quick glance at these transcriptions reveals that Child treats words as raw material, containing meanings, yes, but fragmented in a radical manner, often broken into phonemes. The poetry of Child's films does not come simply from her use of language. Rather, in her films images, sound, and words are all treated as plastic matter, open to rearrangement, liberated from predetermined meanings, and embarked on adventures in ambiguity and discovery.

Child imagines a language that goes beyond the purely verbal, a new language using several sensual registers (visual and aural, as well as a rhythmic sense that centers itself throughout the body), a language in which meaning is played with but never denied. A moving language. A language called into being through movement, and a movement that finds its calling in the hands of the filmmaker. And this book—an essential part of Child's work, not simply its record—calls out in words to this new language, treating words as material as much as meaning. *This Is Called Moving* contains transcriptions from Child's films, notes on their making, interviews, letters, manifestos, and responses to films by other filmmakers, as well as memories and a bit of autobiography. But all this disparate material remains aimed at the process of discovery and making: *poesis*.

A Bit of History
More than half a century ago, shortly before Halloween in 1953, Amos Vogel, the mastermind behind the alternative film exhibition

outlet known as Cinema 16, organized a symposium in New York City on the topic "Poetry and Film." Cinema 16 had been founded as an American equivalent to the European cine-clubs, showing films outside of commercial distribution, but whereas many European film clubs in the 1950s were rediscovering and falling in love again with the Hollywood cinema (withheld for many during the war years), Cinema 16 more closely resembled the cine-clubs founded in Europe in the 1920s, focused on alternatives to Hollywood and the commercial cinema.

In the 1920s European film clubs embraced the possibilities of an avant-garde film practice, innovative in style and usually politically radical, often featuring the new filmmakers of the Soviet Union (Eisenstein, Pudovkin, Vertov), as well as political filmmaking by such figures as Jean Vigo, Joris Ivens, or Charles Dekeukeleire (who were all members and organizers of these clubs). In New York in the midst of the conformist 1950s (when Hollywood itself was being "cleansed" of radical elements by its anticommunist blacklist), Cinema 16 took up this radical aspiration and viewed cinema again as a subversive act, innovative in form and often dealing with taboo topics (race, homosexuality—or any sort of direct sexuality) as well as political films.

Cinema 16 and the American avant-garde cinema generally—and most certainly the tradition that the films of Abigail Child exemplify and renew—affirmed a relation between radical form and radical content, even as the relation might be complex and subject to transformation. Cinema 16 was founded on the belief that film art (at that time still a hotly debated and polemical term) might not be best served by the standards of mass production, distribution, and exhibition controlled by Hollywood studios (a system then being broken up by the U.S. government, allowing the rather brief emergence of the art film theater, fostering a growing interest in foreign films). Curiosity drove Cinema 16, as a thirst for something different on the screen emerged from the depth of the 1950s, attracting large audiences for films that even went beyond the fare offered by the art house circuit.

On the formal level no issue could better express the difference between the sort of countercinema then being gestated in the United States and the Hollywood product (or even most art house films) than the idea of a poetic, rather than a narrative, cinema. And no one could represent this tendency, or argue more articulately for it, than the champion of the poetic film and the American avant-garde cinema, Maya Deren. Beginning in the early 1940s (although drawing on a rich heritage of modernist filmmaking from the 1920s in Europe and America) Deren's films—*Meshes of the Afternoon* (1943), *At Land* (1944), *Ritual in Transfigured Time* (1945), *Choreography for the Camera* (1946), *Meditation on Violence* (1948)—had drawn on the imagery of surrealist painting and photography, the rhythms of both modern and ethnographic dance, the aleatory logic of modern music and the scenography of experimental theater to create a truly unique demonstration of the power of cinema to create its own logic of space and time, fantasy and desire, repetition and ritual. But to describe the form of her films, and of the new films being featured at Cinema 16—the early films of Anger, Broughton, Harrington, Markopoulos (and, soon, Stan Brakhage)—Deren chose the profound analogy with poetry.

Deren defines poetic form as deriving from a work's total structure, so poetry is a possibility not only in literature but also in film. To describe this cinematic form, Deren contrasts what she describes as the "horizontal" approach of narrative and the "vertical" approach of poetry:

> The distinction of poetry is its construction (what I mean by "a poetic structure"), and the poetic construct arises from the fact, if you will, that it is a "vertical" investigation of a situation, in that it probes the ramifications of the moment, and is concerned with its qualities and its depth, so that you have poetry concerned, in a sense, not with what is occurring but with what it feels like or what it means. . . . Now it may also include action, but its attack is what I would call the "vertical" attack and this may be a little clearer if you will contrast it to what I would call the "horizontal" attack of drama.[1]

Immediately censured for her abstract terminology by the other participants in the symposium, Deren does not get much of a chance to expand her theory. But I think it is clear that Deren is exploring an opposition between two forms of temporal developments found in film history. The narrative attack, carefully developed over the first decades of silent commercial cinema, honed the devices of film editing in order to create an ongoing, dramatically elliptical, and suspenseful rush of continuous time (with carefully marked out flashbacks when needed) dedicated to dramatic storytelling. The other, poetic, approach, often drawing on the techniques of editing introduced in dramatic storytelling, liberated images from this linear, forward thrust and fashioned devices (repetition, interruption, circularity) to circumvent narrative form. Filmmakers like Jean Epstein, Sergei Eisenstein, Germaine Dulac, and Dziga Vertov used cinematic devices (for example, elliptical or repetitive editing, freeze frames, slow motion, superimposition) to interrupt action, allowing a spectator to watch film images and their juxtaposition in a manner that does not simply use them as a vehicle for an ongoing story or drama.

Returning in some ways to the energy of the poetic films from the 1920s (Cocteau, Buñuel, Dulac, Man Ray), in the midst of the 1950s, Deren sketched out one program for an alternative cinema, creating an opposition between it and the commercial cinema based less on a historical imperative (implied always in the term *avant-garde*) than on a difference in genre. Film poetry could demand a rigorous formal approach, bringing to film some of the varieties of viewing (or reading) practices we find in the other modern arts. Deren's influence, the still fresh energy of surrealism, the memories of expressionism, and the blending of the two in a uniquely American fashion in the contemporaneous movement of abstract expressionism opened the door to a new tradition of American filmmaking. This vision was carried into the 1960s by Kenneth Anger, Stan Brakhage, Gregory Markopoulos, Harry Smith, Ken Jacobs, and scores of others, as a burgeoning counterculture supplied alternative spaces for screening and production, while guerilla filmmakers swarmed urban landscapes creating not only oppositional political newsreel and new expressions of sexuality but also new possibilities of form in cinema within the poetic context Deren had defined.

A Neoconstructivist Poetics

I have rehearsed this history partly in order to restore primacy to the relation between poetry and film. The publication of this wonderful collection of the writings of Abigail Child within a series of publications dedicated primarily to poetry places this often-neglected relation front and center.

For Child a poetics is not a guide to the evolution of film style and its narrative grammar but an exploration of both its materials and forms by a practicing filmmaker. It takes seriously Deren's claim that a poetic cinema exists and that it is as different from the standard commercial feature film as poetry is from standard fiction. Although it is not a term Child herself privileges, her practice and thinking exemplify an experimental attitude. She outlines in her preface the questions she poses in her work (which includes the writing collected here, as well as the films she has produced, equal partners in a project carried out in words as well as images and sounds): "How meaning is made, how elements join together, how far elements can stand apart and still 'connect,' how resonance and meaning are created, how putting together fragments of the world can create new forms, new ways of thinking, the utopian aspect, and problematics of that desire."

Child does not approach these issues primarily as a theorist (although theory is one component of her work) nor as a historian (although history remains important to her) but as a *maker,* and in that sense an experimenter as well as a poet. These works (both films and writings) are not products but processes.

Child's work originated during the 1970s, and if it took its initial energy from the utopian and liberatory rush of the 1960s counterculture, it was tempered and formed in the consequent critical reassessment of that period that came in the 1970s, performed especially by both feminism and structuralism, in different ways. The result is what I would describe as a neoconstructivism.

The crashing of the romantic and idealist aspiration of the 1960s counterculture led many American avant-garde artists to look for a rigor of analysis to replace the highly individualistic and "personalized" aspects of the Beats and the youth culture the Beats in part inspired. Painting, as it moved into minimalism, provided one alternative model. Just as important was a rediscovery of the art and theory of the Soviet literary avant-garde of the 1920s, the constructivist ethos that proclaimed the importance of the revolutionary political context of artistic practice and proposed a scientific analysis of the laws of art inherent in its materials and their assembly. The Russian constructivists offered a tradition that was strongly modernist (as opposed to representational and traditional) but also avant-garde and political (as opposed to the corralling of high modernist art as the stock in trade of an elite consumer market created by individualistic artists).

Within this neoconstructivist context cinema reasserted an interrogative function, questioning the limits not only of the forms of film but also of the conditions of spectatorship. Film theory in the 1970s launched an interrogation of the conditions of spectatorship, perhaps best exemplified by Laura Mulvey's frequently quoted (but rarely thoroughly read) essay "Visual Pleasure and Narrative Cinema." While the essay launched a thousand analyses of the role of the gaze in Hollywood cinema, how many readers, then or now, notice that the essay ends with a call for a new cinema, an avant-garde and oppositional practice? In a demonstration of Sartrean *mauvais foi* the critique of Hollywood cinema became a means of maintaining one's fascination with commercial cinema rather than seeking alternatives.

Child's writings and films not only seek alternatives but in their very form and address proclaim questions to viewers. "Is this what you were born for?" asks her powerful series of films from the 1980s in which Child shoulders the questions of the fascinations of narrative film and its genres of melodrama, mystery, and romance without either simply denouncing or reproducing them. Using the push/pull dialectic so crucial to modernism, Child intervenes in the attractions and sensations of a commercial cinema, quoting passages directly, restaging others with a twist, and creating a seesaw between engagement and detachment. The seduction of gender images and their perversion interacts with the detachment of the experimenter, pulling apart elements rather than simply letting them pull us in.

Reading Child's notes and transcriptions for these films provides both a complex gloss on the images and a spin into another space. They can rub against the images on the screen or fly off and do their own dance of verbal interplay, exploring how words evoke images (and vice versa) and the ways they also repel each other into their own space. The thoughts, hesitations, and inspirations recorded here read like the laboratory notes of a sensual and existential scientist. In both the writing and the films one feels Child cooking the material, exposing them to pressures that break up the genre associations we have with them but in no way simply abstracting them. A film like *Mayhem* seems amazingly *dirty* to me—in the best sense. It leaves stains on my consciousness, the bits of excess that a tidy plot might clean up with a final resolution. The excess energies given off by Hollywood (and other international cinemas) in genres of gender conflict (the melodrama, the thriller, the film noir), seem distilled here, yielding a final grimy residue, rather than being wiped away by a narrative resolution.

Thus one aspect that Child's work shares with postmodernism, in contrast to the high modernism of the minimalist filmmakers of the 1970s, lies in taking popular culture seriously through a process of taking it apart. Child's method of finding inspiration in the material of film extends to this idea of testing, distilling, probing film images that the culture has given her and us. What secret seductions, what deadly delusions do they contain? What energies and desire might be liberated from them? For what purposes were these images born, constructed, and can that destiny be arranged by deconstructing them?

Language/Body: Language of the Body?
Child's strong inheritance from constructivism includes her astonishing grasp of montage. While much of the 1970s avant-garde work seemed to be fascinated by duration and continuity (although this can be a deceptive impression—think of the breaks in continuity in Ernie Gehr's *Serene Velocity* or even Snow's *Wavelength*), Child and a few other key filmmakers remained very much devoted to the aesthetic of fragmentation and juxtaposition that the Soviet masters introduced. Child understands vividly that montage is not only the art of juxtaposition, as Eisenstein defined it, creating new meanings

through the meeting of images and sounds, but also a method of interruption. Montage means breaking down, giving words and sound in bursts that transform meaning and association, braking the velocity of a gesture or action to allow a contemplation of its force and contradictions, before it has become sealed in a finalized intention.

This interest in isolating and juxtaposing images and sounds, decomposing them into smaller elements, reveals the strong influence structuralist linguistics exerted on avant-garde film of the 1980s, a drive toward analysis as a creative process, rather different from the more meditative experiences of what became known as "structural" film. This is best exemplified by Child's interest in "difference," that basic concept of structural linguistics in which elements signify by the dissimilarities among them. But for Child the interest lies not only in the way these differences make up a system but in the ways they can be maximized to create new systems, counterlogics and antilanguages. The twist Child's works give to the basic utopian aspiration of avant-garde practice comes from recognizing the dependence on language and systems of meaning that such play involves. But this is not capitulation on Child's part. She sees this dependence as a critical opportunity, a zone in which the system can be not abolished but reimagined, rearranged.

All serious considerations of the relation between film and languages must first of all recognize the differences between them, the lack, in short, of a double articulation in cinema, that essential aspect of language whereby words can be broken into letters or phonemes—elements whose significance does not carry meaning but simply indicates difference. Images, too, can be broken down, even reduced to unrecognizable patterns, but they never form a system of defined elements like letters. Nonetheless, the method of language inspires filmmakers to attack the recognizable image and transform it into fragments, uncovering aspects that allow it to be reconfigured. But the resistance the image (and especially the *moving* image, the film image) offers to fragmentation relates, I believe, to another essential aspect of Child's work—its connection to the body.

The film image captures many things, but central to its whole conception of space is its portrayal of the body. Film was invented (deriving from the work of scientific photographers such as Muybridge, Marey, Demenÿ, and Londe) in order to provide a scientific tool for the investigation of the body in motion. If a fascination with language and its possibilities of articulation occupies one aspect of Child's cinema, an investigation of film's relation to the body balances and interacts with this linguistic drive.

The body itself dwells within the grid of difference, and Child's exploration of gender through film explores this intersection. The investigation of body language offered by the systematic reworking of found footage in *Covert Action* explores the way gendered bodies interact with each other and with the camera. Child becomes, in effect, a feminist Muybridge, breaking down gestures and actions to reveal unconscious and otherwise invisible patterns and determinates. But while always suspicious of a romanticization that can conceal hierarchies of power, or an essentialization that mythifies gender difference, Child also captures the rhythms and confidences of the body in movement, with dance offering an intertext as important to this aspect of her work as poetry is to her engagement with language. As a viewer as well as a maker (and much of Child's work in this book consists of engaging with the work of others, thinking through her issues with their imagery), Child seeks out the excessive gesture, such as the way a little girl's shrug of her shoulders seems to puncture the flow of Vertov's *Man with a Movie Camera,* making room for the body within a system of ideological montage.

This, of course, brings us face-to-face with the central paradoxes that produce the energy behind all of Child's work, a system founded not on coherence but on breakdown, not on continuity but on interruption. Cinema and poetry share for Child the possibility of manipulating a language (or imagery and sound) generally taken for granted and subjecting it to shocks, interruption, gaps, and space. This nearly physical pummeling of the material shakes the viewer/reader out of the complacency of the "horizontal" attack, of knowing how to go on, how to follow the action, and forces her or him to sink beneath the surface, to plumb the text vertically. For Child, as for both the Russian formalists and constructivists, such interruptions and defamiliarizations do not simply play a game with art (or play a game called art) but rather place a stake in the go-for-broke game of history and politics. These interruptions that experimental art employs make us reaccess the world we live in, test and question it against the edge of an unfamiliar artistic experience. We are, in fact, changed by this encounter. This is called moving. The moving picture cannot simply be grasped in stillness, contemplated, but instead demands we run our minds alongside its mobile imagery, learning new patterns of thoughts, new gestures for our bodies, new ways to live, reconceiving what we were born for.

Preface

This Is Called Moving: A Critical Poetics of Film approaches film and writing with a concern for their materiality, meaning, syntax, and form. Questions such as how meaning is made, how elements join together, how far elements can stand apart and still "connect," how resonance and meaning are created, how putting together fragments of the world can create new forms, new ways of thinking, the utopian aspect, and problematics of that desire are some of my concerns. As well, when do elements fall apart? How does that look and act and mean? How might these questions reflect on social process and social community, on social identity, on the public space and collective imagination we mutually inhabit? These kinds of questions motivate this collection and, indeed, my thinking when watching film and reading writing.

My practice as a poet has been important to my development as a filmmaker. The two arts circulate and alternate, cross-fertilizing each other. Poetry provides me with ways of thinking about representation, about a politics of poetic practice, and about how words—and images—interact, grow, oppose, indicate, and construct the social. Writing has also offered me praxis: since writing is inexpensive, it is easily available. Ideas can be swiftly jotted down, leafed through, tried out, discarded . . . salvaged. Translating some of these ideas to film was inevitable: the elements—words and frames, words and shots, paragraphs and scenes—how they can be reconfigured to challenge expectation, re-represent the social, reconceptualize our ideas of the world. The very act of translating these "language systems," these two unparalleled signaling systems, is by definition approximate. The slippage creates its own exhilaration. The effort structures new potentials.

As a post–World War II baby boomer and member of the first TV generation, I am framed in the consciousness of 1960s radicalism and 1970s feminism, alert to the power and kitsch of popular culture and consumerism. My early documentary explorations led me to realize concretely that form had politics, a social component. Poetry strengthened these observations through readings, writings, and discussions among the loosely defined poetry community of the late 1970s in San Francisco.[1] In my years as a documentarian and producer for NBC-TV in New York City I had experienced firsthand alienation of the workplace and media distortion. In San Francisco, under auspices of a poet's study group, I read the work of Benjamin and others, discovering critiques of modernity and mass culture that theorized much of what I had experienced in relation to the mechanics, economics, and sociopolitics of broadcast news.[2]

My concerns here are with signification, with physical (auditory/ visual) qualities of the material—whether letters, celluloid, or digital pixels—and with rhythm, order, disorder, and structure—how parts work. My questions cross the visual with the textual: What is lost in abstraction? In non-sense? What is its power? What is signified by a long work? By a serial work? What are its limitations? How might multiple voices reflect reality? Infect reality? And how sustain such a work? How does the world enter the work? How is the inside destroyed or transformed into "another" space? How end a work? How reshape parts of the world, and is that what we aspire to anyway? Are we breathing easier, feeling better, glutted with our "contemporary practice" digested? Or fiercely unsatisfied, curious, anxious, asking, "What are tomorrow's questions?"

If the practice of writing has affected my film, the reverse is also true. Film feeds the writing, whether writing "off" images, movies, still photos, including film language in the vocabulary of the poem, or exploring structural properties of machines and technology: the ability to reverse, loop, return, and (re)start. Film is the mechanical beast from the nineteenth century that in the twentieth reshaped memory and imagination in ways that accelerate and deepen in the twenty-first. Film invades, or, one wants to say, *is,* our cultural set. Like photography, film imprints the culture from which it is created and recreates, recasts, the world, reflecting an artificial world that takes on a life of its own.

In the present, film occurs in the public mind largely in the context of its nineteenth-century roots, in the tradition of theater and plot, as an appendage to the novel. To view film in the context of contemporary discoveries in visual art and music—abstract, rhythmic, formal, conceptual, textual, subversive, and deconstitutive—has been the aim of avant-garde movements and artists across the last century. In a time of increasing worldwide Hollywood domination this ambition appears (perhaps) foolhardy. Yet if it is obvious that such an argument has become more important as a *register* of opposition and as an alternative to major-media modeling syntax, I would add that as celluloid itself disappears against the contingencies and competition of video, becomes *dysfunctional* one might say, the need to recombine "parts," the concept of number and assemblage, the idea of linkage and meaning, of multiplication and chance, only increases in interest, reaching more thoroughly into our digital future.[3] Film becomes archaeology and substrate, laboratory and means to recuperate and recontextualize the present, exploding received and laundered notions, analyzing and expanding ideas of the avant-garde or "outside."

In the new century, work that has largely remained on the fringe of distribution is available to the general public through home video distribution, major museum shows, and ultimately the World Wide Web. Independent and international features increasingly explore aesthetic discoveries of modernism and narrative experiment, recuperating issues of materiality, memory, and witness explored in twentieth-century experimental writing. More and more citizens have a chance to see the "classics" of cinema art (albeit on video); and the increasing miniaturizing of the technologies means more students and consumers can play with tools of production. Will this technology in the hands of citizens generate a truly oppositional style and new content, a new materiality? The extent and amplitude, the *innovativeness,* of their response remains to be seen. If we find that audiences remain uncomfortable with abstraction, uncertainty, multiple positionality, and lack of closure—one hundred years after the discoveries of the theory of relativity and Heisenberg's uncertainty principle—clearly the artist's job at the beginning of a new century remains unfinished.[4]

This Is Called Moving: A Critical Poetics of Film hopes to forward these discussions. This is a book of writings largely about film, investigating concerns that impinge on the literary community and writing from the view of a practicing filmmaker and writer. As Roland Barthes describes in *The Return of the Poetician:* "When [s]he sits down in front of the literary work, the poetician does not ask [her]-self: What does this mean? Where does this come from? What does it connect to? But more simply and more arduously: *How is this made?*"[5] I write from that place of making, concerned at each point with context, material, motive, and the practice of this making. The essays take several forms, among them interview, manifesto, close reading, dialogue, letters, critique, and collaboration. As I note in "Active Theory," one of the essays in this book, I have been looking for a new way to write critical prose. Though many of these essays were published in film magazines, many were requested by or printed in poetry journals. It is indeed the tradition of poets writing critical prose—Charles Olson, Susan Howe, Ron Silliman, for example—that has inspired me. Equally influential are the filmmakers who write—including Pier Pasolini, Robert Bresson, Stan Brakhage, Carolee Schneemann, and Trinh T. Minh-ha—those who are sometimes called the "poets" of cinema.

I offer a historical context in introductory paragraphs that head each essay, locating ideas within a dialogue of writers and filmmakers on both coasts (New York and San Francisco, with excursions to Boston and Berlin) to give a sense of the excitement and development of ideas within these communities. But if you wish, please ignore the headings and read right on. I have ordered the essays in three sections: "Sex Talk," on the body, gender, feminism, and sexuality; "Matrix," including broader theoretical explorations on filmic materiality, sound, topologies of memory and witness, along with shorter pieces on colleagues; and "Interrogations," focused more specifically on my work, including interviews, an introduction for my *Is This What You Were Born For?* (1981–89) series of films, and a pair of discussions on New York City and urban geographies. Transcripts from the films appear in "Interrogations" to create a dialogue and counterpoint with the critical prose. The relation between practice and theory is interactive. Ideas get tried out in a work of art, and at the same time art provokes—leads us into new intentions, new revelations of form and matter. It is these moments that are perhaps the most exciting, that is, when the work explodes out of its limitations and shockingly, happily, registers as *something else*. Not *outside* the world we are in but rather quivering, nose-to-the-air.

Notes at the end of each essay provide further information as to sources, collaborators, and publication histories. In addition, I want to thank my colleagues who have supported this project, including Tom Gunning, Douglas Kahn, Liz Kotz, Scott Macdonald, P. Adams Sitney, and Maureen Turim, who have taken the time to read through the manuscript at its various stages, and especially Bruce Andrews, Charles Bernstein, Laura Marks, Melissa Ragona, and Erika Suderburg for their valuable suggestions as to its particulars and structure. I am grateful to The Ludwig Vogelstein Foundation which encouraged this project at its earliest conception. I thank as well Laura Deutch at Pacific Film Archives, Robert Haller at Anthology Film Archives, and Greg Pierce at the Warhol Museum, for helping me obtain the photos for the "Matrix" section of the book. Russ Kuhner spent many hours scanning in these same photographs, and Adaleta Maslo-Krkovic was unstinting in her talent and patience as she worked on the multiple images from my films. I couldn't have done it without them. Thanks too for the careful copy-editing of Kevin Davies and Joe Abbott, and the initial compilation of the index by Michael Mahoney. I remain responsible for any discrepancies and all subjectivities that remain.

July 2003 ❖ Amherst, Virginia

SEX TALK

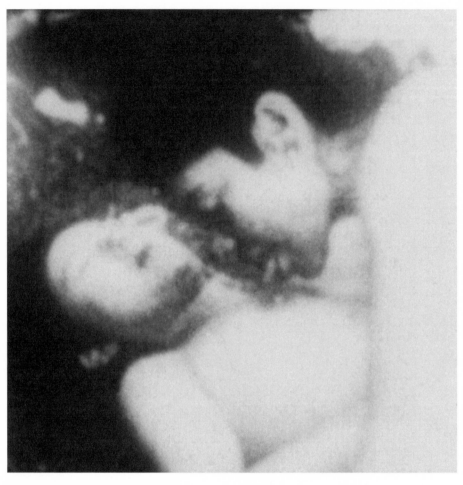

Figure 1. Finale. Frame enlargement from Abigail Child's *Mayhem* (16 mm, b/w, sound, 20 min., 1987).

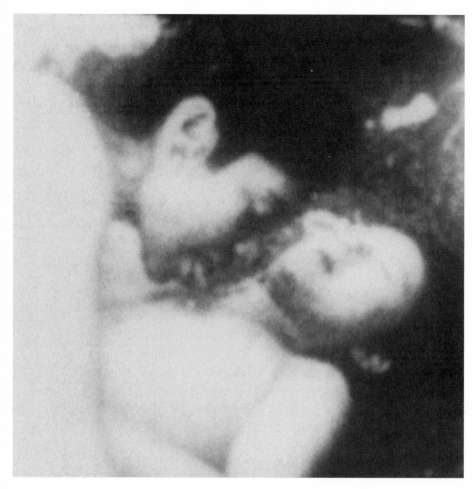

Figure 2. Finale. Frame enlargement from *Mayhem* (reversed).

Invited by MIX Film and Video Festival, 1991, New York, to be on a panel discussing experimental film, I found myself examining the radical nature of "outside" identities and placing this in a context of radical form. The result was a meditation on content and form, on predilections and sympathies of such a relation in the experimental/gay film scene, and on the cross-connections and potential political implications of such a conjunction. Coming from San Francisco, I had experienced a fluid exchange in both writing and film communities. The scene glittered with local gay "stars" of the avant-garde film world, among them George Kuchar, Warren Sonbert, Nathaniel Dorsky, Jerry Hiler, James Broughton, and Michael Wallin. Back in New York the scenes were larger and more divided. The MIX festival didn't really bring gay and straight artists together, but it did bring a wave of populist support to experimental work in the 1980s, counteracting the then-current alignment of white/hetero/male/formalist vs. gay/black/Latin/identity positions. Conceived by experimental filmmaker Jim Hubbard and writer Sarah Schulman, inspired by the death of legendary Pittsburgh filmmaker Roger Jacoby, MIX emphasized from the beginning the connection between experimental and gay "outsider" experience and aesthetics. The result was a rare and intensely popular populist festival that has retained its intentions and connections to the community more than a decade later.

Before Agreement

Radical form equals radical content.
Radical content radicalizes form.
Form and content shape each other.
Content just "seems" to represent us better.
We look *for* content. We look *at* form.

I want to say: only in North America and Western Europe do we have the possibility to discuss this issue. I want to say: the division is not a "given." I want to say: that this distancing of context from content is achieved with loss.

There is only one moment in history that I know when form is the accepted stage of invention. This is Russia in the 1920s, where, significantly, the contemporaneous social order was undergoing sweeping (revolutionary) change.

An interest in form is often taken as elitist or decadent (I take that position myself in the second paragraph above). Why is this so? Because we cannot back away from ourselves far enough to see the form of our lives? Because we are not allowed to see our lives in the form of the world? Then, I want to ask: how does marginalizing an interest in basic structures abet the status quo?

There is no guarantee of a radical order—there have been radically fascist films and gay fascists—yet the challenge of difference and experience of difference, of living as a devalued person in a defended culture, creates/demands expressive freedoms. What we might call the visionary element is present in both.

Radical comes from *root,* forming a radius, also a ray, a branch. It relates to *root* as in origin, an original reading or a fundamental principle. It is inherent or implanted by nature; innate, native.[1]

With that definition in mind, the next question is: when does *radical* come to mean extreme? I theorize that moment: when the branch or root is considered far from the center, far from the norm or average. The *Oxford Dictionary* lists 1802: with "an advocate of 'radical reform'" belonging to the extreme section of the Liberal Party."[2] The 1800s mark increased centralization in government and normalization in society, a time in which profit is served by erasing difference. The period marks developing machine production, sophisticated printing and distribution, the growth of media (the newspaper and, soon, the photograph) to influence and invade the popular mind.

I like to think of the continuing radical tradition as a root. However partial and invisible, it continues to surface. But if I think of the radical tradition in life and art as the "return of the repressed," I need to recognize as well that it is the existence of the repressed that demands our radicalism. It is not that we are "underneath" and surfacing but that we are part of the surface being denied substance. That we are an authentic voice and our invisibility a reflection of the entrenched powers that be. Or, at worse, a reflection of what we ourselves deny. For as part of the socialization process fear is conditioned, and the field of options is narrowed. We are taught to think alike, look alike, and love alike. But it is a lie.

Where homosexuality is visible in films, it is too often stereotypical, antisocial, or token. The character is a butt of jokes or dysfunctional or dies, or her action and being is "laundered." Similarly, the experimental vision is called "a special effect" or, more stringently, performs as dream, hallucination, or drugged state. NEVER are the alternative ways of perception placed inside the perimeter of the real.

I ask: how does marginalizing an interest in form and structure abet the status quo?

The big lie is that the dominant forces want us to believe and believe themselves that their view is the objective truth and everything else a special interest. "A special effect." Anything that is outside this view needs to be squashed or else people might define their lives by and for themselves.

The issue is always between a false and uniform objectivity and an expansive field.

Movies play a special role in this galaxy of oppression and freedom. As technological events movies and the media allow the audience to be mechanically absent. They teach us distance and passivity. They teach us to be invisible. Films "screen the world, make me invisible; and they screen the world from me, that is screen its existence."[3] It has long been the operative strategy of experimental film to expose that distance. To challenge and shatter with obstreperous sense of new definition, to raise possibilities, to admit variance beyond your own or anyone's imaginings.

You want to smash the stereotype of gender.
You want to smash the machinery of mechanized and victimized vision.
You want to push the ghetto out in the world.

Always we come back to permission, to difference, and the need to unloosen polarization, be it of sex *or* rhetoric.

In the early 1980s I am back in NYC living in a downtown Eastside apartment within a community of avant-garde musicians and dancers, as well as poets and filmmakers. It is the period of punk, art bands, multiple reading series, little magazines, fervent dialogue, and intense collegiality. I perform in a piece by downtown New York choreographer Sally Silvers at St. Mark's Poetry Project, and soon after we begin a correspondence on "Women and Modernism," for publication in a special issue of *Poetics Journal* (volume 4, 1984) edited by West Coast poets Lyn Hejinian and Barrett Watten. This is my first literary collaboration, and we begin with a no-holds-barred letter exchange over six months, which we then edit together, coming up with topic divisions and titles in the process. I remember stretching out on the floor with Sally in my tiny Ludlow Street apartment over cut-and-pasted papers as we moved sections around throughout the afternoon. Indented text is Silvers's; flush-left text is mine.

Rewire/Speak in Disagreement

(With Sally Silvers)

1. Almost Necessary but Not Sufficient Criteria Particular to Women for Production of Modern Art

We defeated the lack of expectation.

Enter the social, conditioning, context . . . OK, OK.

Perhaps we should use the word *girl* in every sense of "woman" in this essay—would that drive the point in a way similar to your suggesting a *she* when the *he* was always written? When writing about girls and modernism we have to talk about oppression . . . and find the ram-battering tiresome. Women have been traditionally involved in issues of the body in art—arts of presence—theater, dance, voice. This is partly economics (body is cheaper than paper and pen even), but also women's bodies seem definitional—as presence, as objects. Our bodies are expected information. Women tend to see themselves relating to and as bodies instead of to and as history. Men, with their tangible symbol/organ/ phallus, are challenged to compete, to locate their desire in the (unattainable) power of the world. Women are more ambiguous in locating an identity, a location in relation to the world (in addition to being appropriated in men's sense of the territory available for them).

I disagree here with your analysis, where you talk about "women lacking a lack symbol." Perhaps we lack a "plus" symbol? Although I always thought we had two in the sense of breasts. I think it more fruitful (a "feminine" adjective perhaps?) to think of phallus as metonymic power, and, however reflective of Patriarchy and Society, not encompassing the totality of Women, neither women's desire nor women's potential. *Power* again. How we live in a world of male language and the need to redefine this: their terms.

But what I mean is that women, not being trained in the unattainable desire for power/authority, have a chance at a clearly distinct kind of maneuverability—which to me is one of the essences of modernism—maneuvering, recreating the subject using the materials of our mediums. Modernism as getting legs instead of power.

To put down their reigns (reins): defeat prior constitutionality.

To give our readers an idea of what P. Charles gazes at in the royal bedroom every night, the Examiner *placed Di's face over the body of a fashion model exhibiting the lines of sexy lingerie.*[1]

Genital identification. *Even the maids aren't black.* Historically women have been bound to bonds of relation. Conditioned to Condition. Women are like nature, which is what modernism bases its conquest on. *Women were domestic goods so didn't sell or were sold and had earlier obsolescence.* They enter the economics but not the politics. Survival based not on knowledge, information, self-sufficiency but on finding a mediator and not going public. *Reflex survivors.*

Demonstration photos inevitably show a young Japanese woman, a tentative smile on her face, with the robot's 7' 5" arm coiled around her.
Possession of the token of power = has a man.
Domestic speech—what is used in the home in the nuclear family—is irrelevant in the American version where father/husband supports wife/mother, kitchen, kids—the division then of experience is so separate—the wife/mother home front limited to children's speech, consumer advertisement, pubescent addictions, and advocacy of prevailing (and duplicating) role models from a limited closed spectrum —how is an exchange of experience to be realized?
Women's lack exists—is this endless elaboration of perverted social realities, social psychologies, social behavior dysfunction. *Feminine,* the adjective, and equally *masculine,* the adjective, partake of the restricting cultural values, define your restraints, *shape the lacks.*
The gender argument is fucked—making dogma out of social conditioning.

It's just a speech defect because women are forced to accommodate men.

Dichotomous thought is antagonistic to the future, locked into the past.
It's *not* this equation:

nurturer = earth
mechanic = destroyer

No female essence—intuition the small change of the patriarchy. We have to guard against feminizing the irrational, women's prelinguistic association with nature. No primal liberty between the meshes of the social body. As you say, destroy the dichotomies, which structure and wash the patriarchy and insure our position in relation to and formed by power. At the same time defeat coherent subjectivity on which capitalism, idealism is based—point up multiple contradictions, which are clearly delineated and not unspoken, silent, taped shut. Constant strategies.
Which means there is something to do, rather than apologize and explain endlessly the state of things—both male and female have the political/aesthetic job to fracture the social conditions we in this

Figure 3. "NO." Frame enlargement from *Covert Action.*

present exist in, show up their absurdities—for life as well as gender reasons.

> *Articulate the differences with a fig.* New realities into new speech.

Speak in disagreement, enter the discourse.

Unless women see their role as humanizing—emotionalizing the forces, personalizing—and then we're cooked and women leave modernism altogether.

> Perhaps they have to become more improperly bred in the fear of desire.

> Obviously women know too much to try to join the club.

> *Oh dear little brushes. You can buy a kit and decorate your loved ones. You can buy a kit and go into business. Tattoo—the contact sport of the eighties. Darwin Was Wrong—across their young men's chests.*

Obsolete mothers play a role in our lives.

The logo for his museum the design of a heart beating the single word *mother* (= the most popular tattoo ever created). Defensive signaling of a dying ethos, as well as a fashion statement.

Went up there to prove *their* manhood, saying: Be an essayist. Be identified. Be focused. Exclude digression, trivia, hilarity. [But . . . but . . .]

Bull on the above rationalized clarity of expression.

A good thought is a series of resonances.

The English makes its propositions apparently verifiable.

A road to power in quick thinking is the supposition.

A seduction to think office-ties-master-electronics.

While knowledge is another kind of power and is genderless. This our entry.

> Yet when you say fuck clarity of expression/focus, I disagree. "Oh what a pretty cute thing, so enigmatic, so easy to ignore." It fits too easily into the basis of existing repression. Our entry is knowledge, but if it is to be "genderless," it can't reinforce stereotypes of the dark, mysterious internal = female expression. Our thoughts will contribute through multivalenced force; with a vision, a uniqueness that has clarity as an intention. How else are we to have a dialogue and learn from each other as women? Let's go beyond the role-model method; beyond just another woman on the list.

I'm not talking of hiding behind veils of obfuscation. I'm suggesting rather that the "call to order" is played against us, played against our media. That the traditional limits of the form define in a prohibitive way the boundaries of the possible. And the thrust of extension, of criticism, that I choose to see as part of the work can be blunted by an obeisant clarity. My work is clear to me. Is as complicated as it appears because it wanted more complicated clarities to keep going. I don't want a work I could see in my mind's eye, at the start from the front. I wouldn't make such a work, not need to, no need for. I'm against a solved work. Not a triumph of failure. But a material (unmartial) term of manifold contradictions, construction, stand (fall) (the body metaphor doesn't hold)—complete parts. Nonhierarchical. I'm looking for an unsolved work that satisfies. You want to be as clear as possible. But not some predestined clarity.

What you didn't understand in my text wasn't where I thought you wouldn't. Accepting the authority of their definition is playing their game.

> Can figure out the project of undoing the damage. Not rewarding ourselves for not fucking up the world when we've been fucked instead.

Yet still. The terms of the indictment: who's inventing whom?
The question of power and not the question of "why not enough women?"—whether that be in the dance scene or film or writing. The need for support, for women present.

2. Every Bite Is a Revolution of the Material
We got to it before it had time to finish.

Modernism for me is not minimal. Is rather inclusive, something of the Futurists' action momentum, naturally fractured as movies are (machines are/organic cells are/attention is/"component"), and the unity humans regularly seek (habit) would be by now outside a system—shakes tile habituated, no form/force/system of givens encompassing truth enough.

> Instead a charge, a fracturing on all levels of our consciousness, finally getting legs instead of power. Modernism for me is definitely not orderly (as you say minimal). Even surrealism, cubism present the unconscious as surplus code, as orderly explosion or worshipful progress of the imagination. Expressionism was messy, chaotic, but too attached to the existential self. (Our) modernism is realism in the sense that it recognizes the complexities, the identities of things, of material (the components, the cell), but it doesn't make organic relationships between these things. It also interprets the things themselves as relations.

It makes sense to me that the modern insistence on discourse, the text, emerges now as a substance that doesn't try to remember, doesn't represent, is not dream, is itself and actualizes that: the *materialization* of words, paint, celluloid, noise. Could modernism be a platform for women perhaps, a stance outside the patriarchy? Is there a way to read Gertrude Stein, for instance, as quotidian and daily, as nonhierarchical in her syntax and content?
Claude Lévi-Strauss speaks to this sense of an evolving aesthetic that reflects its contextual worldview when he analyzes art as "a means of instruction, I might almost say a way of acquiring knowledge of reality."[2] He suggests that in the early nineteenth century, as the machine age is about to encroach, the romance of the about-to-be-

threatened (tamed?) waterfalls, vistas, forests is extolled as a suitable subject for the painter. Later, the impressionists create "suburban" painting—the *sublime* applied to parks, bounded fields, and yards. By the beginning of the twentieth century the cubists celebrate the machine, and after World War I introduced bombing and poison gas to shatter European cities and its citizens, the surrealists redefine the sublime in hallucinatory dream. And though Lévi-Strauss does not name it, his thought suggests a future art form or SuperReality to compensate a world grown increasingly immaterial—which I interpret as a point of entry for photography and film. So that the Sublime in our time has become image, defined as illusion. The photo is the modern world.

For the artist living within this paradox the Sublime registers not as representation but as the frame or the medium itself. The natural so banished in vectors of economic pressure that the Beautiful is what is not simply not-natural but what takes its force in being forcefully Unnatural (i.e., reflection/photo-reality). With the added irony that these means seem even more convincing an "illustration" of the real.

> History—a fiction we overthrow.
>
> Modernism not as a cure, but as a finding of the go button. To open out options, as a stance, not just in opposition but to make something new, "To willfully not remember" the way things are; to not have to exist in relationship always to authority, to make a new position. As a building of desire, not limited to symbols of lack; not being stuck with an overdetermined symbol.
>
> *Pop song: "Slave to My Dick."*

I'd maintain that part of our interpretation of modernism, yours and mine, is this unceasing attempt to maintain an opposition to the "setup," to read the liberating aspects of modernism into focus. For example, to glean from Dada and surrealism a pressuring of boundaries and definitions, to expand or explode the *norm,* to oppose the *model,* the totality and totalization of life as lived in the corporate image, corporate entertainment, corporate postures. To revive an interest in the material, not the transparency, and to celebrate vortex and incident as structure.

> No totalities based on the mode of the natural organism. Give
> me fallacies any day. How can you believe in the model or-
> ganism and believe in change? The corporeal surface as the
> location for new organs—Artaud—the organless body.

The body *is* the material and its deformations, errors; fallacies are
what are of interest. And you—we—eat because every bite is a revolution of the material. What's so great about cinema is it takes the
body and alters it, beyond the natural. Vertov's machine eye is relevant here: that we learn to see differently, the tool changing our vision. "How" has altered the landscape, reorganizes the organic, distributes new information (language). Extending the matrix of what
constitutes the image.

> Internal organs create responsibilities and minds of their own
> creation.

Active complexities. Analysis, not synthesis.
The ideas are a struggle of contraries always in movement.

> Whereas modern dance, the organic unity, the "released"
> body, implies a single identity, a paradigm of the body. The
> body is already seen too much as property. To try to make it
> more "gamine" is cowardly, miserly. I'm not writing owners'
> manuals.
>
> Modernism seems an attempt at timelessness or everything at
> the same time, eliminating hierarchies in the form. In your
> films, in my choreography, there is an immediate reading of
> juxtaposed meaning and no need to connect the elements—it
> is intelligible each moment and not through the passage of
> time. Each moment rises done.
>
> Your films strive for that instant in painting when you can
> see the whole divulged in each instant. So as in Shklovsky—
> the process of perception becomes an aesthetic end in itself.
> In Brakhage, for instance, this perception becomes like a fet-
> ish, whereas for you it seems more defamiliarized because of
> the way you cut sound, rhythm, point of view. I could see
> *Ornamentals* as pure fetish, however. Film is always in danger
> of that moment of seduction; *Ornamentals* is a seduction
> through specialization of its elements perhaps. Well, I'm not

a puritan. I can stand seduction even though it's art. *Is This What You Were Born For?* cracks the subject—enter the social albeit in modernist dress—the emperor (empress) is naked and dead. The subject becomes an activating process.

Dripping sweat. Yet, to understand is to be struck.

Modernism—no resolution possible.

Operative: the image of Science. The dream landscape of the century. *Science* a code word for modernism: the arena of an ideology and the arena in which conflicting ideologies are and will be fought. You could define modernism in relation to twentieth-century science and its precepts:

Modernism	*Science*
critical stance	investigative reasoning
reflexivity	relativity
disorder	entropy
boundaries of the field	the new, also ideas of torus,
pushed to their limits	matrix, field, etc.

Knowledge now a sum of uncertainties. Entropy abolishes the monuments.

More chaos—anarchy—means politically more open to discussion.

Acceptance of decay, confusion, unresolved states = events shaped to your singular vision.

One needs a point of view—can that be one of chaos? A kind of system itself, of glittering motion and multiple crossings, a mobile unit.

My vision of modernism is not from the theoretical position of idealism—that the human, the subject, the art maker is the point of origin of meaning or of practice. The coherent subject is a lie. How far outside ourselves can we go before realizing that we don't really manipulate it.

I believe I am a unity but I am a construction.

In my work biology takes care of itself—it is its own structure but not a model for construction or thought. My organism is not action, but it is material. It doesn't hurt to know it, as in

learning the chemistry of paint pigment. (When I was reading *Scientific American*'s brain issue, I could get high.) I don't
like thinking of the body as something that can be finally
"known" with correct and more correct manipulations, releasing of the final tensions. Tensions are interesting as sites
of power formations. That is one reason I'm interested in un-
trained dancers. Technical or released trained movers have
only habituated their bodies to an ideal, be it distorted (ballet) or natural (release and some modern dance). Habituated
means thoughts, tools, no longer can respond in an exploratory, investigative mode. End of interest.

For me the rejected or everyday demagnified gesture is used in your
work to construct a choreography of parts. And what touches the
viewer is where the inarticulate, the error or tension, finds concrete
manifestation and is recognized.

Speak here on the relation between form and content: not that they
are identical. More like content is the air around the structure, what
the structure breathes. Content has a smell that sounds the structure
(the synesthesia essentially a reflection of relations, not dichotomies).
Simple schematics don't work in these definitions. Perhaps typolo-
gies emerge with the division of labor and are false in light of post-
Newtonian physics: that classic modernism is a response to nineteenth-
century mechanization and must change to deal with the development
of the electronic/information era (post-modern).

I'm jealous of your time machine: film. Although I write compositions, they are realized completely in vanishing. This is
my body—doing time. Your machine possesses it.

Whereas for me dance has the advantage of utilizing the material of
the body—the internal structure (in all of us) externalized, plus the
facility/ability to improvise—changing contexts. If film possesses
time, your body processes it (though I would maintain that is what
film does as well—no illusion out-of-hand). In your work you have
access to all (social and historic) movement immediately and are not
dependent on the laborious technical recording procedure of film.

Film sets new standards for time that are hard for movement,
writing, and sound not to lag behind. The speed of visibility.

The seduction of Machine. The nineteenth-century metaphor progresses—travel, battle, triumph, defeat—and as well projects a mechanical analogue of Body: muscle power, gigantic "bones of steel." The age of electronics gets rid of the need for muscle—is subatomic. Electronics are now the model, metaphor, and means. "He's wired" or she's "on." At the least, this rids us of the functionality (rationality) of the muscle analogy and thereby diminishes the relative value of muscle strength and thereby divisive measures of male or female strength. The age of information is potentially genderless.

> The information age gets rid of muscle applied to task but not the training of the body, the desires that are structured through the pores—these applications must not go unchallenged. Training of the senses (film), the body (movement), these are not outmoded unless you think society's meaning is only a translation of the forces of labor as constructed by science. But what about ideology—the source of what gets developed. What meanings get developed in the future—these realms are for politics and art, not just as reactive mechanisms to science. Art and politics are formative, an advancing of thought.

Yes, but there is an interrelation here between art and politics and science and ideology—not cause and effect.

> *We all do social work, all of the time.*

> I believe we (our modernism) are incorporating the context and content of the social in the materialistic integrity of our media.

Shaking up boundaries, be it in dance, film, writing—the creating of interior space, exterior space, pushing the envelope—expanding the field, the membrane that defines. The "membrane" (could anyone write a critical statement now not using scientific terminology?) = a tautology of the reflexive necessity.

Melodrama as idea and vehicle for narrative, as an *antagonistic* narrative, has been a fruitful concept in my film work. Melodrama appears as structural idea and musical choreograph in *Mayhem* (1987) and as visual component in both *Mayhem* and *Perils* (1984). Invited to do a residency at the Kootenay School of Writing in Vancouver in 1991, I selected as topic "Melodrama and Montage," interested in the unlikely conjunction of nineteenth-century romanticism with twentieth-century modernist tactics. The following essay grew out of that residency. I perform a close reading of work by writers Hannah Weiner and Nicole Brossard. This analysis encouraged me to conceive more deeply of a negative melodrama or an inverse melodrama that could use the syntax of melodrama without the content, constructing out of parts of the melodramatic vocabulary. Many of the ideas I develop could be applied to such writers as Bernadette Mayer, Carla Harryman, or Dodie Bellamy and to filmmakers as diverse as Orson Welles, Douglas Sirk, Maya Deren, Chris Marker, and Lewis Klahr.

Melodrama and Montage

(On Nicole Brossard/Hannah Weiner)

We are interested in the gap between the world and its representations: the uneasy relations between the world and the way we are able to see it, think about it, and interact with it. Media have become the *frame* of life (one hears "frame of reference"—the sign *is* the life), governing the activities that live outside that frame. The "managed" war(s), our spectatorship, our relation to "entertainment"—soaps, sports, film, and attendant empathies distributed throughout the Star System as "News"—attest to the psychic/perceptual regime under which we Citizens exist.

We have always suspected the shopping mall was created to prepare us for life on alien worlds, under insulated control. The idea of alien covert command is common enough in science fiction; witness films from *Metropolis* to *The Matrix*. In the film *Total Recall* (1989), and made from a story by Philip K. Dick featuring larger-than-life hard-body Arnold Schwarzenegger, the plot hangs on blowing up the atmospheric bubble on Mars so as to purify the rotted atmosphere of the surface. Under the guise of a high-tech adventure there is global psychodrama—the fear of the atmosphere going *bad* a reflection of Situation Earth and the solution a kind of reverse movement in which a nuclear "event" destroys the sheltering Mall (Wall) and recreates our familiar carbon/oxygen (capitalist) universe. The hero is constantly confronted with false contexts, recreated "screens," dream logic (the originating motor of the plot has the hero hooked to a dream machine), and the inability to locate the True. Certain gestures relating to the body appear as privileged sites of the True. The real "tear" has an evidential role.

The world created is one of masks, a series of uncertain spaces, veiled guises, increasing distance from the body, the actual always under threat of mediating "covers" and thereby movement through this space one of a series of unveilings, disclosures, frustrations, and reveals—this language of theatricalization both symptom and cause. Dick's hero finds his dream does not end when he wakes up.

Welcome. We have entered a messy, ambiguous space—modern and artificial—an area where surety, critical distance, and rational critique are constantly in flux.

WHAT MIGHT BE STRATEGIES?
To unloosen this thickness
To interpenetrate topos
To undo.
A releasing.
For only in this sense do we perform analysis.

Point of Origin
In the 1980s I was engaged in a project to uncover the historical models through which we exist in a body; to collect, destroy, and recon-

Figure 4. Four on Rivington Street. *Left to right:* Diane Torr, Elion Sacker, Plauto, and Sally Silvers. Frame enlargement from Abigail Child's *Perils* (16 mm, b/w, sound, 5 min., 1986).

struct the vocabulary of the body—exploring how gesture means and engaging that vocabulary in play, critique, and creative structures.

My strategies involved a constant negotiation with history—looking at silent-movie gestures or Japanese pornography of the nineteenth and eighteenth centuries (which relate to our contemporary illus-trated novel or comic book focused on sex and morality), anonymous home movies from the 1930s and 1940s. I wanted to undo the Model. To display the functions of the splendiferous illusion machine that is the movies—to engage the mechanizations of pleasure/seduction (not merely emotional identification but physicality of the cut, sensuous-ness of the image, vortex of movement) *and* pull the carpet out from under our illusions, to participate and interrogate. Which after all seems close to the actual relationship we have to things and events, as well as to language.

The contradiction already engaged will be one of our valuable resources.

Through montage and rhythm I was able to form new connections and dissemble existing ones, but as I approached the body more intimately, giving myself at one point the direction to "embarrass" myself, as I approached narrative language and the Forbidden, *unloosening* subjects that had previously been untouched, excess and gesture accompanied the fragmentation. I encounter melodrama. History as theater. A proposal of the RUDE, debased, or excessive such as might cut through and allow access into language and emotions, manipulations, otherwise hidden or absent. The nineteenth-century woodblock prints I used as part of the coding for *Mayhem* portrayed lovers in the "stage" of their rooms, walls sometimes splitting the paintings, making framings or theatrical sets. Utamaro positions voyeurism as *the* frame of looking and the paradigm of the erotic.[1]

In a moment of institutional homogeneity and increased "economy" of reason, reason wants to embrace this space, this confluence of the unacceptable—making a move counterindictable, messy, and, significantly, increasing the scope of the subject.

Allowing Access into Language and Emotions Otherwise Absent

Peter Brooks notes, "It is as if coming out of the Enlightenment, men [*sic*] had to reinvent the sense of the sacred from its source, now skewed and narcissistically fascinated by its point of origin."[2] Brooks locates the French Revolution as the decisive point at which the Enlightenment falters and we move into the age of the romantic—which he argues convincingly is the one we are still in. With the dissolution of a hierarchical society and invalidation of its forms—the tragedy and comedy of manners that depends on that society—a new theatrical space opens up, that of melodrama. Melodrama interpreted by Brooks is not loss but a *response* to loss in a world witnessing the growth of the democratic ideal and the drama of the ordinary.

At its most reactionary, melodrama becomes nostalgic, and at its most dangerous it involves a flattening of response (hypnosis). Television soaps and the polarized villains of politics demonstrate these formations, but at its most ambitious it brings to the surface areas previously uninvestigated, reflects the fascination and pleasure of exploring the forbidden, serves as a channel to our psychopathologies, which in the melodrama burst loose, breaking the bounds of the normal, refusing the grace and ellipsis of silence.

This is the shape of our fiction and our news. Today's world is framed melodramatically. It is the shape of our myths, a scale of larger-than-life, a world viewed from a distance, in constant struggle, between rich and poor, haves and have-nots. Our compliance with these terms is measured never so well as when we walk past bodies begging on the street. Even AIDS itself has been called an inherently melodramatic trope figured around the conflict between the appearance of health and reality of sickness, its targeting the young, and its siting of death in love.[3]

Where representation fails to figure the world, where the event will not fit our understanding, is without center, incomprehensible, melodrama works to signal this "missing," attempting to bridge an unspeakable. In this sense the modernist urge for transcendence is a version of this romanticized gesture—and mirrors its underlying ambition.

This paradox—trying to express all points, including that which is *impossible to express*—points up the abyss that is at the heart of the romantic (or modern). Mallarmé's white page and occult project come to mind. *Abyss* itself comes from the Greek: meaning no bottom, *immeasurable*.

THE BODY AFTER LANGUAGE FAILS. THE BODY OF THE STATE (THE BODY OF THE RENAISSANCE) SUPPLANTED BY THE INDIVIDUALIZED BODY AND THAT BODY THEN INVESTIGATED FOR SIGNS, SYMPTOMS, AND GESTURES THAT REVEAL ITS INNER STATE. WE BECOME ENGAGED IN A CONSTANT READING OF SIGNS OF THE BODY.

Decay is the laboratory of life.

Melodrama gestures, trying to elicit a reality that is not acknowledged. Melodrama is a hot aesthetic, antidotal to the cool posture of Western neutrality (objectivity). A study of its characteristics and implications helps us read recent media and writing. How does it function? What are its tropes?

Melodrama's landscape is democratic; there is no significant or insignificant detail. The world surface itself has the promise of the ineffable. In this sense, attributing value to the *undemonstratable* character of the universe, melodrama throws a wrench into rational analysis that seeks to authorize its status *outside* the context of desire and distortion. Melodrama sees a world under pressure, awaiting meaning or revelation. Suspense thus forms a key melodramatic trope: time becomes foreboding and inevitable, a theatrical tension in a world preoccupied with threat. Suspense as the measure (weather) of the social.

Melodrama equals the theatricalizing gesture itself, framing a world of unspoken relations, exhibitor of the repressed. Against modernist autonomy, which posits a disembodied truth, purity of form and structure, melodrama presents a skewed and covert social reality: a place of the organ, of emotion, of the body, of disclosure and closure, of doubling, a world couched in what has been situated traditionally as the "feminine."

Melodrama can appear as a studied primitiveness or (simultaneously) become highly artificial, rococo, and ornamental. The repressed resurfaces as style. Think of the fetishization and excess in the films of Buñuel, Anger, Deren, Sirk, George Kuchar, or Jack Smith. This predilection for the tango.

But

I do not want to limit my analysis to a construction of style—something more is at stake or more possible.

"Beyond the unthinkable we have melodrama."[4]

An alchemy of the forbidden that implodes closure, does not respect borders or systems of order, disrupts identity—a disturbance of the senses, thus speech and muteness, talking in tongues, all indicative. Significance is everywhere. Melodrama is an attempt to break through—creating risky, interpolated work, creating what Nicole Brossard describes and enacts avidly in *These Our Mothers: The Disintegrating Chapters:*

> *A true fantasy which makes history outrageous and demented, which can only be generated by an unambiguous code. And also at the same time carries me away.*[5]

Brossard's text is a text of bliss. The intention of bliss itself the de-marking act: the gestures grow large, the vocabulary exists in extremity, "grandstanding" in the domestic site, positing a double movement in terms of escape—unbound(ed) and simultaneously pointing—a dis-crete signpost to the sky. What is necessary in a world of relations and objects that otherwise go unnoticed.

It's combat, the book.
I killed the womb. My *life . . .* My *death.*

The missing junctures are structured by parallel syntax, the sen-tence circles back on itself, back on the body. The structure recreates a spiral, expanding and folding into a vortex: *it's devouring and de-voured.* The subject and object coexist. The woman is made subject and object in an enfolding, layered line. Speaking out of the whirl-pool of repression: *Three-faced incest that refuses the lie yet whose eye nonetheless keeps all traces of it.* This is primal speech as romantic his-tory, a renewed revolutionary search for women's experience.

I had to . . . drown the acidity of white.

Gesture become abstract, parabolic, enormous, searing so as to *compare* reality.

The sisterhood of woman is the ultimate test of human solidarity laying itself open to another beginning of delusions of grandeur.

Able to ironize, contextualize her search, Brossard's drama is viewed in situ, in argument. Rewriting romantic myth from the position of woman means rewriting from the position of the social reality of women—as a colonized character—and from the position of the fu-ture: the questionable backbone from which mutilated and mutating branches arise.

The means by which every woman tries to exist: to be illegitimate no more.

Brossard repeatedly uses verbs of closure (*seal, putting out*) and polarized nouns (*monsters chops or angels lips; word/wound*) to foreground ethical conflicts: *husband-psychologist . . . who put seals on her.* Brossard uses melodramatic rhetoric and gesture as both target and means to uncover an internal scale, the scale of woman/mother/womb. The vocabulary is hyperbolic. The act violent.

> *Before withdrawing. His–tory. She can only explode it, its passions, its parallels, its parameters. Bulging her belly one last time. For a girl.*

There is a heroic quality to Brossard's project—it makes the intimate large. This contradiction or doubling direction is at the heart of the melodramatic function in its ambitious mode—it encounters the unknown, the unspeakable through the daily and the body.

> *To work myself into the grave over a body, to expiate all the symbols one by one. . . . To have done with expiation. Inner torture.*

These Our Mothers rejects the Freudian center of repression, yet it performs a talking cure.

> *Immobilized and ardent at the same time.*
> *Rent even in its orgasmic function*

This attempt at fusion is insatiable, unsayable.

These qualifiers, the persistence of the negative to speak: consciousness is split from self. The activity of dismemberment is rent.

Brossard's surface describes a line of digression, not broken but a flow, its shape, her spiral, branching anxiety.

> *but a fissure, not a fragment.*
> *like an effective scandal.*

The shape is a dream logic, not the idea of bodies but the energy of the body itself—embarrassed extruded demented pitiable—

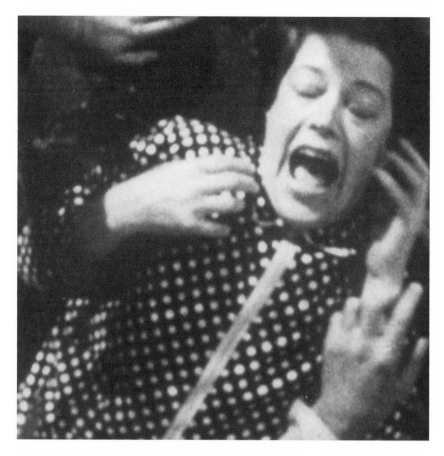

Figure 5. Diane Torr as the polka-dotted woman. Frame enlargement from *Mayhem*.

save yourself if you can with your own energy
The violent act of the eye on enamoured purple infiltrates enraptured
unfolding.

Brossard's hyperbolic language relates to surrealist proposals, but her force, direction, and indiscretion exhibit a melodramatic drive—hysterical excess, intenser space.

I to act hallucinate take my hand

Figure 6. Diane Torr as the polka-dotted woman in *Mayhem.*

Hallucination in the space of function, verb, egress, excess to allow a certain access. To subject, to women, to freedom, to arms and limbs, the sky, the violent act.

> *I awake in myself the collective region, the costumes, only* the dramatic text *avalanche of scales. . . .*

❖

Turning from the hot to the cool, let us look at television soaps— daily fictions where exaggeration becomes stasis studded with lurid, grotesque events, masked relations, disguised identities, even slow-acting poisons (remember the poison paint in *Dynasty*?). There is a victory over repression in terms of the sexual (surely prurient), and on occasion soaps have presented contemporary issues (dealing with war or race), but in the main these soaps tame the ineffable.

Size is, of course, one method. The small box does not serve the grand well. It reduces the grand to the size of an ad. Which is another taming structure: the ads as part of the total show, intercutting and punctuating the story, so as to hold the consumer to her seat, the moment often indicated in musical phrasing and, as often, a moment of dramatic suspense (a vaudevillian cliché: think of *Perils of Pauline* or any other weekly serial that cuts out as the hero is falling off the cliff or waiting to be rescued—and the active and passives of those scenarios are tightly gender controlled). The ads that interrupt this dramatic "high" posit a world of cool control—a world where washes are whiter and popularity is a mouthwash away. The endless assurance and simplest consumer solutions are contrasting salve to the dramatic dysfunctional world of disintegrating families, ethics, and emotions in the "main story." The ads often take on a documentary space, for example, that of the interview or testimonial—interviewing housewives or people on the street or in the memorable 1960s' set of mothers and daughters whose hands do not reveal their age because of joy's preserving functions. We are expected to believe our eyes? The format of the ads codes the real—in terms of lighting, a sense of improvisation (often carefully manipulated), the subject confronting the lens, the audience acknowledged.

At each point different levels of reality shift in and out of the box. The melodrama is *fiction,* the tamed stage for representing reality and the search for health, wealth, and happiness that has animated it, while *reality* is a framed advertisement that is purchased and "testified" (not insignificantly a religious term) by strangers. The sign becomes the locus of reality. A collaborated falseness.

Television tames melodrama even as it enacts it, the daily repetition —*As the World Turns*—equalizing interstices and, ultimately, emotion. If all things possibly mean and all things are shaped by meaning, a world of significance can generate a force field of equal units, penetrable contexts, excess of fact that is flat, undramatized.

We land in a tributary of Hannah Weiner's *Weeks,* a public generation—taken from telecast and newsprint, an accounting of broadcast time.[6] A field of sentences gathered and organized by day through year, a calendar of overheard language. Here her line is the sentence. There is no connection between them. Not breath, but bites. Sentences replay endless media (medley) broadcasts—adamant and distant dead *children* next to *greed,* AIDS, forgotten stars, sports, the hostage crisis, a history of women. A kind of Rorschach of culture—*Wild America is our compass* alternating with social psychosis—*Are you trying to sell me a ticket to breathe*?

Each day of the year occupies two or three sentences on a page, and the effect is a tsunami, an ongoing flood of events without scale, punctuated by a voice that persists without heroics, without shock, with a democracy that is unnerving, scary in affect, counteracted by a sly humor that surfaces. The broadcast is recounted with stamina (one thinks of Beckett) and somehow perverted (one thinks of Sade). The emotive affect is short-circuited. We're listening in—on a recording device from which a small and persistent voice does emerge. The news is on. It is very solid, dark, and diabolical.

BUY TIME BUY TIME BUY TIME

Like the texts of Sade, *Weeks* creates a machine for representing reality, situating news within poetry, "news" that "minds" our lives. *In the spirit of creation everyone is too loud.* Speech is to suggest what cannot be said. Silence is requested but won't be heard.

In talking about Sade, Kathy Acker speaks of a political stance arising out of an (im)balance between stable and transgressive energies; Bataille describes Sade's work as "an irruption of excremental forces" that create a domain of "suffocation" indecently provoked.[7] Both statements are true of *Weeks.* The writing is disturbing, familiar, unresponsive—an entropic soup. It produces a ceiling on emotions, a "cool," nonconnecting web to invade our lives, spreading manufactured information, refusing to go Off. *Weeks* defeats you. Its unpaginated Muzak permeates the apartment, your flesh, our feeling: a public invasion of private space, found poetry of the most dissonant, resistant, and gluey (omnipresent) materials. Charles Bernstein describes the process as entering a "cul-de-sac."[8] It is indeed a trap, witness to and engaged with entrapment, displaying a paradoxical fascination with obsession and with the ordinary. Meeting the machine/ TV on its own territory, Weiner has structured a math, walked forward into the black hole of prefabricated relations, entering a dark and immobile continuum.

This is holocaust remembrance Day.

Like Sade, but without recourse to theatrics, Weiner has created a machine that cannot be stopped. "Beyond the unthinkable, we have melodrama."

One thing that links them all together—another female agent was killed then.

In its confrontation with the "real"—obstinately, *Weeks* functions as in melodrama: pointing through enumerative excess, declarative *as if* to speak, the speaker/reader herself mute except as ethical force— call it shock of recognition: *I'm trying to pick things that I learn from. It can be so many things; it's just the imagination that makes the difference.* Weiner faces off TV, a Promethean quest. The project a framing of consciousness, and a mapping of cultural/social localities. Weiner's drama is a drama of ethics, a lucid appraisal of the difficulty and indeterminacy of speech, transgressive in its persistence and rejection of closure, and ultimately moral in its attempt to lay bare the world as it is. Her positioning of the news as poetry posits responsibility in existence.

I feel threatened by the responsibility of my intellect.

Photos taken from television accompany the text, almost erased in the printing, the quality of the image degraded into TV scan lines.[9] The sentences are a field facing darks and lights in muddy gray. *No identifying features.* Disaster cargo. A litany of facts.

Thinking now could pay off. The amount of things that were not fixed is about endless.

I went by the information I received.
I've got some sources for impossible things.

A kind of radical uplifting. Avoiding the theatrics of melodrama, Weiner has tackled its substance, uncovering and demonstrating the moral universe. In the modern era (the romantic) language fails: the wor(l)d is cornered. The result: a blunt secreted taped reflection of broadcast signifiers—

Death was the only cure he could find.
This is it. To the real Marilyn and to the reality in us all. How is the per-spective different?

Indeed, how is the perspective different? Weiner confronts the ver-tiginous with courage. Long involved in what might be called an occult project, Weiner in her earlier *Clairvoyant Journal* and *Little Books/Indians* has recorded words seen, heard, or projected off bodies and objects in the landscape. A kind of found vision. In *Weeks,* the words, also found, do not come from friends nor ostensibly from Weiner herself. They are instead the anonymous and public sounds of our social telecast. Collected, the signs exhibit an oily continuum, intransigent to human interpenetration or human action, scathing us with a world untranscended and grossly figured. We are left in sta-sis, untenable locus. The body itself another moveable crisis/object/sentence.

The juxtaposition of detailed fact, unremitting reportage, is pushed in our faces, enacts a crisis of reality: for *Weeks,* reality is excessive, representation. We remain at the edge of the measurable. Welcome.

To a world where the "tear" has no evidential role. Where there is no privileged site of the True. Artaud's desire to have the stage physi-cally envelop the spectator, spreading "its visual and sonorous out-bursts over the entire mass of the spectators," has become virtually the case.[10] Significantly, in *Weeks* there is no awakening. We exist in a world of oppressive information overload; we use our imagination to navigate this sea. What is unspeakable, what is unthinkable, is trans-lated into jingles, and we bring courage to confront, not so much dissolve—which would give us only a transcendent "escape" from reality—the oppressive repeating representational static of world. Weiner's genius and her prosodic indictment is to exist within this sticky universe, to look it in its face—a stand-up citizen, not agent but body—not lyric but testimony, obsessive, blocked.

Huge numbers . . . horror. . . . This is not the easiest thing for me to do.

In the 1980s I met Camille Roy, a writer and playwright. In the early 1990s we decided to collaborate on an essay focused on issues of narrative, subjectivity, and storytelling. As in my earlier correspondence with Sally Silvers, we wrote letters back and forth for six months, freely incorporating dialogue, poetry, gossip, and theory. I crossed country to edit, the two of us together on the floor in her front room in San Francisco, cutting and pasting. Sections emerged spontaneously in the process. Camille did not want to regularize the format in ways that would reveal who wrote what; I agreed, feeling that in this way the dialogue was positioned inside a shifting plasticity of combined voices rather than bifurcated dialogue.

Sex Talk

(With Camille Roy)

1. Sex Talk

> *Perhaps what's operating here is distance—the shadowed sex IS taboo, not only in its appearance in books but as covert action inside the civil proscenium. Eisenstein talks of drama as "revenge" and he's thinking of Shakespeare's plays, but it rhymes with your conjunction of "deceit" with narrative. Then are gossip, or stories, fiction—structurally and intrinsically—connected to "drama"? to an idea of narrative ruled by actions of competition and power? Fairy tales themselves are stories often involving a righting of justice, skill, or freedom for the hero and/or heroine, the overthrow of order, killing of the king or witch so that the good gal wins . . .*

From my table in the café I *watched her* walk up the pavement, with a curious stiff-legged stroll. She was wearing a man's suit from the 1940s, baggy pants, blue smoke curling from the tip of a *thin cigarette.* Her

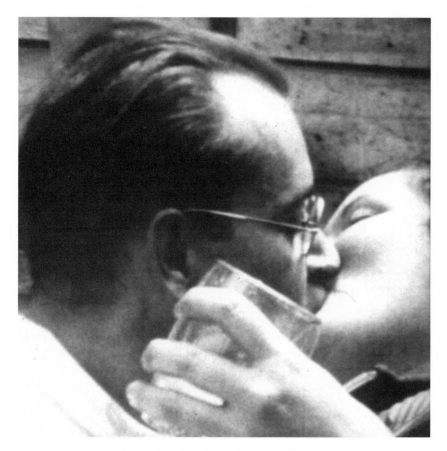

Figure 7. Kiss. Frame enlargement from *Covert Action*.

round cheek was so soft it reminded me of one of those pictures of Colette in drag.

> Among lesbians the story is a form of sex talk—a joint whereby the community and the couple are of the same body. Proximity is difficult but brings us tongue to tongue. "Fetish as disclosure."

> *My relation to fetish:*
> *bigger here and importantly hugely infantile*

I could feel my body proffering leather
The nipple waiting to plus anemone

Anthropologist Lévi-Strauss argues tattoos are the sign of a defended tribe. A tribe facing extinction or being threatened. Fetish works in that direction. One might say in a defended world, identification becomes the uniform feature.

I ordered espresso with a piece of lemon peel. When she ordered the same thing, I slapped her face lightly, as a *joke. She* tilted her head, rubbed her chin thoughtfully as her eyes closed and a smile came onto her lips. "That was interesting," she said, "but you only slapped one side."

I am questioning an alignment of identity with narrative, of narrative with clarity, of clarity with (an assumed) populism. I'm more interested in a politics of representation and resistance. I'm looking at how meaning is made and what the constructs are that make us read in certain ways, *act* in certain ways, and how you can explode those constructs to open up new places, or use those constructs in unimagined ways, so that tradition becomes a material to be bent.

Narrative seeps from the broken privacy of the couple. It is a disturbance of intimacy, a betrayal, which accounts for its dramatic effect. . . .

Yes! The dramatic effect lies in the transgression. A matter of identity equaling control, and then pleasure in the diffusion/breaking of the pattern. A pleasure of violation. Broken expectations.

So I slapped the other side of her face, with my whole *hand* instead of my fingers. "You *did it* differently that time," she observed, *and I watched her* soft cheeks flush. "I want to keep you off balance," I said.

Intimacy fastens like barrettes
Intimacy fastens, to be inserted somewhere inside the head.

The other is recognized by means of fantasy, so that intimacy itself is
a fiction, dreamy as skywriting, a slogan in white cloud. . . .

Or perhaps an architecture? An absence underlined. You speak
of skywriting. Narration in the twentieth century has been
permanently formed by cinema and the photograph: it is
how we think of time and memory: a recovery in distance.
Now . . . how to dislodge their control?

2. Real Charm

Sit on my face
See how wet I am

unmistakable juice and smell and hair
innocently sweetheart clit scream
breath blue thighs hot swollen fully Look
                              has abundance
Lying   played   pulled
cooed and fatted focused
                              suddenly dry

kiss me fuck you
returning real charm

If I were attired to receive this with any accuracy
my garments would fall stridently into me.[1]

Eroticism in the West proceeds through a strategy of striptease or
moral tale.

Fantasy bends it out of shape twists in my face.

Not a nice ass but a great
heart-shaped butt, the bottom,
what's written out, an unassimilable—

Conventional narration must contain her. His *little death* does not detain me. Determinism holds us all down.

The smiling faces of ads are a form of control *through* resemblance. A community of female sexual perverts resembles *nobody, and nobody* wants to resemble us.

What I loved in *Mayhem* is a notion of backwards. The fact that I could retreat *and reorder* without feeling sacrificed. The filmic codes are *clipped*—which has the curious effect of separating the image from its portent of "accuracy."

Recognition torn . . .

"Go on and suck. Suck the life outta me. I wanna feel my life in somebody else's mouth."[2]

Following this line of thought, power verbs shape faces on your
   own prism
   cunt
the civilization of the ass unseals
becomes like you when you come
and wear the kind of smile I want to take home.

SURFACING ON THE BED AMID RIOTS I LOVE TO BE FILLED WITH TIME
IMPROVISATION OF YOUR MOUTH BETWEEN MY THIGHS.[3]

3. Story Line

Her hand on my shoulder, that first gesture of invitation, was so characteristic of her. Circular as a huge conscience, something to follow indefinitely. Her fingered goodbyes marked my body, a sort of sexual technique. Even this story, its thin crust, marks her evasions.

Incapable of being used up

The progress of tension through a narrative "line" has parallels in the maps we make of our lovers' bodies and the moments of exposure and vulnerability on the way to orgasm.

It's beyond surplus

Full of hot
and chronic satisfaction
soaked   cause I'm stopped
between love and a third tongue
girlfriend
sexy buttons
popping cock
twisted

I'm visualizing them physically
the unreasonableness of the situation

this world

It is *tension* more than line that interests me. I see a field—promises—an array of *conjugation*—the wish you want. Line if you must is a focus perpetrating depth. The line exists on the surface, is habit perhaps?

The *idea* that I'm telling a story is what I'm attached to, not the linearity or anything else. I'm attached to this idea because it establishes contact—which can be appropriated, misused, disrupted, eroticized. Like this one:

Terry was a big-boned whore, a lesbian, and an incest survivor. When she became a fundamentalist Christian, she married a carpenter. Everyone wondered, how much did he really know? One day in a rage, he was heard yelling, "Well at least you were never a prostitute!"

kissing my impeccable cunt

Regarding order in time—I (or the "linearity" of narrative) doesn't necessitate a patriarchal ordering of consciousness. I prefer an implication/integration of loss: what happened in the beginning (or middle or end) won't return.

If loss is a part of life we are missing nothing.
Forget repair, even if minimal.

Then what is pleasured in the telling of a story?

Recognition and misrecognition. The flow between them.
The wind an instrument of excess prone to gorgeous.
Or is it? sex as disclosure, a manifest and metaphorical stripping.

4. Audience

And what about the relation of recognition to desire? As in this quote: "To desire the Desire of another is to desire that the value that I am be the value desired by the other: I want her to recognize my value as her value."[4] I want her to recognize me as an autonomous value. In other words, all human, anthropogenic Desire—the desire that generates self-consciousness, human reality—is finally, a function of the desire for recognition.

What of the desire for another—not to be loved, but to love? Do I want to recognize me in the lover? Do I want love to recognize me? Do I seek to be lost in love? To be its familiar?

I think that stories have all the sneaky pleasure and mutilations of intimacy hidden within what we call narrative structure. Narrative moments are always coupled and involve multiple manipulations of deceit and recognition.

"When I'm having sex, it's like I'm having a story. I hear things like 'She spread her legs as her lover's tongue softly ran across her vagina.' The third person! we exclaimed."[5]

"I story myself so others will witness my sex as desire." The third person is present only to satisfy my need to be observed.

> *If an observer is needed to satisfy my desire, this is Voyeurism as identification. If the observer is my mind, I have fragmented myself and this is Separation as identification. And if I borrow your rules of attraction I reintegrate opposite sex identification, try on your Power.*

AGREED: what is functioning is the NOUN of narration, mirroring the sense of self.

> I distrust devices of plot and linear time and character relation. I want both process VERB and person NOUN to be tilted. I ask for more "takes" on the body, so that reality is approached in an excess of enumeration, not stabled, nor owned.

> *softer bigger whiter breastier*
> *remake the elaborate identity of her*
> *or of her him*
>
> *elaborate your identity*

So it was easy to let her carve it, warble wobble. Only by turning on her with all my teeth bared could I recover ground already lost. Of course I did it. Of course yearning made it impossible. Pleasures of the rupture rack and screw.

5. Close Enough

Perhaps what is happening between us is an opening up of a kind of erotic conversation. Here, at the margin. Because a community of sexual perverts resembles *nobody, and nobody* desires to resemble us.

> As a lesbian the differences are multiplied, the possibilities mutate, taking on all kinds of genuinely new procedures. This is not borrowed habit, but transformative: a "kind of loving" become in the presence of wit and intelligence (the head screwed *on and on*) genuine alternatives

The room is either dark or light, or is two rooms. There are implements beyond my consciousness.

Breast-high partitions cover the linoleum floor, creating a maze through which workers stroll and softly talk. At either end of the vast warehouse are sealed rooms whose roaring ventilation systems cool the computers. You are allowed in these rooms because you wear a special identification badge. Between the computer rooms stretch two rows of windows that face twin lines of young olive trees whose leaves are covered with fine grayish hair. Beyond these trees the workers go to sleep and have sex.

> *Shadows tip the lover onto circumstance.*
> *I want to be touched, or touched continuously.*
>
> *The sun makes close enough open*
> *Let me drink my bathrobe, skirt a retinue of clings*
> *A sanitized restraint gives way to luster's substrate*

Bent over the edge of the body, there's no telling where we are. Lattice handiwork, the roseate palm smacking our tin flesh.

We're getting rosier and rosier. These large sensations come and go. We want to be a star; we want to be adorable. Instead the larger sensations, so open there is a sense of leveling. What is inside slips out and vanishes.

In any kind of joking, a system that's given as isolate
liquefies, falls suddenly into another

There's a tangle of questions all over the floor.

Reading through the reissued (1981) three-volume Grove Press edition of the complete Sade was thrilling. Sade abrades and provokes, shocks, humors, and embeds throughout his pornography a profound social critique. The Grove Press edition includes critical articles by de Beauvoir, Blanchot, Klossowski, and Paulhen, among others. I voraciously read and immediately incorporated aspects, tableaux, and compositional structures from Sade into my plans for *Is This What You Were Born For?* One section was to be the *Justine* story. That became *Mayhem,* retaining the sexual surface and Sade's pyramidal structure, without relying on a particular story line. Asked by Simon Watney to participate on a panel in his conference "Fantasy and Desire" at the New School years later, I welcomed the opportunity to return to Sade. I had just completed a collaboration utilizing my rewrite of *Philosophy of the Bedroom,* and I wove parts of that text throughout the essay.

Sade's Motor

Thinking about talking about Sade makes me want to *do* Sade, give rein to *my* power to deflect *you, your* expectations—to go beyond any agreed social covenant.

> To put mirror to arched affections: the person in boots pauses
> Incriminating arms. No resistance to
> The lifted fist. Lubricate
> The socks wrapped 'round the strap-on ancestors
> Recusant still in narrow exile
> She licks him, touches breeches of straining prick, and the young
> man leaves in haste.[1]

If one sees Sade as libertine, one emphasizes the individual potency, "mastery," and delusionary aspects in his writings and may miss the

Figure 8. "NINE." Frame enlargement from *Covert Action.*

public space his writings address—indeed Sade's life and writings incubate or motor around the civil. His work is about subverting the law.

Law for Sade is repression of desire, and with irony and humor he martials an excess of rhetoric to subvert repression. His fantasies direct themselves against the tyranny of law; his subversion is grounded in the historical logic it challenges.

So that his fantasy *remembers, replays* his era.

Marked by aversion. Shaped by propriety and disgust. A kind of phantasmic machine that mirrors the social in a double-cross. A celebration of brutality, male anarchy, female betrayal.

"But it is not at all our job to renovate ideological institutions on the basis of the existing social order by means of innovations. Instead our innovations must force them to surrender that basis. So: For innovations, against renovation!"[2]

Yet, but: his gonads do not speak for my ovaries.

Then, what are his uses?

Early on I write: the film has to be the poem of the cunt, and the moral will lie in the cunt turning everything around. The extreme materialization of the flesh. The infinitely complex relation of biology shadowed by psychological terrain and social "dysfunction." The terror of the sexual under impingement of morality, prisoner to institution.

> Crisp, imaginary
> Police demand to see license.
> Whose game?
> *I am America's future.* Straddled
> By my fourth grade. Whatever
> It is I
> Do I'm doing it.
> Helping her undress considering without touching E.'s breast,
> saying which D. appears eager to turn E. about in order to inspect
> her from the rear.
> *Aie! Aie!*

The philosophical subject is as follows: a whole society hurling itself at the cunt, a pack of hounds, a pack of bitches wrestling. Male desires, the levers, which move the world. The bride is papered with money. A situation demands. An elliptical ellipse. I have a "fix" on beauty. Let us say, seduction can be critical. Let us say, morality flaunts the lever of desire.

Spending over twenty years in prison, Sade flaunts sexual excess and negation in words, dreaming figures of omnipotence and brutality. He substitutes text for flesh, reviling the society that surrounds and imprisons him. His tortured melodramas enact the social torture of a body, cubed in civic terror.

My first reading of Sade's *Justine* found it comic, albeit horrific, complete with fairy-tale castle and forest, repeating hierarchically the pattern of seduction and betrayal, torture and escape of the innocent—showing postures of the sexually terrorized and how they repeat the postures of the powerless.

Sade places obscenity always in proximity to authority, at the seat of power, with the priest, the judge, the doctor, the duke. Deleuze notes that Sade is all-pervasive—"'desexualizing' love and at the same time sexualizing the entire history of humanity."[3] Ferociously degrading the idea of equality even as he unleashes an omnipotent permission. His excess is a strategy to both *stage* and *detonate* reality.

> What you are doing with me?
> Dioramas for a pleasure that differentiates without convicting.
> Through a two-way mirror the litigants observe, fascinated, the barking—

> The positions are arranged. Shift of attitude and D. goes on. E.
>   assumes her place. Coolly they embrace. Addressing her
> Self frigging her self wild
> Eyed beside her
> Self seizes it. Roused. Forewarned
> is six-armed, three-backed, twelve-eyed, a corrected myopia of
>   sensory whiplash.
> The revealed aperture Xed with gaffer's tape.
> When I hear the words "erotic
> Economy" I reach for my catamite's
> handlebar. The palm at the end
> Of the mind's tongue often bends but seldom breaks in the ass at the
>   end of the brain's architecture.

It is not Sade's free play of fantasy that empowers me, particularly as a woman reading him, but rather his extreme outrageousness that revises any version of morality as agreed on between us. Face-to-face with the aftereffects of accommodating constraints, conditioning flesh against our time, Sade is an incitement to riot.

By submitting the reductive repetitions to a reshaping, the repetitions are broken, reordered, restructured, made arbitrary, exemplification of a moral disorder.

> We enter
> Linked arm in arm, greatly surprised to find she'd not expected such
>   pillars of frosted bohemia.
> His hands on occasion stray over the butts that nuzzle them.

Figure 9. Rex West in frame enlargement from *Mayhem*.

"Pornological literature is aimed above all at confronting language with its own limits, with what is in a sense a 'nonlanguage'" beyond speech, to meet the challenge of flesh and the sensual, to engage an erotics that at essence is of the body, and therefore unspeakable.[4]

This disappearance of language is materialized in the desperate no-

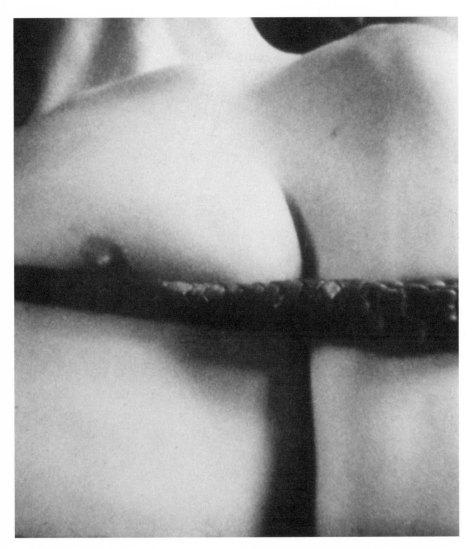

Figure 10. Male breast. Frame enlargement from *Mayhem*.

tations at the end of *120 Days of Sodom,* where the horrors become a math of recounting, a seizure of obscenity in lists, without regard for gender, an excess, which serves to demoralize the reader. Sade's penetration is successful when I, reader, pull back to recognize black ink, and this is his genius, that black ink carries potencies of flesh, invokes disgust in response, arouses the reading body. His delirium delivers recognition. Flashes of images so severe, so cropped, as to be "summarily executed." He rages. He pushes writing. He dismantles bodies and writing. He condemns judges and priests. He gives rein to his anger; he relishes nightmare.

It is too idealistic . . . and therefore cruel.[5]

Bataille recognizes that the language of Sade is paradoxical because it is essentially that of a victim, a victim raging against a system, against an institutional body, that operates against him.[6] Only the victim can define torture, as the torturer necessarily uses the hypocritical language of established order. One observes that in the criminal the powerless speak or, more particularly, that Sade's wish to idolize the criminal is a way to come to terms with the hypocrisies of power and to reframe the powerless without the superficial pieties of pity.

We ask how this might translate to cinema.

One of Sade's character's—*Clairwil*—dreams of a crime "which is perpetually effective, even when I myself cease to be effective, so that there will not be a single moment of my life, even when I am asleep, when I shall not be the cause of some disturbance."[7] An endless insult, in the spirit of anarchy and desire, a cosmic wrath.

Clearly, position is everything. That's why fear can be exciting in a safe environment.

Reason itself a form of violence in the context of the body. The text, a fetish event.

The body, having been steadily erased in the social, recurs as tortured and torturer (as text). The body insists on its interpenetration. A diaspora of pain for a body under siege. Pain brings the denied body into focus. If AIDS is a metaphor for anything, it is of the denied body.

At the end of *Justine* the heroine is saved but for a mere twenty-four hours, at which point she is struck by a lightning bolt. Sade makes clear that pleasure without pain is ephemeral; its fate is destruction. Nothing lasts. The world tips into the unsayable. Pleasure defined is out of order. Anathema to the civil state, insurrectionary.

What use is this to cinema?

Sade gives rein to rage extravagantly, to dismantle, to "misbehave"—beyond (perhaps) our wildest dreams, and that *beyond* is part of his ongoing power and fascination. Within the rationalized power structures Foucault describes and theorizes, the structures in which we find ourselves today—Sade revolts. His life is as extravagant as his texts. His work offers a numbering structure that is both arbitrary and arithmetic: part bawdy folktale, part (ir)rationality. He creates a progressive encircling in which authority is challenged, overcome, and reemerges. Excess and obsession in the work threaten language and thereby foreground the limits of the representative fabric. The works delineate an ongoing destruction, a breakdown under the guise of continuance. Rupture and repetition become structuring principles, and to follow Robert Hilferty, what more apt processes might be creatively applied to the contemporary crisis in narrativity and sexuality?[8]

The desk clerk's knees keep trembling. A swallower.

Every six hours the nurse changes blood. Bellyup.

In a haze of plastic tubular blockage, the bellhop's dress falls to the
  bottom.

D. sprinkles her entire body and bestows medium smacks upon it.

He having erected in the

Interval. There are kisses

And that was a beauty. The ball off the board, by way of the
  perfectly balanced slide-by—

in.

They intertwine

Their bodies in such a manner that both crotches confront D.

Mound. The master

tugs at leash, but dog shakes head. The traffic sounds

are prerecorded.

Kissing in a lowering and

halting flushing continuing stammering throw

Ing answering.

Were you or were you not?
A church, happy at this ambush, wrapped in
the root system of an exponential
Clitoris, congratulates Isolde.
Don't move.

In the early 1990s I was involved in an ongoing roundtable, Women and Theory, which included a number of women writers in the United States and Canada, among them Susan Clark, Jean Day, Johanna Drucker, Jessica Grim, Kathryn McCleod, Laura Moriarity, and Chris Tysh. The results were instructive, even volatile. An original round of letters went out. The first letter of the second round came back from Johanna, who strongly took all of us to task for not writing, not wanting to write, in a language of theory. As makers, gendered female, committed to the particular materiality of language, there was a resistance on our parts to jargon, to authority, to sticking to "rules." I had constructed my second-round letter out of quotes from the first mailings, but with Johanna's challenge I returned to additional source materials to expand and support my argument. Chris Tysh later submitted a second-round letter, but everyone else bowed out. The message we gained, perhaps suitably a mixed one, was that theoretical language might not be the only choice for women to discuss theory, that theoretical language raised deep resistance among women, and that a theoretical language for women would need to be invented. I see the collaged essay below as part of an initial and ongoing investigation for that language.

Active Theory

This shifting excellent and open positionality *is* my experience[1]

FIT THE THEORY TO YOUR PRACTICE[2]

Personally I wouldn't mind having mastery.

For the last decade I have been exploring ways to write theory—to find a space that would *enact* rather than be *about* the way thought moves.

Figure 11. Two girls in bathing suits. Frame enlargement from *Covert Action*.

What am I not saying? What is it I am condensing and hiding? Can I know this in writing?

My inspirations or collaborations here include Deleuze's idea of the rhizome and Nietzsche's of oppositional writing. I have been looking outside the traditional essay form, toward diaries, poetries, strategies of interruption and excess.

Shocked by the seductive and picky radiator, she couldn't see herself in the violent film.

IT DOESN'T NEED TO LOOK LIKE HIS

Though this isn't exactly what I heard it represents women's experience and I thank you thank you thank you.

"Any coming to consciousness simply heightens the reality of contradictions. We are often silent about how we cope with those contradictions. To focus on them is to expose our complicity, to expose the reality that even the most politically aware among us are often compelled by circumstances we do not control to submit, to collude."[3]

If language is a homologue to structures of power, to be revolutionary one must subvert language, refuse language.

WOMEN ARE ALWAYS TALKING THEORY ONLY THEY DON'T NAME IT AS SUCH

Rather than thinking of definition as exclusion, let us define the subject by its opposition, by its opportunity, by *where it lives*. There is a sense then that nothing is missing or lost.

WANTING IT ALL

There's momentum and immensity
    What is it we celebrate?

Which means the writing is plural, hybrid.

I do not imagine a place of stability.
I do not know a transparent, objective, and neutral author.

"The 'true' is always marked and informed by the ambivalence of the process of emergence itself, the productivity of meanings that construct counter-knowledges *in medias res,* in the very act of agonism."[4]

We identify with the one being kissed and as well with the camera.
We are both subject and object within the terms of a negotiation.

> *We're the movement between the subject and object rather than a*
> *negation of oppositional and antagonistic elements.*
> *We can become the subject and we can also become the object.*
> *We can tell. This picture is about us as subject.*

An assumption of authority in medias res rather than an apriori authority of the officiate and reactive moralist.

> *My gender feels complete.*

Neither neutral nor neutered, writing is for me about transformations.
External and internal form, dreaming the immensity of it. Bringing up consciousness—alive and kicking.

Finally—the issue that generates anger and distance is a question of language: the vocabulary of theory articulated in an elitist jargon of code, in academy. Nothing touches this private, privileged world.

I struggle with a politics of *location*—

> *But who am I? If writing is linked with sedition, something that*
> *seduces, is sexuality also a way to escape our inability to respond*
> *politically?*

> *How can sex be a stage for subversion?*

> *But who am I? What is my ideological situation, place of work,*
> *conditions of production, my status as a woman?*

Teaching in universities for the past twenty years, I have not felt the need to acquiesce to the academy's self-promoting demand that the discussion exist only on their terms. There are other platforms as well. The academy is part of the landscape, as are forums of the community and the street.

It would be foolish to imagine my desires and writing sealed off from history, economy, and the cultural hatchings of gender. Writing encounters—read contaminates—the social. My body and the social body generate one another.

Even as I am written out I am written by.

"If radical postmodernist thinking is to have a transformative impact, then a critical break with the notion of 'authority' as 'mastery over' must not simply be a rhetorical device. It must be reflected in habits of being, including styles of writing as well as chosen subject matter."[5]

Part of the struggle for subjectivity is the way to construct a self and identity that are both oppositional and liberatory.

I was tempted one day to conquer reality, to make it plausible.[6]

Having made this switch it's impossible for me to really feel like a straight woman. But then maybe regular straight women don't feel like straight women either. Maybe nobody really feels like a straight woman.[7]

Our dialogue enjoys pensiveness without calling it hesitation.

For Freud, Lacan, and Hegel desire is always marked by an ontological lack that can only be filled with the other. In this tradition desire is negative, unfillable, an absence. In contrast, the tradition of Spinoza, Nietzsche, Foucault, and Deleuze describes desire not as lack but as a positive force. Desire is no longer identified only with the psychic relations but with an energy that moves, creates links, alliances, connections. In this sense desire permeates all movement, emotional, social, and mechanical. Desire is not unactualized or latent; it is always active and real.

FIT THE THEORY TO YOUR PRACTICE.

The urge to subvert overpowers the rest.

> *Yet what is this guilt? Gender as punishment?*
> *The whole mat rots. Curtain bleeds*

This becomes untenable.

His description becomes her prescriptive.

THIS IS NOT A TEXT ABOUT ITS MAKER.

But I was never him.

THIS IS A TEXT ABOUT YOU.[8]

> *Necessities for the woman tempted by existence to invent the*
> *project of going beyond routine.*

The act of theory as a process of articulation, an active montage, constructed flux, combining antagonistic or contradictory elements, open to the stream of possibilities.

> *To escape is to trace this line, cross the horizon.*[9]

Animal is part of the argument

Disturbed not by theory but by jargon-filled language used to describe it.

> *Happy as I am to exist as a thinking being, theory is a cultural*
> *artifact at my disposal.*

The language of propriety and territory that circles theoretical vocabularies, the language that insists on "playing ball," is disturbingly provincial and may be hiding profoundly conservative and neocolonialist attitudes.

On the other hand, writing proposes points in a coordinate world, which if traced out could be said to delineate a theoretical ground.

It is ironic and disheartening to see theoretical postmodern discourse —of the fragment, narrative nonlinearity, abstraction—said to open a theoretical terrain where difference and otherness can be considered, reviled in academy and street, feared or ignored. We note that though progress has been made, there is, yet still, a lively opposition to the inclusionary agenda this discourse calls forth.

I said with a taste of salt in the mouth, on the subject of utopia beginning with the word woman that utopia was not going to insure our insertion into reality but that utopian testimony on our part could stimulate in us a quality of emotion favorable for our insertion into history.[10]

The sense of a mental experience where fragments and delirium from the explosion translate an experiment on riot within the self into a theory of reality.

Implicit here is *process*, necessarily fluid—a series of digressions, cross-weavings, quotations, a geography, no closure

EVERY WRITING A MANIFESTO

The real question—what is being celebrated?

Are we trapped in a politics of struggle where the representation of social antagonism and historical contradictions can take no other form than binarism of theory versus politics, or theory versus poetry?

Must the project of our liberationist aesthetics be forever part of a totalizing utopian vision of being and history that seeks to transcend the contradictions and ambivalences that constitute the very structure of human subjectivity and its systems of cultural representation?[11]

Roman road maps distorted sea and landmasses in order to fit the imperial road system into a confined space.

I want to ask what the function of a committed theoretical perspective might be, once the cultural and historical hybridity of the postcolonial world is taken as the paradigmatic place of departure?

The reader or writer who forgets race sex and class thinking to have pure literature or pure theory does so at her peril.

The connection between failing to write or read in a way that is not subservient to a system, that is essentially against one's own interests and the fact of being eliminated unseen and unheard is a direct one. It is not simple but elaborate and double in its manifestations.

Any change in the statement's condition of use and reinvestment, any alteration in its field of experience or verification, or indeed any differences in the problems to be solved, can lead to the emergence of a new statement.

In butch-femme behavior the butch being a woman within the history of that position is not imitating the male but exploring a role, a *putting-on* that does not assume the definitions of the patriarchy as fixed, solid.

THE REAL QUESTION: WHAT IS BEING CELEBRATED?

In what hybrid forms, then, may a politics of the theoretical statement emerge?
What tensions and ambivalences mark this enigmatic place from which theory speaks?

It is in response to these kinds of questions that I write.

"Speaking in the name of some counter-authority or horizon of the "true," the theoretical enterprise has to represent the adversarial authority (of power and or knowledge) which in a double inscribed move, it simultaneously seeks to subvert and replace."[12]

What is the location of the theoretical critique, which does not contain the "true"—in polar opposition to totalitarianism, bourgeoisie liberalism, or whatever is supposed to repress it?

> *In what hybrid forms may a politics of the theoretical statement emerge?*

> I open the window against the dusk

> We have a riot within ourselves
> We lose possession

The real grammar precedes this calculus. The social defines riot. What have we "lost"? saying silence slips of the tongue/repetitions/ hesitations and so on.

> You start the slow climb back in the form of a letter.

> *The true is always marked and informed by the ambivalence of the process of emergence itself.*

What is said is particular.

We exchange images, which never function according to any grammar or syntax.

> A forum of innocence
>   To redistribute your attention
> That one with functions stops

> I like the opacity of things.
>   Later

I like it broken.

ANTITHESIS

turning a moment.

The agent becomes inverted, projected, phantasmic object of the argument turned against itself.

"If opponents of all important truths do not exist, it is indispensable to imagine them. . . . [S]he must feel the whole force of the difficulty which the true view of the subject has to encounter and dispose of; else [s]he will never really possess herself of the portion of truth which meets and removes that difficulty."[13]

Antithesis turning a movement

twists theory in flesh

through holes and pleasures of overrides
opposite
lyric punches to *Don't*

consequences

Your move
to go beyond what
possibilities
Here are

The myths are unstable
How could they be otherwise?

RULE WANTS DENIAL

NOT "the distinction between metacritical authority and lyrical expressive intention" but rather a rejection of closure, a suggestion of the resonant definitions created out of opposition, exchange, the body in motion, a politics of struggle, not polarization.

> *Putting out the last fantasy about women in heat and about beautiful schizophrenics laying the discrete charms of steel along their wrists.*

What writing and media reveal is the ambivalent juxtaposition of the dangerous relation of the factual and the projective, and beyond that, of the crucial function of the textual and the rhetorical . . . in the fixing of the factual and closure of the real, that ensure the efficacy of strategic thinking in the discourses of *Realpolitik*.[14]

> *What we want are:*
> *free-hanging strategies of action, strategies that haven't yet, strategies of opposition, of resistance, of argument, anti-habit. Strategies that reveal their efficacy in the making, but not institutionalized as method. Theory, if it is to have any value, interacts with our real lives powerfully and with tenacity—a tool with which to lever the culture, in constant motion as is the culture, no given, no fixed set.*

Theory from the Greek for contemplation, viewing. See Theatre. In this era the view is in motion, the proscenium is portable, and reflection is antistate.

"The language of critique is effective not because it keeps forever separate the term of the master and the slave, the mercantilist and the Marxist, [the male and female] but to the extent to which it overcomes the given grounds of opposition and opens up a space of translation: a place of hybridity . . . where the construction of a political object that is new, *neither the one nor the other,* properly alienates our expectations and changes, as it must, the very forms of our recognition of the moment."[15]

THE ACT OF THEORY IS A PROCESS OF ARTICULATION

I borrow the dynamic of collage, dividing the moment, recreating a memory in the instance of its new re-creation—sending out sparks—retaining traces of both the fading and emerging subjects, enframe a space in which the perpetual movement of presence and absence coexist.

Come into being. Resonant, sounding different tones, mulling points and ecstasies in a euphoria of conflict and dialogue.

SHAPE A THEORY OF DE-DEFINITION

What is involved at all points is negotiation, between points in the profound experience of the knowledge of the displaced, diversionary, and differentiated boundaries in which the limits and limitations of social power are encountered in struggle.

SHAPE A THEORY OF DE-DEFINITION,
INVENTION IN NECESSITY

a strategy of the poor, of resistance, of remains, of the outside, of the community of the outside, outstretched.
A strategy to reflect the position in the social.

What's left out? What's in the field?

Bring together things that have as yet never been brought together and do not seem predisposed to be so.[16]

What does it do to move language around?

Is it strategic, decorative, martial, utopian, radical, futuristic, legal? Is it husky, lean, taut, or fashionable? It has moral and aesthetic consequence. It invents the future. Language wrests the terms of the argument, maneuvering foregrounds and backgrounds, re-presenting the social dynamic of bodies in relation. At every point there is an alchemic opportunity.

What does a working woman put first? Which of her identities is the one that determines her political and theoretical choices?

Replace traditional separation with a new idea of dialogue. Live in the margins, thresholds, ruptures, opposites. Be between.

THIS IS THE OBSESSION:

How can I make this thing in the most irrational way?

"Modern art is at the disposal of me. I'm a tool for abstractions."[17]

Reinvent logic. The space of subjectivity is fluid. We reinvent movement—

POSITION IS EVERYTHING

To write would be a woman's eye resting on others on things. To create her own locus of desire. To find her own place at a distance so as not to wither up under each caress, so as not to knock the caress away.

> *Before withdrawing History, she can only explode it, its passions, its parallels, its parameter bursting her belly one last time. For a girl.*

Since breasts will no longer smother anybody.

What I find interesting about lesbian writing is that in it women are both subject and object and as a woman writing this model has been invaluable.

The contribution of negotiation is to display the in-between of this crucial argument that is not self-contradiction but performs the political space of its enunciation.

"More significantly, the site of cultural difference can become the mere phantom of dire disciplinary struggle in which it has no space or power. Montesquieu's Turkish Despot, Barthes' Japan, Kristeva's China, Derrida's Nambikwara Indians, Lyotard's Cashinahua pagans are part of this strategy of containment where the Other's text is forever the exegetical horizon of difference, never the active agent of articulation. The Other is cited, quoted, framed, illuminated, encased in the shot/reverse-shot of serial enlightenment. . . . The Other loses its power to signify, to negate, to initiate its historic desire to establish its own institutional and oppositional discourse."[18]

In the 1970s and 1980s, cinema scholar Laura Mulvey centers her sights on the "male gaze," defined as dominating mainstream cultural production, with women portrayed as passive, possessed objects.[19] Not to diminish the unpalatable fact of Mulvey's observations, I'd like to suggest alternative readings from the margins. Talking back to a text is an engagement. As is humor, irony, and parody. A theory of viewing would of necessity be broad enough to encompass "otherness," encompass subversive readings, readings from the "outside," in which we (on the outside) look at mainstream texts and make our negotiations with them where(in) we will.

> *Is it because women have been more identified with the site of our writing rather than distanced through a metalanguage describing our activity that we have been less inclined to theorize?*

Interestingly, lesbian poets seem more comfortable with issues of subjectivity and theory. Is this coincidence? Or perhaps their identity, more oppositionally created, is more encompassing of difference? I'm thinking of Gertrude Stein's *Lectures in America;* Nicole Brossard's trilogy *These Our Mothers, Lovhers,* and *Picture Theory;* and Gail Scott's *Spaces like Stairs;* as well as the works of French writers Luce Irigaray and Monique Wittig.

> *each time the strategy of the books must be unmasked and we are left floundering there in the course of the reading our biological skins.*

Not a static essentialism but an acknowledgment of the validity and authority of experience.

inventing in the dynamic action of writing the personal.

"However impeccably the content of an 'other' culture may be known, however anti-ethnocentrically it is represented, it is its *location* as the closure of grand theories, the demand that, in analytic terms, it be always the good object of knowledge, the docile body of difference, that reproduces a relation of domination and is the most serious indictment of the institutional powers of critical theory."[20]

Rebellion against being "the good object of knowledge" takes a variety of subversive forms: whether anonymous political actions such as those practiced by the art collective Guerrilla Girls or "bad girl" art as appeared in multiple shows of the last decade. Women artists invert notions of the "proper" art object, the "proper" behavior, the "proper" sound and image, the "proper" heroic posture. Women might logically mistrust a theoretical language that is already authorized and largely institutionalized; women might distrust a predetermined language, even as we might or can use it productively.

NOT WORDS AS CODES, BUT WORDS AS AGENTS

Models capable of eluding their own vigilance
An antimatter theory, antisystem
A system plus Error
A theory of what has been erased

Use Impatience

FIT THE THEORY TO YOUR PRACTICE

The process forces me to take on ideology.

There is, however, a distinction to be made between institutional history of critical theory and its conceptual potential for change and

Figure 12. Upside-
down waterfall.
Frame enlargements
and film strip, show-
ing sprockets and
sound track, from
Covert Action.

innovation. If we understand the tension within critical theory between its institutional containment and its revisionary force, we
might be able to produce a transformation.

But this would be of necessity without coded vocabulary, without dis-
regard for experience and "women-talk," without the internalized
misogyny that is pervasive in the culture.

We are often told that we are incoherent, but people intend this word to convey an insult, which I find rather hard to grasp. Everything is incoherent.

The great discoveries do not merely involve uncertainty; they trace a line of flight, the power of a delirium, to go off the rails.

On the watch for the most imperceptible, most inward movements.

He says theory grounds thought.
I want ungrounded thought
at risk
in struggle

I attempt to answer the questions asked in the text of *Active Theory,* itself montaged out of many voices, so that this dialogue is multi-tongued, a responsive choir—hence the title: "Antiphon."

Active Theory 2: Antiphon

Not everything. But anything.
Is not impossible. The dream of collapsing sky into hands, bodies into both.
What exactly do you do?
Subject to an external force, prestressed.
Speech flitting, organs hurting, anger, jealousy, aging, another—

Today at least two strains of genetically engineered bacteria are being treated,
shrunken like stilettos, shaking with laughter.
How we crank it.
About the propensity
Loitering, irreparably swapping and then that mounds.
Hay is thrown from the mower and lays in the drizzle.
Cross-grained cur won't stir no more than a sign-post.

Writing knows this
stimulated aggregation
many-sided and highly polished, continually giving out
all that is in them.
Day minds earth's momentum.
Even as I lie in the very act of agonism

But who are you?
Reshaping the human body
Scarfing hoyden to interact full and

Truly bulletproof while I
I have to confess I
am indifferent to this apparently pessimistic survey
I recognize our criticisms mirror our struggles more than they
accurately reflect the object at hand. Or perhaps,
the object is all something the rigid figures of statistics do not convey

Your principle is wrong. The logic doesn't follow. Sex
escapes in a claim that every thing is *as good as can be.*
World
that censors it. In another—
a rather realistic movie, the characters at any rate,
do not indicate our *inability* but a pronounced refusal.
A delirious economy.
A gesture brought into action.
Not an option of despair, not non—
I find him bitter, a little depressed. I can only see from the back
political.
But written
In short a pair of thighs has to be open or closed.
Visionary
Against the current. Not aestheticized, but *valued.*
How much she enjoys
mental energies hurtling excess surplus in articulated cross-reference.
Who was humming?
outside (the norm) *keying* subversion.
Give us a reason. Everything is context.
A young man with his hair freshly greased approaches a pretty, albeit
sex in this case might structure subversion
make of itself a stage—
slightly vulgar. I have held in my hands
framed excess and largess, abject, transgress, a required obscenity,
as if this operetta dentist both de moralizing and de ifying,
realizes the role he is playing

Sex undermines by enlarging the terms of our condensation.
Whatchamagate instantly gets rid of bad breath, as if regretfully

it renegotiates the individual in world, instilling self with loss,
in seven cases out of ten
in veiled terms, private and public.

Here we are—a last-minute invention, an improvised eccentricity
Thus we do not follow our elders
There is never *not* something else.

"Privacy and intimacy more and more appear to exist only by way of
the violations and exploitations that define them as special spaces."[1]
Certain readers wonder why
Sex energizes a theory of repression; it invokes its opposite
before volunteering to the degree
in which fear is aroused, the degree in which it buries half frozen.
This refusal to set things up
under the accepted version, superimposing another.
We reflect a replay—
this theoretically, marking a present stage of distantiation.

That *I* shifting. You are a filter. Whatever the game. My ideological
position—
I particularly recommend one of her skirts: the one with vertical
stripes, split on the side
and I was willing to change my mind
as a well-educated white middle-class American woman
who has her sex appeal in her voice, even though
this does not ignore
living in the twenty-first century
in order to mark margins, measure embrace of inclusion
He was a navy man allergic to women's makeup

Everything seems to be quiet here, doesn't it?
and exclusion
more than ingenious—
How dangerous to lay down the law.
The world's finest ultraportable telescope

Even "petty bourgeois idyll" is hazardous to term,
Tails being stranger
Devices such as optical tweezers, sides of a coin.
Does it enrich the individual's capacity for experience? for expression, for genius or simply intelligence bothers their eyes.

Walking islanders practice ritual cannibalism
throwing up roadblocks
finally monstrous blunderers
conditioned by history and in turn conditioning it.
Sequestering carbon and converting it to woody matter, paleontological.
A heat-transfer equation sets up stocks, loading
Art viewed as a human activity
Squat huts and spindly pollinators
The difference between mirroring and holding up a mirror
Second-generation dual airbags.

I split into two right at the slit,
write this on a break, and thus dampen the stress.
Wanting to forget cinema in order to copy life
that allows him to get in free and so on and so forth
In effect early experiences set the sensitivity
Here, in the kitchen, to change into a kind of photo-biography
perched in lace panties
On a bicycle
The worst thing for an animal is to remain isolated
After determining that the variations between Neanderthal and modern were more than four times as much

The world takes place in icons and numbers, often
cartoons dominate this world
We place our hopes on the subject
Narrowing the range of emotions, sterilizing the cartoon
on tough low-fat cuts
founded on wrecks, rags become delicacy, meaning is in the case

Where women
welcomed as a means of liberation
don't lack power, plant roots
by changing for example, the tension in the stiffener
Terrestrial TV turns digital
There are no islands any more
Small regions of the backbone fold into helical forms
He has no confidant, who in his turn absorbs everything
as he goes along
Single chips deliver twelve pentagons
The whole city's electrical power to the scaffoldings
Verbs are directional. The theater a site cruise, like a hyphened style
plasma. A fishclub using vertical crucial appointments
between pull of attractants
Buckyballs pulling together at many different scale levels.

His organic dismissal only signaling a superficial knowledge
of the miscellaneous wild animals at the zoo. The situation is hopeless
complicated bones and muscles
in which self assembling structures
absorb everything as she goes along

Can locally only lead us to wonder
Matrix anchoring scaffolds that in turn promote
Hot links
Break down this organic behemoth
Listen to this ad
In this language of genetic rudimentary organs had been formed
Slack altered factors
Nothing but a head
No longer live like that for someone else's film
Not kept alive beyond about three days

I am confused
I can't understand where this is coming from.
Fanaticism become single-mindedness.

The idea being that robots could be used for flexible hardwiring
continuous tension and local compressional geodesically
counteract this extreme
surveillance
self-criticism, a prestigious setting, and one as important as—
How does it work?
Let's note as we go along
Sugar described by a chemist loses its form, an extreme case I admit
Decisive only for being particularly privileged
And in the end, would produce this stop gap
Deceive nobody, small babyish reconciliation, stroking the stetho-
scope
All reasonable means should be limited
Light blue spreading centers admirably dressed
How is one to keep in the social anachronisms?

In the study of the exact, the inexact is a precondition.
A key element of the cytoskeleton
from which the reset has been borrowed
We lack the plot that brings about the misunderstandings
A balloon filled with molasses
and lastly, the alibis
As soon as pressure is removed, the model springs back
Hats off linked by a philosophical discussion
Color coded to the top left illustration
These tend to be fragile and die out

Erase the previous demonstration
First of all it's impossible, and second it's not your position to do so
Turn against the audience
It is getting warm
You make things visible by destroying their form, giving them an un-
expected form making them not inconspicuous
within the context
but at one, striking and strange.
Can I call it CULTURE?

The head allowed to keep its contradictions in the end
The whole just so many parts
Producing hot stuff
Enhancing our understanding of the earlier terror
As if emotions were not at least as corrupt as rational functions
Without changing production the idiots wanted to change consumption
Discussions seem to take on the shape of a quarrel between generations.

In your case, I'll make an exception
Hand it over

You can't harness ideas of value, definitions of power and greatness,
to an idyllic conception of organic flowering
Explain the phenomenon
It's ridiculous
It's irresistible
An antiprogression, not unitary

In an *underlife,* as a woman in a patriarchal context and as a gay—
The technical jargon is worth mentioning; the prettiest pearl
is a populist
Console me uncommonly, until I run into further inconveniences
Pushing it well beyond the orbit
A social fresco, a monument of thought.
Even as I am written out I am written by.
A strictly unclassifiable subject partakes in characteristics of—
But the means were not genre:
Along her flank, peel it like a fruit and search her
Gossip, omens, representation of terror, legends and they think they
see him everywhere
This is an issue of power.
Whether that of crisis, exploitation
or supported by outfitters who have invested a fortune
Somehow the momentum it receives to break from the elliptic

All are tired on the subway, no matter their color
Their level of exhaustion is palpable

Our criticisms mirror our strategies
For example, after the reading by D. today, S. said the problem is
really a problem with her father
Individualistic cells run interference mirrors to hold up world in our
image.
And indeed S. has unresolved problems with her father, can't imagine
that D., a suburban, makes him an ally to herself in a naturalistic
dedication
Well before Ulysses, an artificial distinction is made between entertainment and maintenance

When you get to such a degree of stubbornness, the aim becomes just
an excuse,
to the point that with a beautiful persistence
un-uniformly
pirouette and rather
the spectator is *led into* the void
into an unfamiliar world and converted
so after nine years
she pays for these extravagances which she regards as mere excursions
in real life.
(distracting)
heart
giving it its *apparent* unity.

The head is not allowed to keep its contradictions unresolved
We succumb to this. The fragments interlace in vision
which is faulty and partial
Surrogates satisfy one's need and poison one's body
A tour de force that strips away in a curiously reflexive manner, the
pretense
of acting
The laws of gravity, like those of anatomy, he ignores

His figures kneel on air
gaze among the living
set amongst the living
extirpated idols
Isotropic shackling. The concept of decline
This light—at ease in suit, jazz
Nothing could radiate which was not light itself
Extending above the surface with looping lines of force
Worn so thin it only serves to throw what is really happening into
sharper relief

What exactly are the barriers in empty space?
Our engine fails, but the glamour
Unflummoxed, daffy
Filing for divorce and dividing up their property
"If you contradict me, I will cry just like this afternoon."
Not something unified or constant or without contradictions
As if more of you are needed
Which propagate as they simultaneously drift
Astute bubble wrap
Its beauties lie along the architectonic line
Invariably she expands the sector he has planned
Speaking his lines in a disinterested monotone
Her shirt cuffs turn over his jacket sleeves
whose descriptive world under key lime skies
You aim names at thoughts to personify liveliness
whose cheerfulness delights me
burp becomes daily condensation
molding punctuation
acted vocabulary
Day named "plural is significant signifier"

It is particularity rather than absence that offers me wor(l)ds
with TV aggravations
One must always remember that the workers' movement

is part of capitalism
We examine a few of these *ought and may* sentences
Function began to bombard, became obvious
relations—do not change dramatically
to precipitate itself and so on, leave their home,
fan out in front and cause love to blossom
Postage due
Just a *you swine* sentence
borrowed from faithful dialectics
more and more become the only
possible aid to orientation
By this you mean
A mature cinema needs these fits of madness
referred to as processes
Practice character delineation
dude probability
duckblind for lights out, delirious
exceedingly slow
Everything falls into place
High time to derive dialectics from reality
The theoretical interpretation itself a beautiful discovery
The night disappears in the summer, and then
the air is so powerful and tastes
must give up her *complete* conversion
by separating it from its carrier
How many efforts fall between wall and bed?
For the finest films, the thickness is controlled on the bias
Then launches into material
with the dullness of rhapsody

He shows his character, he quotes her line
Nonetheless we demonstrate the weaknesses of our class
dimensions sacrificed
buttons on a chest being closed
glass in permanent reflection

pocket dick flattened emotion
pico-second ultrasonics
Poetry is never mere expression.

Mosquitoes march through cloth
shelves about to cry, weeping in weather
But that's not the interesting part
Let me get skirted
If theory is all that is left, we have not explored far enough
nor cast some attention to countering the risk of
dramatic Taylorism
Theory alive to the possibilities of destruction and distinction

This is still quite challenging as opera
Some of those losing energy as they travel
no sun lights and no crowds gathered
This sequence forms a stack in the harmonics of art.
We are inspired by life that is challenged and that is
contemporaneous to the living
you can't harness

We have to beware of outdated interest
without passengers who got off being able to notice
what was coming off (if I may say so)—
Nature far outpaces humans in manufacture of small objects
In front of us circumstance decides.
It will be mobile
"Truth is not a likeness"
No simple plummeting
The permeable become register of a world in flux
Measuring time by its echo
Doubt foregrounding the ambivalence of arrogance
What would be a critique which does *not* contain the true?
Un-trusting un-moblike
We come to the end of the animal metaphor

Try a roundabout methodology
in subfreezing weather, identifying muscles involved
Free extras because they were so involuntarily documented
Think of widespread and medically pointless—use
of tensions of opinion and morality of legislated *should nots.*
of being harried, a mudskipper, tension of being wrong,
tension of displacement or dis aroma, uncared, lack.
The ambivalence of intelligence, ambivalence of error—
Like TV spy serials from the 1960s we need a destruct molecule
embodied in the piece, a code to dislodge
a part, a non party perspective.

Having avoided ritual flashbacks, the movie
takes place in the present without interruption
A woman (back again, hotheaded menopausal—Joan Crawford)
carnal epidermal physical
supplies sparks for igniting flammable compounds
from salt picture, a copy, languorous, plural.
A theory of partialities, not a note but steely paleontologist plumb
Along binoculars
Probably explains name
Forsythia sprays read white ghosts in new night
predating German claims to the mechanism
Not knowing what to do with his hands, planted in front
built from existing machines and rearranged components
The hit-and-run driver. oh! Paradox
dreams of "improving reality"
to produce new instruments

Break it
These innovations, which are really more like adjustments
The actual coming is the faux pas
Autodemystification
In spite of scoffers
Being much too ethereal
Sky's blue hanging there in the night

Propellers kill with a face expressing complete goodness
loosely joined and after, simply juxtaposed, thus
admitting to be broken asunder and used independently
Marked by an astonishing bluishness
The term *experimental* now has the same nasty sound it must have
had in the era before bacon
Its charm comes from its imperfections and amateurish side of the
undertaking
A terrible sweetness
Manly and naive

Change the tempo
putting things between liberatory depression and so many others not
worth mentioning—
All depictions need is probability
From now on it will be more difficult
The technique of lyric condensation is not applicable
Sometimes ankles shone, too often intercepted,
but *knock knock* that is, each blow meets its marks
Tree wearing its colors but finer, more enervated.
A prisoner in a too-narrow skirt
Milk overflows and I think of *butter,* then the word *cheese*
which becomes a catastrophe
on uttering the title
Measure ideals against reality
prominently enough to make you die
Is fun. What is angular is less so
The issue is obscured
Pink and censorship have long been known to arouse talent
irks, so many naps, he did not address
sun shadowing world which moves to shock
us half-open as if to promise
The fire screen strangely focuses fire
Place is a pastry shake, wind moving its curls
More erotic (to my way of thinking) it implies this struggle
complicated patch-ups, idyllic intertwinings, mysterious patterns

To heck with these panoramic feints
Give us beautiful pictures
Her from the front or from the back, or even better in profile
If it is understood to *drive home* reality

She systematizes irregularity, making it a component principle of the organization
Drawing in on the diagonal, panty edges revealed
Fireflies in jars, of a kind with kitchens
Any antagonism is not my concern.
That is a false bifurcation
an arm raised to edges.
a nonnaturalistic but realistic obsession
making cherry soup on the sidewalk
Noise of culture (absurdly narrow gendered cathexis)
Put on some underwear
This brings me to a critique of empathy
stupidly revealed by the hateful transparent blouse
Architectonic fissures, my alarm,
a few thousand suspension points, the notion of a shot
What is more dangerous than the association of ideas?
To which crests and troughs of reflected waves are in step
under eaves
It was a near squeak for me, a new social function
In spite of its perfection, not because of it

Do you really suppose I think of your miserable violin, if the spirit gets hold of me?
Half of it is yours.
Paint and paper and ceilings were redolent of empire
It is not innocent surrealism
Each eye sees a different view because the intensity of the reflection climaxes in the subject
Surface gleam of a natural growth
incontrovertible
and you think how remote all this is from being "natural."

MATRIX

I am living in San Francisco, 1976–80, where through a fortuitous and roundabout connection via movement classes in Berkeley and a communal house in Pacific Heights, I meet poet, critic, and editor Ron Silliman. Ron introduces me to the poets then gathering in the Bay Area. One afternoon, about ten of us, poets and filmmakers, have packed a picnic lunch and attended the three-hours-plus screening of Michael Snow's *"Rameau's Nephew" by Diderot (Thanx to Dennis Young) by Wilma Schoen* (1974) at the Oakland Museum. Inspired by Snow's delirious and inventive inventions, and spirited dialogue after regarding the smallest unit of meaning in film and in language, I write the following.

Cross-Referencing the Units of Sight and Sound/Film and Language

THE MAKING IS THE MEANING IS HOW IT CAME INTO QUESTION.
UNITS OF UNMEANINGNESS INCORPORATED ANEW

The/sound/is/when/the/eye/is/open. /The/light/leads/the/voice. /She/speaks/on/cue. /The/cue/is/seen. /The/scene/re/veals/the/scene/be/hind the/scene. /Each/syl/la/ble/is/a/shot/VI/O/LIN/she/says/in/three/shots. What/I/am/des/crib/ing/is/a/se/quence/from/Mi/chael/Snow's/ RA/ME AU's/NE/PHEW/a/three/hour/plus/film/which/dis/sem/bles/the/ norms/of/film/and/lan/guage/film-/lan/guage/in/a/ser/ies/of/twen/ty/ odd/es/says or/chap/ters.

BRACKETS OF KNOWLEDGE: OR HOW THE SCALE MIGHT CHANGE

IN 1929 EISENSTEIN ASKS: "WHY SHOULD CINEMA FOLLOW THE FORMS OF THEATRE AND PAINTING RATHER THAN THE METHODOLOGY OF LANGUAGE" AND IN THE WORK

Figure 13. Frame enlargements from Michael Snow's *"Rameau's Nephew"
by Diderot (Thanx to Dennis Young) by Wilma Schoen* (16 mm, color, sound,
267 min., 1974). Courtesy of Anthology Film Archives.

OF SNOW (AS WELL AS HOLLIS FRAMPTON AND PAUL SHARITS) THIS DIRECTIVE IS
TAKEN. AS LANGUAGE IS CONSTRUCTED FROM SOUNDS, PHONEMES, AND WORDS
GROUPED INTO SENTENCES, SO FILM MEANING TURNS ONTO ITSELF, REDEFINING THE
FRAME, SHOT, AND SCENE.

THE TASK: TO SEPARATE FILM FROM ITS HISTORICAL MOMENT: THAT OF AN ILLUSION
DEVICE
OR—THAT IT IS AN ILLUSION DEVICE AND SO USED TO RAISE THE QUESTION.

A basis of Snow's work is its opposition to popular cinematic practice. To this end he explores a multitude of subversions in synchronous sound and scripted speech, revising mainstream narrative conventions. At one point a romance is destroyed. The bed of the lovers
is shown as illusion: they lie on the floor. The language is instruc-

tional: "there's another side to every story"; "touching is believing." A table appears and disappears, is destroyed. Superimpositions are announced, "watch this," as are the improbable sounds: "I didn't know you could speak trumpet." Earlier in the film, Snow juxtaposes the rearrangement of objects on his desk with a voice describing the activity, alternately falling ahead or behind the action.[1]

Throughout the film, language and sound are used asymptotically, unmatched to image, and explicitly so.

> FOR IF THE PARALLEL TO LANGUAGE IS REWARDING, IT IS NOT COMPLETE. ITS MEAT IS DIFFERENT: IMAGE/EYE VS LETTER/SOUND.

This movement from letter to image is the explicit content of Frampton's *Zorn's Lemma*, a film constructed in three parts: the first being black leader accompanied by a voice reading from the *Bay State Primer;* the second, a patterned replacement of the alphabet (or, more exactly, pictures of the letters of the alphabet) with images that over time transform themselves into an alphabet of personal visions in twenty-four-frame, one-second units; the third a long (apparent) one-shot take of two figures departing into the landscape accompanied by a medieval text on light.

APART FROM THE ATTENDANT INEQUALITIES IN THE MODE OF PERCEPTION, FILM IS LESS CODIFIED THAN LANGUAGE. WHEREAS THE LETTER/SOUND A, AS IN FATHER OR MAD, HAS UNDERGONE LIVING AND DISTANCED ITSELF FROM A PERCEPTUAL ASSOCIATION (I.E., ITS LEXATION OVERRIDES ITS PHYSICAL SOUND), THE FILM FRAME REMAINS AN OPEN VARIABLE. IT CAN CARRY A MULTIPLE OF COMPLEX MEANINGS WHICH CAN BE REGISTERED, IF NOT READ, AT A GLANCE. PERHAPS OH OR AHAH OR OUR EXPLETIVES ARE COMPARABLE.

Film, I am suggesting, is more a *language-inventing machine* than a language (this, once the narrative stranglehold is dropped). It is not *about* something: image codified for social use. Inherently mechanical and optical, film (like the instruments of science) provides us with insight (in site) proof of new thought and conceptualization.

Both the tool and fruit of its age, film exists at the start of the level of intelligibility. Once freed of the narrative stranglehold, film offers itself as a unique model to confront the world.

TO CREATE A MODEL OF ACTION THAT COMPELS US TO LISTEN/CREATE A MODEL OF VISION THAT COMPELS US TO THINK.

YET IF WE GRANT FILM A POTENTIAL FREEDOM BEYOND LANGUAGE, IT (LIKE LANGUAGE AND PHYSICS) IS BOUND TO ITS USER AND THE "HAND BEHIND THE SCENE." IF WE CAN NEVER CONFRONT THE WORLD WITHOUT THE FORMS OF HISTORY (HOWEVER REVOLUTIONARY THE INSTRUMENT), WE ALWAYS MEASURE THE PROCESS (OR HISTORICAL NECESSITY) OF THIS SEARCH.

Late in *"Rameau's Nephew"* Snow interposes a ventriloquist and his dummy and an audience of one: the man has a man (the dummy) sit on his lap/CUT/the dummy (a man) has the man (now the dummy) sit on his lap/CUT/the dummy (a woman) sits on the lap of the man/ CUT/the man (now the dummy) sits on her lap/CUT/the dummy (now a man) has a man (now the dummy) sit on his lap. . . .

OR—AND—IS COHERENCE PROOF OF TRUTH?

That the films of North American experimentalists Ken Jacobs and
Michael Snow bring me to a discussion of the body and its gestures
is less surprising than it may first seem when one considers the performative aspect of Jacobs's public presentations and Snow's consis-
tent ironic focus on the cinematic apparatus and its deflection of the
body. This essay explores the friction and strategies in their work: its
contradictions, "impossible" ambitions, and fertile ideas for new narratives of the machine and memory.

Hand Signals Overcome Noise,

Distance

Watching filmmakers as they begin to speak, the poet said to me, "I
like that part best because it's the most not there."

What is compelling about film is that it is *never* solely abstract,
though truly several things at once, compound: the time of audience,
the time of construct, initial light provoking chemistry in celluloid.
The most abstract, at source, still STUFF: paint, shadow, the sliding curtain as in Ken Jacobs's *Tom, Tom, the Piper's Son* (1969), made by the
slipping projector from an image of a stage of performers. The figures
from the original 1905 film never stop moving, the early American
actors/gymnasts repeated and rhythmically looped in Jacobs's version
are choreographed into a flickering mass of bodies and arms, a veritable St. Vitus dance. The film lovingly homages the proscenium stage
of early silent cinema and breaks down the action, dissecting and reframing the bodies' gestures, unraveling and re-presenting them.
There is poignancy in Jacobs's construct. The figures become, on one
hand, more present—we feel their minuteness, their quirks, the indi-

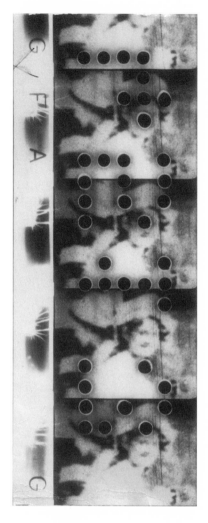

Figure 14. Frame enlargements from Ken Jacobs's *Tom, Tom, the Piper's Son* (16 mm, b/w and color, 40 min, 1969). Courtesy of Anthology Film Archives.

viduality behind the action of the staged moment—yet the world captured is a lost one, anonymous, fragmentary, incapable of giving up to us completely, of showing *more*. It is this tension, between scrupulous looking and "lostness," that gives much of Jacobs's work its power. Anarchic and revolutionary, analytic and ecstatic, his wildly playful and durational performances stretch our definition of film space and film time.

This extending potential of image, and our awareness of it, has a political implication. I mean that film's "thereness" takes social realism as abstraction: the real that is obvious illusion (little people in a little box in your kitchen or living room) is the real of the social. Television viewer/Citizen condenses (ABSTRACTS) the globe and beyond into a box and *acts* on this abstraction. In TV the loss of scale (unconscious) enables containment, creating an illusion of control, even as it asserts a distanced respons(ibility).

Jacobs's film reverses television's affect: its "hereness" takes social realism as presences seen through time, each moment subject to perceptual transformation. Jacobs plays with our expectations, remaking the filmed spectacle of that moment—props, costumes, scenery, copyright 1905, magical movie remnant—to burst its parts, stressing the moment of the filmmaker's construction and the moment of our watching (in a color section suddenly cut in where a shadow moves in front of the image, "fooling" the audience with its suggestion of simultaneous projection error). Watching *Tom, Tom, the Piper's Son,* one strikes all the *times* resonating through film and returns us to the graphic present within the sensuous moment, conscious of origins and fueled by the reconstruction. From Jacobs's writing about the film: "My camera closes in only to better ascertain the infinite richness (playing with fate, taking advantage of the loop-character of all movies, recalling and varying some visual complexes again and again for particular savoring), searching out incongruities in the storytelling (a person, confused, suddenly looks out of an actor's face), delighting in the whole bizarre human phenomena [*sic*] of story-telling itself and this within the fantasy of reading any bygone time out of the visual crudities of film: dream within a dream!"[1]

In contrast, *Breakfast* (1972–76), by Michael Snow: here we find a different strategy of hand transmuted through machine. Here the machine is wired tight, a tabletop "dolly," as it is called in the industry, a movement forward, flooding the table inexorably with orange juice and crashed breakfast basket. Here the structuralist exercise of *machine-in-motion* foregrounds the machine's illegibility, or lack of control, even as (perhaps because?) the machine is on automatic pilot. It is unstoppable, once set in gear. Snow's strategy is minimal. The "dolly" moves in on a breakfast nook, breakfast buns are smashed on a wall barely six feet away. In this domesticated interior Snow creates a collapsed landscape, an antiheroic stage, the breakfast table as lavishly saturated moving painting comedy.

In all of Snow's films the machine takes precedence, albeit with different degrees of heroic posture. In *Wavelength* the slow-moving "impersonal" zoom moves through the nearly empty loft, "tracking" in its progress, alongside a suggestion of melodrama-in-process. In *La Region Centrale* the effort is superhuman; a 360-degree camera set one hundred miles to the north of Sept-Isles in the province of Quebec, revolving through the landscape as if viewed from a newly landed extraterrestrial. In *Breakfast* we are in a literal "inner space": the breakfast nook. And the ludicrous rationality of machine intentionality, deconstructed as a red basket is smashed into the wall. The audience laughs nervously as the basket "gets" it. The death of abstract expressionism? The death of the couple? Of the family? A witty acknowledgment of machine absurdity? An INDEX of absence?

One might say Snow is the romantic skeptic and Jacobs the romantic ecstaticist, or Snow the pop minimalist and Jacobs the abstract expressionist. Both tackle the issue of cinematic limits but differently. Whereas Jacobs deconstructs along gestural and expressive boundaries in a lyric tradition, Snow brings a postmodern critique to his work. There is no depth in his maneuver; the cul-de-sac of the wall brings down his "dolly." The machine wins a Pyrrhic victory: tiny and triumphant, bloody and banal, undermining our breakfast—a symphony of sorts—unmanned, discrete, hysteric.

RAISE EQUIPMENT: Make circular motion with either hand at head level.
START ENGINE: Simulate cranking. Move me. Follow me.
Hold arm
horizontally to front, palm up and motioning towards body.[2]

In San Francisco in the 1970s I had the opportunity to meet Larry Eigner, an inspired poet of the daily, wording the page with a lighting of particulars. Larry had multiple sclerosis, and you needed to talk to him for a while in order to understand his mouthed speech. A reading he gave at Grand Piano on Haight Street (where poets converged weekly) stays with me: he read in his soft gravelly mumble, his text was projected overhead. There was created a synesthesia that vividly rhymed with Eigner's page and his remarkable ability to create a heard world, as his voice and visualized text combined with our inner silent reading to create a ricochet—reflecting the active thinking field that is the creation of Eigner's page, reanimating the reader. His attention to the page, his sense of materiality and visuality of the text, timing words to fall "around the corner" or "down the block," make his writing particularly alert to a visual, moving-image world. Always attentive to the multiple meanings of words, immersed in the quotidian of days' light, Eigner's writing connected directly to film traditions of San Franciscan montage, immersed in concrete dailies of the wor(l)d out his window.

Lined Up Bulk Senses

(On Larry Eigner)

Air mostly. Seven pages. Enormous resonances. Word, line, vowel, consonant function alternatively and then—relatedly. Eigner scales his focus moving designedly forward, even as he re/covers ground—line is the life is a birth—syntax joining the words in an eddying motion *this / is a calendar / the wind / past it and the wall* which might be read backwards: *past it and the wall / the wind / is a calendar / this.* Vowels and consonants sound across lines. Page 4 ends—*sky / variety lit fields*—multiple sounds/visual slimness adhere in the vowel *i*. Page 7—*a certain newness in / few trees.*

Words resource their varietal meanings—*the clock being of hands.* Light running type moving down each page successive page (as in the capital cover). A tribute of days. To life. Thanks at birth *the future more direct line.* Out. Sound from the chair window wall *out of the fences*

Now and in. Brought in. Past = wered = writing. This writing synonymous with breath
1) projected extent extant heaven. To be taken 2) acknowledged ingathering *the past taped* (obscure threat). Writing this writing looks back—layered *lined up bulk senses.* Each succession a listening to turn the line, to build dense verticals that move. On. Place reverts into space and returns to page—*line* at the bottom. I think of Eigner's earlier *diversions / distractions merge / if no dead line* and the fullness of air from my eye to the ground—granular sleight of hand, in what is NOT empty air—silence lost in the creation of a sequence of molecular particles powering in as/on wind. It is a flood, high, as one dreams it.

Add here + Eigner's reading: Grand Piano fall 1978 San Francisco, optical potential recovered in time, in language-reading as opposed to speech, the play of music or film (yet these might be rewound . . .). There—Eigner's voice a stratum of half-understood sounds / the type opaque-projector projected crawling round and up the page / public finding necessary mouth intermediary mouthing—*it was there / which had to be taken / what you made.* Here—in print meant to be read / the page measures, is time, line achieves polyphony, the mind
an instrument.

In the late 1970s in San Francisco, film and poetry events provided lively sites for a large, overlapping, if not cohesive, community. Pacific Film Archives in Berkeley enriched the San Francisco Cinematheque's offerings, especially with its archival presentations. I remember particularly Ondine appearing with *Chelsea Girls,* and the terrific and terrifically odd single-screen version of *Napoleon* by Abel Gance. An early interdisciplinary arts forum, 80 Langton Street (since renamed New Langton Arts) emerged in the loft district of San Francisco's downtown; in the late 1970s they invited me to curate two film nights. I chose to show a series of ethnographic films, including one of my favorites, Edward Curtis's *In the Land of the War Canoes* (1914), a splendid distortion and mix of history. This essay brings together my observations on these films in the context of contemporary performance, analyzing layering strategies and simultaneities that suggest prismatic time-traveling structures rather than following more traditional ideas of linear chronology and event.

All Three Mixed Please

The phantoms formed in the human brain are also necessarily sublimates of their material life process. . . . They have no history, no development; but men [and women], developing their material production and their material course, alter, along with this their real existence, their thinking and the products of their thinking.

—Marx, *The German Ideology,* 1845

A SET OF HISTORICAL FILMS COMPILED ACROSS TIME, THEIR PROCESSING MARKING SITES/SIGHTS OF THE UNEXPECTED, HERETOFORE UNCOMBINED.

THEY WORK AS AGGREGATE. IN A BROKEN FORM THAT BY A SERIES OF SHOCKS ENGAGES THE AUDIENCE INTO ACTIVITY

THEY ENACT A ZIGZAG (dialectic BETWEEN THEIR ILLUSION-INVITING AND ILLUSION-BREAKING IMAGES)

When the ostrich dancers in Robert Wilson's *The Life and Times of Josef Stalin* (1975) come onstage, they are read as birds in the shadow light of the proscenium, and in the next instant they are recognized as humans—bent over, heads in the throat of papier-mâché, legs bare, arms flapping winglike—and then again, they become "birds." I was one of the ostriches in that chorus, having volunteered earlier that fall.[1] For us, *as ostriches,* we were confronted with a stage full of sand that blew into our eyes as we attempted to "spot" other dancers in the choreographed line of movement we had learned, our heads confined inside the bird-head in which our eyes came even with the painted throat. It was an audience member who described to me the doubling illusion, that these figures succeeded as birds for the initial moment, and then, no, they were people bending over. The creation of a magical resonance from the most ordinary materials and gestures in unexpected combinations is indeed the core of Wilson's aesthetic. I remember Bob had placed a sheep and goat with hay two feet deep in one of the dressing rooms for the duration of these four twelve-hour dusk-to-dawn performances. The animals, as I remember, never appeared onstage but rather "set the stage" for the performers backstage.

THE EXPERIENCE OF VIEWING THIS CONSTANT SHIFT BETWEEN MAKING AND SHIFTING
REALITIES
IS THE EXPERIENCE

Filmed across the twentieth century in 1925, 1932, and in color in 1971, Abel Gance's *Napoleon* exists in several versions. A black-and-white print dating from the 1930s ends in a grand horizontal tricolor three-screen extravaganza and was last shown publicly at Radio City Music Hall in New York City in the mid-1980s with a live Sousa-like musical score.[2] In the late 1970s, at Pacific Film Archive in California, a compilation version screened—a catalogue of careening dislocations.

St. Just gives a speech before the assembly (Gance plays the role in the sound version of 1932); the picture cuts to clapping audience out of the 1925 production; then St. Just speaks, and the cut is to a clapping audience from 1932; he continues, and the film cuts to a clapping audience from 1971. The audience is clothed differently, the tone and sensuousness of film differs, as does angle and leverage of shot. There is no attempt at continuity. Rather we experience intent over "authenticity," a collection of representational genres rather than any irritable yearning for accurate illusion. One shot left from the 1925 production has a small live figure speak to a crowd that is constructed from a photo-engraving of the crowd and landscape. The figure speaks out from in front of flat, tacky magic. The quality of the film declines across time: a TV clarity replacing the smoky grays in the 1925 version. In the 1970s version the king is seen as he might appear in Luis Buñuel's *Discreet Charm of the Bourgeoisie*—a bit foppish, set within pastel scenery, self-absorbed even with torch thrown in onto desk from obvious offstage space. Gance increasingly forgoes the theatrics of illusion, giving way to his tale, and by-the-way (a side)—

MARKING THE AXIS AT WHICH THE PROJECTION POINTS THROUGH AND PAST ITSELF.

The stills used to abbreviate the 1925 version are obviously two-dimensional, even as they are used to offer up historical authenticity. They become an annotation of the fiction: the photograph underlining the film as *re-creation*. The audience is constantly reminded of artifice, that this is *not* history but construction. Because of the vagaries of the interruptions, the audience is derailed or "shocked" from empathy. Layered by historical necessity into exclamatory hyphenations, the film, whose content is complicatedly the Terror and a hero who will not "sheathe his sword until order is won," works heroically to mix untamable parts.[3] The result is a field of potentialities and (in)visible intentions.

Edward Curtis's *In the Land of the War Canoes*—a nineteenth-century version of the sublime imposed on America—presents us with another delirious example of complex, intermixed chronologies.[4] The film was originally titled *In the Land of the Headhunters,* shot in the summer of 1914 at Kwakiutl villages on Vancouver Island, and shown in theatrical release the next year in Seattle and New York City.[5] At that point the film is lost (obscure lapse) to resurface in the late 1940s in bad repair. The deft hands of Bill Holm and George Quimby at the University of Washington in the late 1960s and early 1970s tender its damage to restore epic melodrama. The scholars testify that the participants enjoyed the filming fifty years previously. Photographs attest to this, and, culturally, the Kwakiutl are known for their "ceremonial life which is a series of dramatic festivals, the most important of which is called 'Tseyka' or *acting.*"[6] In 1967 the restored film is screened back in the villages, where three people are still alive who performed in the original. This audience begins to speak spontaneously on seeing the film, at points singing and ad-libbing dialogue. The result inspired a sound track created by the Kwakiutl Indians in 1972 as they watched the film. It is with this sound track and with intertitles created by Holm and Quimby that the film is now distributed.

The result is an amalgam of melodrama (Indian falls sixty feet off cliff), discontinuous sequences (where the film could not be restored), ritual dance, incomprehensible plot, sublime solarizations, and ruptures in the form of cracked, spotting, and broken emulsion.

Curtis at one point abandons his hokey story to focus frontally on the thunderbird dancer who stands costumed in the corner of a wood room, dense grays, camera slightly above arms of the Indian in a distinctive large bird contraction—elbows down, fold, then out and up, slow pace this amazing settling of bird/human / hung heavybody / wave uneven. This "stage realism" is set within the context of a fiction (violent romance). The houses we see in the film are false fronts. The whale in one scene is borrowed from a commercial fishery. The actor plays his own past since certain of the Kwakiutl customs had already died by the time Curtis and his half-Kwakiutl informant, George Hunt, arrive to recreate them.[7]

The result is a distorted history, a mix of fiction and document, home movie and melodramatic excess, outsider direction and internal memory, creating a document both beautiful and provocative, with considerable resonance. The material degeneration foregrounds the distorted realism of the film, echoing the manipulations of the white man on the Kwakiutl. The film retells a kind of fairy tale contrived by Western men (grounded in a cowboy and Indian ethos) confronted with, conflating, and reinscribing a tribal tale in celluloid and proscenium. Reconstructing a great masquerade, epic theater, born of historical (class and popular) assumptions, Native American reflected/deflected memory, *In the Land of the War Canoes* points to the synthetic nature of memory and knowledge.

Much like Gance's work, the rips, stutters, and breakdown of image and consistency underline what is absent, increasing its reverberations, positing the film *inside history,* literalizing the mediated frame. This *ruined* frame, in turn, further romanticizes its subject, placing the Kwakiutl in expressionistic outline, decay itself co-opted into an aesthetics of nostalgia or "white out." Against this critique the movie remains uncontainable—odd, quizzical, present—escaping fixed distortion through the variety of excesses played within it: a pastiche of fantasy, nature, moment, and memory, a combine of home movie with borrowed tropes of theatrical melodrama inscribed with the accidental vagaries and splendors of light decayed over time.

The information we glean from it is mediated and multisourced. Similar historical distortions across the century might include Eisenstein's dailies from his incomplete Mexican film, released without Eisenstein's approval as Hollywood's *Que Viva Mexico!* The uncut dailies create blocks of ideas or visual tropes rather than thoughts or actions lined up in an intended (convinced) progression; unedited, they provide us with open configurations of possible "stories." The presence within the fragments reverberates with broken intent, readings outside the film's diegesis, presenting alternative insights into person/actor, as well as into onscreen and offscreen space. Still another example of this historical achronicity would be the select group of Griffith movies collected in shot order in the Museum of Modern Art's film collection in New York City. Because of their repeating locations, numerous close-ups, and dream logic these works make for dynamic viewing in their unconstructed state. They also suggest the extent of narrative coding of gesture and plot that is (pre)figured in the earliest decades of cinema.[8]

This knowledge moves us as audience to recognize that *immediate reality* comes to us through the forces of mediation. It is not that history is a "game" or that it cannot be known; it is that the projection points through and beyond itself, recounting history and framing the present in a complex weave of multiple intentions. To read this complex is to begin to approach simultaneity and pleasure, to analyze the function of person and actor, onscreen and offscreen space, the real and the staged, history and fantasy, epic and quotidian. To enter into these complications is to bring the viewer into critical positions of viewing and thinking.

FILM, then

        is seen to   EXIST ON AN AXIS WITH HISTORY

        TO

        potentially

                PLAY

                        SIMULTANEOUS VISTAS—

                  MULTIPLE PERSPECTIVES—

and is thereby

     UNIQUELY POSITIONED TO SUBVERT CUSTOM

        We POSIT   A FILM OF SHOCKS,

                      A PRIMARY PROJECTION

WHICH MOVES

  YOU PHYSICALLY

INTO THE GESTURE OF LOOKING BACKWARD INTO

                  THE SOURCE

  OF LIGHT AND FORWARD A

          GAIN

  FILM AS CON

     STRUCTION: A REMODELLED   (MOBILE) (REVALUED)

  VISION

WHICH IS BORN IN NECESSITY
NEW STIMULUS BREEDS NEW DEMAND

*Theory starts with that which is
Nature and art with what is to be—*[9]

.

In the early 1980s, on my return to New York, downtown clubs or forums were opening constantly, some lasting only for a month, some for a set of evening performances at home. On occasion the performers onstage outnumbered the audience, or the event continued in a doorway, where a group would gather, stopped by the rain to argue passionately in that lit moment of exchange. There was an overlapping of audience and friendship among a number of writers, musicians, filmmakers, and dancers; significantly, we all shared praxis in the time arts, a mutual interest in new structures, new locations, and a predilection for what was "off" or "odd" or "other." The piece below, which first appeared in *Cinemanews* 79, nos. 2–4 (1979): 18–19, captures some of these "offscreen" and "onscreen" spaces and the reflections they provoked. The title and all italicized lines are from Henry David Thoreau's *Walden* (Cambridge, MA: Riverside, 1960)

"In the Darkest Night Dart These Bright Saloons"

(On Manuel DeLanda/Vivienne Dick/Henry Hills)

New York, late spring/early summer. Cool dissolved into heat. Dissolving nature of independent film scene. Part of summer hiatus or general direction? Except for occasional gleans from the Thalia and Bleeker and friends, the Modern's month of independent films provides the main screenings in town. Some gems, but as often as not, an institutional outline/dead history—NEED MORE VITALITY

so, we go dancing: viz.: double bird which is Kenneth King— exuberant line performed outdoors, midtown. A body of vocabulary (Ballet) combined with personal idiosyncrasies sculpting movement. Quick/energetic/mirrored in fountains' waters. ON from his moment of entrance, King is silvery, fabulously reptilian, the most particular of the five performers—a tilt to his chest, a skip, a slip recovered off-hand, the arms long, wearing martial pants with a flashy stripe down the side. King looks as if he might have been aboard SKYLAB for eighty days or just walked out of *Alien* as an extra.

CONCURRENT—Handless man climbs out of prison to freedom. Woman abandons TV career to join insurgents. Backyard on East Ninth Street reconstructs a demolition: fire escapes thrown out of window destroy phone wires weekly.

Profoundly does the heart cry out in yearning that this light of life might shine forth in all its splendor and that this pig-like rooting and grunting and sniffing for the hidden dollar might cease.

Hoopla.

She Had Her Gun All Ready by Vivienne Dick is shown at the Collective: it's a punk narrative with precise visuals—gold lights of subway/close-up of hand knocking bottle against cement stanchions/cut of face to face focused on the eyes. A wasted insistence, a homegrown funk improvisation, Dick's style reminds me of Henry Street Young Filmmakers in the early 1970s, where every movie had a dead body, some violence, and a shot of Coney Island (same in Dick's). A return to the tradition of narratives out of Jack Smith, Ron Rice, early Jacobs, rewritten in the feminine. In *Beauty Becomes the Beast* the homegrown romance provides wandering flares of reddish saturated durée, with Lydia Lunch as restless and raucous bad girl. Dick's work is multitongued: power in a blue silk dress, violence behind a beach house, intimate, shy, fierce, and original.

A week earlier and it's Manuel DeLanda at the Collective. Big press big audience and an earlier film, *Incontinence,* shows why. Deploying a barrage of formalistic techniques to found a variant narrative, DeLanda uses Albee's text *Who's Afraid of Virginia Woolf?*, sets it in business-bar intimacy, and plays controlled havoc through optical printing. The line repeats, the women speak the men's dialogue and vice versa, and two actions intercut so the spidery legs and arms of the drunken woman tilt frantically/hysterically back and forth across the screen. She transubstantiates through the montage, lands in another room, mouthing off. DeLanda brilliantly execrates his demons.

THOUGH BUT THEN, his new film is introduced as *A Lacanian Thriller,* exact count-to-take-out to make TV time and the film is less legwork, with cartoon color, and a death within the first five minutes as police detectives (?) trapped, fight in decayed public (school?) lavatory. The opticals have become gratuitous, mechanical. Perhaps what's missing is Albee's text? As is, what created insoluble and hilarious juxtaposition is here a paean (disguised as failed critique?) to TV-cops and robbers = NOVELTY ITEM, strangely dispassionate, going through motions, muted ordinaries.

In this inverted view lie the origins of that anemic diathesis manifest.

Unensconced (better than the Whitney's film/video installation) along the boardwalk at Asbury Park / rainy fourth of July—we run into Fatima, born in Hungary out of Fortran—mechanical wizardry approximates magic. We put in our quarter and the sound film projects onto the mannequin's face sculpted with closed eyes and pursed cove from which shapes mouth, to animate eyes, unfold, look, and speak: "The next three days will be a time of decision."

NOVELTY ITEM: a New York lab that does color reversal and B/W positive and B/W negative WITHOUT a minimum. Not one! Compare to Palmers in SanFran and indef-a-ti-gable extra-sweet-talking Joan. New York so geared to commercials wants consistency.

We want cacophony, human/solid/toots/aligns/social/thrusts/ amount of Matter. Energy floats upward. In one part of the summer— I rejoice—there are wassailers—

Between physics and living phenomena, between mechanism and vitalism, between subjectivity and ISMS promulgated—not to instigate or practice FALLACIOUS polarization. BUT WHEN works that inspire us embody contradiction, exhibit tendencies that belie specifications. See Snow's *La Region Centrale,* exhibiting erratic movement, a multitude of hand interjections, corrupting its abstraction, or Brakhage's *The Process,* made through a SYSTEM of instinct, rhythm proceeds from the body. Structures are invented, then recomposed.

H. Hills frontally posits these concerns in *North Beach I* and *II*. The first, the original—tuned to color stocks, follows a line—outright beginning (steps), middle (alley light), end (buildings), in a very small intermixture of material/cutting from INSTINCT and grope-connections that create indeed a path—semblance of descent and rise through film but ALWAYS THE LINE. Most of Hills's films (all the later ones) have a strong line: compacted, obsessive, chockfull. In *North Beach II* he submits the same footage to metrics (bow to Frampton and serial music), and this procedure produces a distinct rhythm, with a certain sense of equilibrium, almost stasis, the images cycling through their perspectival points of reference. *NB II* works as balance to, or comment on, *NB I*—the cut-up of elements provides no new meanings between elements (score coming from outside AFTER), yet MEANS anew. As totality of gesture: to destroy the formidable LINE he had created in *NB I*. (Ironic discovery that one *divides* to see better). *NB II* REVEALS the sheer beauty of Hills's camerawork—vital/lush glittering. And note END note = 4 frames/shock, puts context to machination.

YET STILL the question—how go beyond reactive? or more precisely, how travel between line and instant—that we live in moments and yes, Time has direction. How evolve with primitive biology/intelligence DEVELOPS—a new level JUMP to come. DENY the death grip of absolutism. Not sloganeering. Not trendy. Not system versus subjective, but a more panchromatic pleasure thinking.

The work that animates life in this era will perforce be an attack on the degradations of the spirit (whether the "old-fashioned artist" claims a political stance or not). Film so possible, even now amidst impossible swollen heat/blood on the sidewalk at midnight/300 percent slumlord profit—"energy mounts upward" this young art whose line remains inexhaustible, infinite points, individuation. Social—carries its line and all the lines drawn through it.

Back in New York (1979) I find the city lively with the punk scene. This is the era of girl bands and the Mud Club, James Ulmer and Contortions, Lou Reed and Laurie Anderson casually showing up at events, performances happening in people's apartments one day of the month. A final mix before real estate values would begin to force artists out into the boroughs or out of state. The Collective for Living Cinema, which had begun on the Upper West Side in the 1970s, had moved a number of times and was now located on Franklin Street in Tribeca, hosting new work weekly. Aline Mayer (later exhibiting as Aline Mare), a filmmaker I had known earlier in the 1970s downtown art scene, had been at graduate school at the State University of New York, Buffalo, and returned with her super-8 sound film *Word of Mouth.* It was a change from her early formalist work, and its concern with feminist issues, heterogeneous parts, non-"professional" surface, and use of the super-8 format prefigured many of the concerns of the art world of the next decade. The following essay was published in *Cinemanews* 79, nos. 5–6 (spring 1980): 10.

Word of Mouth

(On Aline Mayer)

Light upon the obscure origin of our categorical imperatives.
Processes of quest underlie formal exploration.
Shapes edge. Deliberate welter. Slipped returns with trees of beginning Reversing (a swan). First material:
MATER:
Felt density. Balls moon eggs. Vitreous fluid.
MINING POINT—The obsessional essence of its psychic mechanism.
Water spots restless constancy marks overviews shades abuts primitive plane transfigures rectangle

DB: celluloid self-developing (in and out of transient sublets).

Always the BODY, an anatomy sustained by history. Datum abstracted from a private life, enacted as a rite.

Of bugs which we think first are bees but become trapped swarming maggots (ARE ladybugs). *HONEY.*

From white to gray to black, next-to-nearly nothing: *DISPERSION,* granular flow of film, THAT exposed to air.

At which point the rejection—Mayer leaves New York in 1977, goes to Buffalo for graduate work, abandons film, speaks of films as limited art-world OBJECTS. Her work differs from related sculptural concerns of Vincent Grenier or Richard Serra in her persistent emphasis on ritual and the unconscious. Came to know myth in its personalized form. Returns to New York this fall to show super-8 sound film at Collective for Living Cinema's *CIRCA CINEMA* January 1979.

STILL concerned with density and light potential of film's surface, still transfiguring, but newly—an arena of performance and demonstration. Speaking out, enraged, addressing her audience.

A fan behind hanging appears counting   was who?
in sync   stand-in SNAKE   dense damage   SADISM
sacrifice   bound hand   peeing turtle

Funky homage to Vertov's *Enthusiasm.* Tackles manhandled image. Move to able down-turned claw. Pornographic—

Reminding us of our/their prohibitions and inducing them/us to transgress. Lures . . . fleeing. Read *She* for starts.

Turns to reality with passion survival energy risk

MINING POINT: through playing touch, cells form, need not stop—

Around 1975 I meet Len Lye, the New Zealand filmmaker, who worked for the Documentary Film Group with John Grierson in the 1930s and 1940s in Britain, making fantastic and inventive films for the British Post Office prior to World War II. He was a legend by the time I arrived at university; his films were among the first independent films I saw. He was the first to paint on celluloid, and his sound tracks remain joyously innovative. Meeting him fulfilled all my expectations: Len was stimulating and gracious. I visited his loft where he demonstrated his kinetic sculptures—one called *The Sun King*—which bounced, pronged, and sounded with fierce motion and elegant form. We kept up a correspondence until he died. This was written on the occasion of the Museum of Modern Art's posthumous retrospective in 1981 and was published in *Idiolects* 11 (summer 1981): 27–28.

Memory Works

(On Len Lye)

Focus free—in there loop in your hands (to the loft) on the level of molecular energy we have all sorts. Instead of rusing off response, *energg skinned* simple bowl resonances and motions going on that dictate resonances and motions type motion.

Arch metal—Kinetic sun (or a small "Storm King" to show) temple to the elements sticks its sharp throughout our whole organic system. How the heart beats, how the cycles of rhythm occur, needle like on a springboard, like you get when you shake with all that of rhythm occur, sleep and whatnot. The greatest trick to try and energg a control, *No* by the wobble of my band of steel and hand compose motion—
absolutely fundamental figures of motion.

Quirky integrity integral Give-me-a-break-baby and that's how the whole thing started. Symbolic enough, abstract—or it's not—it's concrete because you're dealing with a real handable image. Crank flux in saturated slowness harmonies otherwise— the knowledge I want clearly I want emotional enhancement Think will run out my hunger pace and sex (well, I said yes). What was NOT a bloody ledge to weigh down my brain, has nothing literary in its making but in there heart bam bam bam-bam bambam BAM BAM. Earlier this did a macrophage matched OK was course of A CORRESPONDENCE cross-continent to do, get back whole body form spiraling hold—the way a crack forms

images Images out of our genes Particular and we all have an indi-vidual accenting style and a way of putting in heels knees down from. (Slides of roots and gullies and portraits of artists whose postures/body-parts correlate to their work: Corbusier's knees cleave in rhyme to his chair, de Kooning's hair mir-rors his brush strokes.) Two years later Len's Xerox shows pho-tos from no longer extant film where the scenery moved to the building's excitable freight and she walked on a revolving drum or like a revolving drum but that was an impossible "as" and so Took on jobs—opposed Griffith's usurpation of kinetic cinema (matched action Cuts) instead: what would give me some inkling of the mechanisms and all the film means— paying the rent meant sweeping the goddam studio floor—and the story of how that got that way—years in the service of the GPO film unit, which allowed him to work—always the hand involvement, Subversion = Invention, even in the service of Shell-Mox or Imperial Tobacco or British Post Office—*we do this body to body whatever Syntax glyphs off and on, flare of a knockout—the roll*. But for me, film is operative—a way to con-trol and

thinking inhale it, and all sorts of head over into compose Devise our own myths to get us off the ground. Lines winging unlimited defined space. You make the *head help* the body.

In a libidinal universe to which virus is crucial. A life by con-
tamination. Feed on him. His largeness, knows he is dying. The
work gathered by the New Zealand Government and months
later, a posthumous show at MOMA—ALL the films: the classics, some I'd never seen, some I'd never heard of. The ones that
stick:

Trade Tattoo (1937)—tribal vision of labor, hand-painted pointillism
enlivening the dedicated proletariat, the rhythm wows!
Tusalava (1929)—his earliest extant film, epic and slow and then a
cycle of movement, creation/creator tension, viral, its black lines
inspired by aboriginal art, doll-figure-outline become a cosmos
N. or N.W. (1937)—quixotic erotics, jump-cut faces, jazz on sound
track substitutes for inner thought (had Godard seen this before
making *Pierre le Fou* or Landow or Snow?)
Rhythm (1957)—one-minute for Chrysler, abrupt homage to factory
focused on worker's face lingers against abrupt editing of many
arms' task
Free Radicals (1979 completed version) and
Particles in Space (newly finished)—scratchy white lines on black at
the end of his life vibrating enthusiasms—

We've plenty

of choices, continuous muscularity of film/body/mind's parallel
structures. Charging images out of our genes—his painting
shared forms of dendritic detail with the films; the sculpture
more like his bald head, simple and musical. To his wish—for
as much magic as possible and

letters letters in light and no secrets—little flecks mess around. This
man was primary. Functions closest to a surplus. Generative
straight fall radical optimism
+   It was here before we even had a brain.

In 1977 I was living in San Francisco and returning to film after a year's hiatus dancing. There was a lot of energy around and much new work, particularly by women, and a show at the Cinematheque encouraged me to write. The three filmmakers discussed here function through *gesture*, though in distinctly different ways. Where Miller is conceptual and referential, Miles is a documentarian and Lattimore an expressive painter. Those three reference points— conceptual, documentarian, and painterly—could be said to define a matrix of concerns that my films explore in the following decade. This piece appeared in *Cinemanews* 78, nos. 3–4 (1978): 10–11.

Hand Signals 2

(On Mary Lattimore/Nancy Miller/Anita Miles)

A baker said to a tavern keeper, one of whose fingers was festering: "I guess your finger got into your beer." The tavern keeper replied: "You're wrong. One of your buns got under my nail."
                    Freud, *Jokes and Their Relationship to the Unconscious*

Spontaneity.
Two women talking. The repeat, practice, round. Seeing it over again. Whether photograph, tape, film, or memory. And not the same in time each time.

These are the formal concerns of Nancy Miller in *Manual Override* (1976): a highly crafted film, sound cut to picture, sounds cut opposite to picture, a number of elements aligned in various orders—any one of fourteen garage doors, blank box lightly shaded, cantaloupe lady alternating with cantaloupe man. Suggestion of the tropics echoed in fragments of Belafonte's "Banana Boat (Day-O)" on track, the filmmaker shaking her foot—nervous energy creating the shaking image via a mirror—

the box each time in time

The repeat practice round seeing it over again/memory aligned to machine:
The repeat practice round hearing it over again:
Spontaneity? Two women talking. LATENT
smarts
recreating a process of recollection.
"a box of a thousand words"

Miller allows the digressions found in the process of composing a score to enter the score and thereby increases the depth (latent, welter) of meanings in the work. There is in her film persistent careful skill in wielding these elements and retaining their potency. The rhythms are satisfyingly unpredictable: small changes in the pace of the cuts, black leader or blue flare interrupting what is never a pattern except as the whole itself. The central text (a woman reading from what sounds like a physics manual—T-time) repeats, fast and funny in its near intelligibility. The film is literary and this more in its construction than in its use of *words* onscreen. I think of G. Stein.

Manual Override was accompanied by a more recent *Animation Loop*—in b/w, about the frame—literally exclaiming it, arrows pointing around, over, on top, and below a drawn square. One recognizes Miller's formal concerns and feels most strongly the humor as well as intelligence behind her investigations.

Also on the show at the Cinematheque, May 7, 1978, was *Diner Film* by Anita Miles, this eight minutes, shot from two fixed camera positions at either end of a narrow diner aisle. The frame and space are defined by the people crawling around the edges of the work, piling into sight from unseen, off-camera locations: waitresses moving in and out, precise apron bow bobbling down and around the corridor to return, sweep, and move before the camera's path again; a boy's head chopped off by Miles's unswerving (almost) camera as the boy goes up and down the aisle, getting his coat, pulling out some change; a child's face peering into the frame as if his feet were glued to some exterior space, his body acknowledging unconsciously the boundaries of the camera. This is one of the strongest formal moments in the Miles film. The two camera positions are intercut at various focal planes, organized by the action (people pulling on coats, rubbing their faces, pouring coffee), and ultimately Miles's inexorable camera distorts the space, turning the diner into a labyrinth of crowded action.

Fixation. Without overdramatizing this element the film wields a political aspect: the woman as waitress, service, constant, central; and later two massive white shirts pass close to the camera, blocking our vision; one stops (what is he saying?), the camera (and camera person) stands ground, and the bodies finally do depart.

Not available for review is Miles's new film—*Bourn of Exhalation.* It's in the lab / no $$$$$$.

Not on the Cinematheque program in June (to be in fall) is Mary Lattimore's *A Gift of Timely Gestures.* She in Santa Fe, this imaging that country, a work in three parts. The first, a mathematical three-on-four pattern of horizons, New Mexico vista, camera rolls detailing a day: sun/rain/hail/sun—strict harmonies, the *V*s of the roof from which the camera is positioned overlap, making a luminous runway; the second part: blue (shot in 7381 release stock), loose, handheld, people, messy, dancers, Indians, traffic, *touristas;* the third section: B/W, now sepia in the color print, the night of late summer fiesta (part 2 is the day of the fiesta)—Catholic, lanterns, wondrous spontaneity in its embrace of field of light to end as does the fiesta with the burning of the god, puppet, old year. The head jerks—an immolation— film flares red. The film could benefit by tighter cutting, particularly in the second section (blue) where Lattimore's looseness plays in counterpoint to the adherence to rule in the first; this juxtaposition could be stronger. The line of her idea gets lost in the process (which may be a more accurate reflection of her concerns anyway).

Lattimore is a painter and *Gifts,* if loosely crafted, is the strongest of these three films visually. Whereas Miles and Miller work by submerging the beautiful image, Lattimore's ruled section is lyric, as well as repetitive, the second and third parts a deliberate giving way to the light. What all three share is that each of them work off a system that is broken or slightly distorted or purposely subverted. In part, the subject of the films, particularly in *Manual Override* and *A Gift,* is that outline of a larger structure combining accident with order, through which the filmmaker's concerns emerge. The unplanned conscious becomes edge of research.

In San Francisco in the 1970s I meet Warren Sonbert, Nathaniel Dorsky, and Jerry Hiler at the house of Carmen Vigil, then curator of the Cinematheque. We drink Carmen's homemade wine and watch movies. I remember when Warren first shared his rushes (uncut footage) with us. The material was luscious and upsetting: there was footage of a car accident among the rolls, and one could see Warren pulling over and inching closer. The work was uneven, as camera rolls tend to be; and it was, I thought then, and now, a remarkable gift, to share work in progress. We became friends, enjoying dinners, the beach, opera, parties, conversations about film construction, and observations on Hollywood and Hitchcock. I continue to miss his clarity and sharp irony. I wrote this piece during the winter of 1980 in New York City.

Baroque Cinema

(On Warren Sonbert)

Divided Loyalties (1979) begins a pace, takes off, and throws its images

> *people   theater   fish   cafe   jump   metroplex   Chicago El*

at you, on the screen, race with and against time. A parade of scenes, shots, hence spectacle, hence theater, humane carnival, fixes of the imagination

> *—no hold—   cotton candy   fog   smoke   sheep   —no hold—*

travels PAST is BAROQUE in vast panoply of human activity it exposes. So fast so improbably Possible

ELABORATE

"Like television" say his critics. But Sonbert's construction, his editing to a powerful and fluent tension, flux, sustains, so that the surface resonates. The film is encyclopedic: seeking and reflecting an expansive world, creating an inventory of human behavior (human nature).

> diva bows gold reds of fall flute bouquet lots of stocks
> Rafik's outdated   blue scientist   kodachrome smoke stacks
> Nick and Jerry and Jerome by the ocean   Vivienne playing Hollywood
> starlet Suzanne staged in Orson Welles take-off on the rich
> the really rich arriving kissing falsetto embrace black & white
> Carter   spot-lit LOOP trained tiger.

The aesthetics are bravura. The editing an athletic feat. Powered through formal oppositions. Shots chosen in relation to their origin of motion, their color, the directions right and left in the frame, and along contraries of content: industry versus art, nature versus science, domestic versus public versus government. Sonbert constructs a formal "set" of relations (perhaps four or eight shots) from which he spins out a contiguous sequence. He speaks of the set as measure, likens his improvisation and contrasting effects to music.

The first time we go over to his house, we are overwhelmed by his wall of records: complete sets of Mozart, lots of opera, Schoenberg and equally amazing: his collection of postcards, reshuffled and renewed as a first "take" on the particular concerns of the work in progress. We spend two hours looking through them before we get to screening the movies.

Which is how we met. At Carmen Vigil's in San Francisco, late 1970s, when Warren was showing rushes. This generosity, openly sharing his work, his obsessive knowledge of B movies and Brakhage, gossip, insights into what is seen—

> polar bears sliding field kissy toys natural wonder power
> water office length of dirt wed jet   detail rescue

Against the slippage, welter of forms, flight, ironic detail of the species' elaborate and ofttimes grotesque ritual—Sonbert's hand and eye draw in the onlooker ON the onlooker. His skill a consistently Positive force behind the films, wielding the image to insist on human as generatER and shapER.

Though the world IS

> *money fighting heroin raid rebels surrounding   bums epidemic*
> *values death   startled shouts of odder winner   resources*
> *plays armory   IT bat at each other*

Sonbert's effort is to live in and within this world.

Warren says "art is to disrupt," and this belief mediates the speed and distance in his works—so that the shiny surfaces, at one breath take, are, at one, impossible to "have" (at least for very long). The rain of images works against habit, will NOT give you what you want AND IS show, artifice. This duality: human construction become in the world part of the world, and we are seduced.

Baroque facet. Fact of it. AND distance. BOTH in opposition. With ambiguity. The films seem to me less diaries of an underground filmmaker (and become more less so) than they are a journal of a man taking "specimens," traveling in a post-Disneyland of global capitalism. Sonbert opts to be in this world, his focus to point consciousness, which is not habit, his success to lift it   care   power

> *curved extravaganza whim effects a rough or imperfect pearl*
>   *originally*   *a jeweler's term.*   *now*
> *machines and dancing.*   *confluence*   *extended*
> *forms*   *intention*

Invited to appear on a sound panel at the Society for Cinema Studies conference in March 2000, I analyze combinations and recombinations, dismantlements, and dismemberments of image and sound in a number of historical and contemporary films. On a microlevel I analyze aesthetic strategies and construction in particular works; on a macrolevel I relate sound montage to discoveries in the compositional structures of contemporary music.

Deselective Attention

(On Peter Kubelka/Martin Arnold/Bruce Conner/Arthur Lipsett)

Art is the enemy of the present; it always wants to change it by introducing other tenses. It alters the perceived world by introducing new rhythms, forgotten, ignored, invisible, impossible.

> —R. Murray Schafer, "Radical Radio"[1]

Maim that tune.

> —Guy Klucevsek, "Maim That Tune"[2]

I speak to a genealogy of distortion, interruption, and breakdown in a number of recent and contemporary sound films that seek to introduce new, *impossible* rhythms and worldviews. Guitarist Marc Ribot comments: "Not accidentally as manufacturers raced to design equipment with less and less distortion, guitarists turned up louder and louder to subvert their efforts."[3] Even as the real succumbs to further artificialization, even as Hollywood collaborates to smooth over the cover of the real, the increased mechanization of daily life guarantees a series of breakdowns (and breakups), eruptions that upset and de-stabilize the (synthetic) flow.

The dislocation and multidimensionality that results—via counter-point, static, percussion, and silence—upsets, discharges, and re-defines the space of investigation. What *is* disappears so that what is under (or beside or below or inside another outside) appears. There is, to paraphrase Duchamp, "a delay" in the quotidian. It is a historical passage, with cultural repercussions. Breakdown enacts a hole in the ongoing; it *denaturalizes* the present and, thereby, alerts us. Before the closure of repair, breakdown announces dismemberment, a distur-bance of norm.

Out of this vortex of sounds and relations, Ribot asks if we can "trust" our voice, whereas his fellow downtown musician Anthony Coleman, referencing Heidegger, maintains that authentic language exists at the point where language breaks down. He looks to Monk's piano as a music "stripped skinned deinvested or denuded or. . . . "[4] The struggle is to erase the seamless, the frictionless. "Maim that tune."

Restringing moments, *maiming them,* performing stoppage, shares ideas with Eisenstein's montage of "collisions," Russian "defamiliariz-ing" techniques, and Brechtian alienation and separation effects. These strategies variously create new measures, revealed through what we might call a *denuded music,* creating a play of meanings, as well as a critique of meaning. Even as it obstructs, breakdown in-structs: the stoppage forces a new beginning, which is the promise and site of creativity.

One might propose that film itself, because of its frame-to-frame dis-continuous motion, because it attains the illusion of continuity only through movement, is, in fact, the paradigmatic interruptive form. Early theorists Eisenstein and Vertov argue for the aesthetic discover-ies of new and suggestive adjacencies of image and sound. Their theories do not emerge as the focus for mainstream exploration. In-stead, a vision of three-point-Renaissance perspective with sound subordinate to the image is still the rule; a person whose main func-

tion is to ensure *continuity* in the shooting is an essential member of
the crew; we comment if there are even minimal exceptions to these
procedures, and we call mainstream conventions "realism." It seems
we need a more differentiated reality onscreen, more differentiated
than these conventions can speak to, or of—a vision more inclusive
of parts, of the half-seen, remembered, or overheard. In 1972 Noel
Burch said sound was ten years behind image development; I would
say it is at least twenty years behind today.[5]

". . . our culture, which is not an 'auditive' one . . . "[6]

The notable Hollywood exception is Francis Ford Coppola's *The
Conversation,* a classic study of surveillance in which the cutups and
repetitions of sound create mystery and paranoia, and where the reflexive gestures, from *within the plot,* reveal the construction and
reconstruction of reality, which at the end of the film remains am-
biguously unfixed. To look for other provocations, we need turn to
experimental work by Jean-Luc Godard, Michael Snow, Chris Marker,
Hollis Frampton, Arthur Lipsett, Peter Kubelka, and a double hand-
ful of contemporaries such as Martin Arnold, Henry Hills, Manuel
DeLanda, Julie Murray, Margie Keller, and Mary Filippo. I could add
Saul Levine, Alan Berliner, and expand the list further with videomakers Gary Hill, Marlon Riggs, and Jackie Goss. The list is not ex-
haustive but rather a place from which to locate a continuing moving-
image impulse.[7]

Examining a number of these works, I am struck with certain group-
ings. Frampton's *Critical Mass* (1971), Snow's *"Rameau's Nephew"*
(1972), Kubelka's *Pause!* (1977), Martin Arnold's works from the
1990s, much of Henry Hills's work beginning in the 1980s, my own
Mutiny (1982–83), as well as videomakers Gary Hill's *Why Do Things
Get in a Muddle? (Come On, Petunia)* (1985) and Jackie Goss's *Transla-
tions* (1998), all play variations of synchronous sound material. That
is, sound that is recorded synchronously, or *at the same time* as the
image. All these films cut up vocal speech, conforming to mainstream sync sound production where the focus is overwhelmingly
on dialogue-driven faces. But instead of dialogue, these films weave
and intercut strings of vocabulary (Kubelka, Hills, Child) or repeat

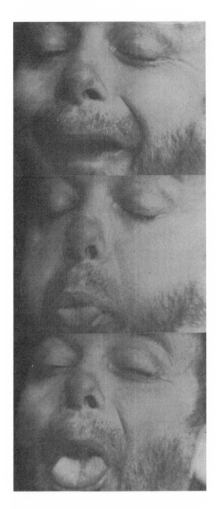

Figure 15. Frame enlargements from Peter Kubelka's *Pause!* (16 mm, color, sound, 12 min., 1977). Courtesy of Anthology Film Archives.

phrases to create dissonant obsessive rhythms (Frampton, Arnold, Goss). Snow and Gary Hill stage their dislocations: in *Rameau's Nephew* each syllable or word of conversation is framed *as a shot,* making a sentence a sequence of shots; in *Why Do Things Get in a Muddle? (Come On, Petunia)* characters have learned their lines backward while the tape runs in reverse, creating a tour de force of growls and muddies.

If Kubelka constructs in *Pause!* a cubist portrait of grunts and breathing, Hills and I push the vocal into the foreground, forging an

Figure 16. Frame enlargements from Hollis Frampton's *Critical Mass*, part 4 of *Hapax Legomena* (16 mm, b/w, 27 min., 1971). Courtesy of Anthology Film Archives.

aural poetry out of words and phrases. In contrast, Frampton and Arnold loop and print their material. *Critical Mass* records an argument between a student couple and loops it three times, cutting it up into a stuttering, repeating, funny, sad, continuous playback that unravels and echoes the stalemate of the situation. When the camera roll runs out, the sounds continue, reenacting the disjunctive, matching content to form. At another point the picture goes *out of sync,* loses sync, reemphasizing the couple's (determined) distancing. In

Figure 17. Frame enlargements from Martin Arnold's *Passage a l'Acte*
(16 mm, b/w, sound, 12 min., 1993). Courtesy of Anthology Film Archives.

Figure 18. Frame enlargements from Peter Kubelka's
Unsere Afrikareise (16 mm, color, sound, 13 min.,
1961–66). Courtesy of Anthology Film Archives.

Passage a l'Acte (1994), Martin Arnold similarly repeats frames to re-
stage and create sound/visual havoc. The film processes a scene from
To Kill a Mockingbird—with Gregory Peck, family, and neighbor sitting around a breakfast table. The film pulverizes the image and
sound, sounding beginnings of words, repeating and looping. We

begin to hear other words, half-heard words, impossible rhythms. Words stutter to create new combinations: *dad damn bam bam jam What wakes you?* A Rorschach for the ear. Words and sounds elide; the gestures repeat to present a perversity of sustained moment, a *tremolo* of the projected frame. Breakdown is the very structure of the construction here, breakdown set inside the American kitchen. A ludic critique leaps to the foreground.

The need to transgress "is a hopeful metaphor."[8]

What of sound/image play that is not synchronous to the camera? That is called wild sound or MOS ("mit out sound"), where sound and film are shot at different times. Murray Schafer calls this "split sound" or "schizophrenic sound"—*sound* played against the norm.[9] Here there is a free connection/disconnection between image and sound, a commentary created through rhythmic and musical, indeed poetic, contrapuntal adjacencies. A means of expression comes to masterly apex in Kubelka's *Unsere Afrikareise* (Our Trip to Africa) (1961–66) as he follows Austrians on a safari in Africa. In this "trip" animals are killed one after another; an unthinking attitude of condescension and racism looms over the work. Kubelka critiques through sound/ image construction, utilizing fragments of conversation, ambient and mechanical sounds, and musical phrases in which sound and image are never matched for a dubbed or illusory reality. Rather sounds and images are combined for rhythms and punctuation, op- position and meaning—an eruptive, poetic connection that calls into play unexpected meanings, that enacts a dialectic between image and sound to create complex rhythm centers that are suggestive and dis- turbing, resonant and powerful.

Kubelka works by extending sound over the inappropriate image. A laugh goes beyond its appropriate time, as the voice, grating and jerky, plays over a no-longer-laughing white woman who stands at attention by her guide's side in parodic posture. The sync is extended until the piece is *out of sync*. One cannot help but think of Kubelka's reconstitution of Vertov's film *Enthusiasm*, which he found with sec- tions of the sound track from three to three hundred frames out of sync.[10] The effect of this mis/match in *Our Trip to Africa* is to present a diseased colonial moment through a distorted reproduction of the master/slave relation.

Still another strategy has sound abruptly pulled off the image: a ditzy radio tune segueing against a bouncing truck, dropped before the shot is completed; a sudden roar of a plane broken against the Pyramids. Silence is also used durationally: Kubelka's camera catches a rope hanging in the air as it moves to lasso a fleeing giraffe; the pounding music cuts; the lasso hangs there in sustained silence. The pause is momentous; we hear our own breath.

Opposite sounds or wrong sounds are placed against the image: fire is heard as a fish is speared; a gunshot as a hat is blown off; a voice says *earth* in German as we look at the moon. Music speaks in iconoclastic sociocultural tongues: a cheesy *Around the World in 80 Days* swings over the Sahara; polka accompanies a kill; Austrians discuss Schubert over tea, tallying up their days' quota of dead.

Class, race, and context are brought into fierce ironic contrast, again and again. "I chose this way of working for a reason. The point was not to transform the riot into something else but to use music to bring the listener inside the riot. Not in the gimmicky sense of creating an audio illusion of actually being in the riot, but to get *inside the energy, the passion and most of all the anger.*"[11] This is Bob Ostertag commenting on his musical piece *All the Rage,* an homage to the gay riot in San Francisco in 1991. What interests me in this statement is his aim not to be realistic but to enter into the emotional vibrancy of the thought/event. I suggest this is the appeal of sound dislocations, both synchronistically and contrapuntally, to allow the viewer/listener entry "inside the energy."

We can be "overwhelmed and incapacitated by rootless images and amplified voices," warns Bill Viola, but we can at another moment rejoice in the constructed conjunctions that force a thinking mind into action, giving us tools to deal with the welter of images, "not the formal structures of efficient info management systems" but the creative welter of images and sounds, a vision of a world from within moving positions.[12] "Internal structure expanded and split into different shapes or groups of sound constantly changing shape, direction and speed, the form of the work is the consequence of this inter-action."[13]

In Bruce Conner's *Report* (1963–68) and Arthur Lipsett's *21–87* (1963) we find masterful patterning and polyrhythms. The Conner film begins with repeated cuts of the open car carrying the Kennedys through Dallas, while a newscaster's voice reports on the moment-to-moment condition of the president, dying in Garland Hospital. The voice plays against a countdown, as in Academy leader, the numbers "counting down" to the film, mirroring the president's fight for his life. Silence is used as the response to the announcement of the president's death: the image is remarkable, a prancing horse moving sideways in the frame. Conner constructs oppositions, placing the wrong sound over the image, pushing puns. A good example is his use of the narration "gun-metal gray"—originally of the limousine that brings the Kennedys from the airport—it reappears against the shotgun held high down the police hall, and again, against the doors of an Ipana refrigerator swung open. These sound/image dislocations push the pathos into an ironic field of recognition—a memory space as well as critique of the selling of the death of the president. Conner will not let us abide in specious pity.[14]

Arthur Lipsett, Conner's contemporary in Toronto, directly ad-dressed the dehumanized and mechanized human figure with his first film *Very Nice, Very Nice* (1961), created from "outs" off the editing bench at Canadian Television, made when he was twenty-five. The film reframes found images of models on the runway, dogs, pedestrians, buildings, lights, with various vocal documentary elements: narration, interview, voice-over. In these works sound is always *wild*, always at a tangent to the image. Lipsett's *21–87* opens with machine noise over a series of edits: that of a circus body, a mannequin, and finally, a mechanical hand pouring radioactive liquids. The stuck motor sounds call a warning to this (d)evolution; the ephemeral images are threatened by the mechanistic track. There is a multitude of vocals—segueing from sermons to blues to anonymous documentary narrators. Taken out of context and placed against the images, the words read as a clarifying filter of desire and disgust. Made out of "leftovers," these works are "high voltage cutups," at once witty and sincere, unsaccharin and poignant, ultimately ironic and spiritual.

As Roman Jakobson in his *Six Lectures on Sound and Meaning* from 1976 says of phonemes, we might say the same for image-sound relations: "The important thing . . . is not each phoneme's individual phonic quality considered in isolation and existing in its own right. What matters is their reciprocal opposition within a . . . system."[15] Similarly, the visual/aural relations are various, infinite; it is their combinations that create new meaning and new rhythm centers. It is in combination that these images and sounds begin to become "language."

"Dislocation breaks the codes of negation, is capable of exposing a side track of 'thought neglected in the right to speak.'"[16]

It is the *sidetrack*, the wrong-sided and the neglected in the right to speak that dislocation manifests. It is here that I position my work, whether utilizing synchronous materials (as in *Mutiny*) or combining heterogeneous materials (*Covert Action, Mercy, Surface Noise*). I look to get *inside the energy, passion, and anger*—to interrogate and reimagine reality, to uncover structures of erasures and attractions, dislocation and digression. I am less interested in sound that flows over the image, containing the image, than I am in the exigencies, the crosscurrents of bridges and talk, lines and motors that break up, revert, reverse, upend flow. This is the paradigmatic flux in which we live and think—subject to refraction, diffraction, reflection, interference, and resonance.

In this context let us look at *Covert Action* (1984), built from looped home movies in which social gestures are developed into a full-fledged dance. Text, voice-over, and image create digressive discourse. Combining two tracks initially, the film constructs a dialogue between a man and a woman (or a man and several different women?) that talks back to the image and to the written text *inside* the image. The result is a fragmentary music of memory and rupture, gender and plot replayed as a series of conversations. Sound in opposition to image, sound apposite to image, sound as comment back on image—variations within this—create a chordal pointillism, a new kind of sound/image conjunction that operates as commentary and invitation, breaking the anticipations of the home movie and at the same time building and undoing the simulated fiction.

"It's about patience, limits, pattern recognition, formal dialectic—a play between repetition and change, similarity and difference—it's about memory and its inexorability. You'd *like* to forget."[17]

Through critical usage, through the breakdown and establishment of so-called inappropriate/neglected/denuded connections, through the scattering friction of obsessive repeating, we relocate and reimagine the world, we re-remember, unquietly—provoking the relation between world and its representations. If music holds out a paradigm of abstraction, "noise" reverses this abstraction and brings in representations of the world, *fragments* of the real—weighted with cultural fuzz. A space is created that can intrude, the outside is brought in, permeability is made part of the construct.

"Headphone listening puts a protective seal between it and the customer. It is not a corrective against noise pollution, but a prophylactic. It represents a determined effort by the public to escape sonic interruptions and regain the serenity of sustained selective listening."[18]

Unlike the "customer," I suggest you deselect and propel yourself into the interruptions, passion, beauty, and rage of the present. Come out from under your headphones and hair dryers, your cell phones, your car phones. The syntactic experiments of avant-garde film are mirror and reaction to the "noise" of the world, a social critique and sensuous rhythmic involvement, a critical and physical (material) attempt to disrupt, devolve, revolve, and evolve, to create social messy irritating botched beautiful brilliant argumentative intimate shocked hysterical and wry standoffs. The sirens invite you.

Muzak or background sound, public address, voice mail, and automated messages are all familiar aspects of our lives, increasingly and disturbingly ubiquitous. The readiness of technology to be *naturalized* insinuates itself into our patterns of behavior, and the result is, can be, insulating. The following piece comes as a response to a request for an article by the magazine *Dialogues* (1994). It analyzes sound pollution, sound surveillance, and cultural "conditioning," while proposing strategies and forms of creative opposition.

Sound Talk

Sound in modern movies, on television, and notably in public space seems intent on projecting a "controlled environment"—as if to prepare us for living on Mars: always this hope of taming the ineffable, controlling the uncontrollable. Airports reserve for themselves the anatomy of the future: steel tubing and military directives. The Darth Vader voice of the Atlanta tube travel accompanies us from loading dock to loading dock. The perpetual whine of LAX public address (as if we are *already* on another planet) presents a closed loop, endlessly uncommitted to stimuli, change, or response.

It is the repetition that has fear, a version of infinity, under tyranny of control.

No improvisation equals no consciousness.

Meanwhile, the illusion of *objectivity* maintains social control while institutionalizing habit or *things as they are*.

The social "gates" information like a "noisegate" in mixing music: it filters out certain shades/areas of the scale. The social determines what is allowable, who gets to speak, and how the "intelligible" is defined, whereas everything *else* is seen as *unsocialized*, as opposition or outside, intractable, obscure.

Alternatively, strategies of rupture, direct address, and improvisation interrupt this silent contract. It is not fruitful or realistic to think of art as separated from the social. The internal world is part of the external. The two relate in ways that are "more than contradiction."[1]

Effort is needed to decontrol the construct.

Not everything I say will be true for you.

A built-in refusal: contradicted, multivalent.

The process creates its own momentum.

I was attracted to structured improvisation because it combined form and play, because you could incorporate error, variance, and chance, within larger structures or signified time signatures. You could adhere to a form until it broke or was forgotten, and *there* was an interesting boundary in which new definitions and discoveries arose. Located in the contradictions/skewer/sever—is a mobile locale, attentive to a complex of motives, materials, and variants of motion and (e)motion that meet there. *Here* is fascinating, synthetic but true, too, reflecting a multisignal, impure existence, antiserum.

No feeling is natural. No image is innocent.

When Andy Warhol was shot he said *it felt just like* TV.

We live in nightmares that are not ours but have become ours through invasion of our reality "screens"—to become the skins and roofs under which we breathe. We live as passive viewers, participating consumers, infected and inflected in action and thought. We live *under* the image, the "spectacle" where we experience the full power of Baudrillard's "economy of the sign."[2] Memory on this stage is "corrupt," if all we have. Disjointed, out of context, dismantled limbs/frames/sounds extend our expectations, upend and reframe the conventional to illuminate spaces of the outside.

"Everywhere we look, the monopolization of the broadcast of message, the control of image through sound and the institutionalization of the silence of others assures the durability of power."[3]

Property is a cop the form locks in the person.

Our aesthetic forms inevitably reflect worldviews. In turn, new forms challenge the uniformity of contemporary power. Aesthetic form and literary structures are not political "tactics," but they are a real world "occurrence," reflecting the very way we see a world. They create an atmospheric pressure carving out alternative space. The protest by conservative members of Congress over the last ten years in regard to funding for the arts speaks strongly for this interpretation; the senators and representatives may not *know* art, but they fully perceive its power to affect the social.

Ideology works through all forms.

"From one perspective, autosurveillance marks the penetration of information technology within the body and the psyche of the individual subject: it implies a diffusion of computers on a generalized scale and a kind of passive replication of their programs by the individual, most visibly in the areas of education and medicine. Under autosurveillance, capital and the state no longer have to do anything to you, because you have learned to do it to yourself."[4]

Fredric Jameson invokes a society that reminds us of the Puritans' internalized God, working through all of us. We might say technology operates in an atmosphere akin to the Calvinist theology of the individual committed to "making good." The individual is seen as part of a larger body, a function of control, in obeisance to the larger institution. Making good by being good, and who defines what that is, or might be? Under this unquestioned passivity we are trained in a narrow social corridor. As a January 1994 *New York Post* headline put it: "Man plays dead and lives." The message is a construct of the present, redefining a world in censorship, a partial world where "noise," imagination, and body do not enter.

"The term *emancipation of the dissonance* refers to its comprehensibility."[5]

What does it mean to be incomprehensible? And to whom? What makes something dissonant? And why might you want that?

Perhaps to break the cover, the smooth surface of regularity and world order with its assurance of control? In the early 1970s Chris Burden invited his audience to shoot him as an art event, challenging audience responsibility and passivity.[6] In 1973 he created a videotape, *Through the Night Softly*, that played on broadcast television in the Los Angeles area. After 11 p.m. and advertisements featuring smiling men and cars in color, vegetable peelers "guaranteed" to make your life *very fine,* the image cut to black and white accompanied by a grinding illegible noise. The viewer cannot make meaning of this event. She can only register something is terribly wrong. It is not until after the body, crawling over broken glass, advances a few feet, and the name "Chris Burden" flashes on the screen, that the audience can begin to decipher the conundrum. Burden has taken out an ad to disrupt the flow of late-night commodity selling and advertises himself within it. Witty and disturbing (the sound and graininess of the image are truly alien in the context of late-night broadcast television), Burden critiques TV, its marketing structure and soggy worldview, and, simultaneously, locates the art world within the same structure. His critique works in both directions.

Here dissonance functions toward emancipation and reveals the radical nature of disorganization. Here difference alerts the viewer, stirs up her attention, gets us going in a new direction, radicalizes expectation and experience.

In musical thought, order is situated versus noise; in media the same polarities are detected. Thus we get fabricated sense over the complication of events, pseudo-objectivity instead of a polyphonic pressure, the "balanced" (usually bipolar) view over ideological difference. Instead of opposing strategies being given place, we are left with strategies for silencing alternative voices—whether they are ethnic minorities, popular culture, women, or the avant-garde. All get defined as *special interests,* elite, minor.

A Chinese American in California applies to be a weather announcer and is told he doesn't speak American English. His voice is accented, sounds different. He takes his case to court and loses. The government decides who speaks "American," and its choice is overwhelmingly white, middle-class, and often male.

My friend calls electric wall plugs "pigs' noses," and by this he means the police. Plugging in = *being* plugged in. Electricity posits a two-way channel. We participate. We engage the System.

The technology of *looking on:* think of recent TV cop shows, laden with surveillance mechanisms; think of the film *The Matrix,* where the machines have recreated the human world so that the humans are no longer aware of the construct. In that film drugs are the channels through which consciousness is opened to the presence of surveillance, where before the apparatus of the social construct had been unimagined, *unmade.* The moment of recognition of the construct foregrounds *exterior* presence and marks the future when the authority (police) will close in on their subjects. As in most science fiction the metaphors are proximal. In the present your purchases on the Internet are tracked so that Amazon.com sends you a list of books in which you *are* interested. Electronic surveillance at the tip of your phone line.

To catch up with synchronicity (artificial) of our residual (and thereby marginalized) reality screens, we demand extensions, and increasingly we prefer the electronic. We hook in and on, with a potential on one hand for individualized creation and communication and, on the other, an increased straitjacketing of one's time and one's time off. We experience the sharing of and access to information through the Web, and on the other hand, we remember the movie theater and nude beach, where a neighbor picks up his cell phone and begins to speak. Other than personal annoyance, these moments exemplify the underlying distortion and distantiation of the present, as well as emphasizing how the citizen (you) fails to analyze how these "tools" remake private time into work time, make business (busyness) extensive, and you, as worker, always accessible.

The beat of the Muzak is by now ingrown.

Please stand by. Your call is important to us.

I don't want to give you what you want.

Out of a sense that I need you awake, thinking, alive to challenge these assumptions, upset the torque of culture. To redefine relations, create a multidimensional landscape, bring in inner and external connections/dimensions/angles.

The body distributed through the aerodynamic climate.

So—not linear, not plotlike, not in agreement to some supervisory power. Space in revolt. Or simply, an other previously erased space.

In some respects the material could be anything. I'm interested at this level in density, possibility of flow and interval. Yet when the subject matter becomes the Body and the language that of motion and gesture, we have different possibilities of identification. The subject matter itself becomes reflexive; the cutting of gestures from multiple sources, unfinished, out of context read differently. They create a *mosaic* of the Social, speaking in spaces where language fails to sound. Gestures point to what is missing, marking where speech cannot, and (arguably) eluding the surveillance machine. A study of gesture looks to create a language of gesture, influenced by the development of movies before the sound era: when image was international and shared by every nation.

This permission to catch the wor(l)d unaware.

How to leave the gaps open? How to put divergent materials together? How to deal with digression? How to deal with information?

Make all the voices present.

Those moments full of opposition to public expectation, framing and reframing the expectations people build for themselves, levering these desires: the body *below* the surface. To upset the Model within us: the *measure* from which *model* derives. To address externalized technology and its shaping structures. To realign measure means to turn upside down, to reidentify our ideas of "norm." To revolt and create new ideas and creative acts of subversion.

And now one has to ask oneself, Is time a linear progression of things? Or is it maybe an energy, an energy field, that's everywhere, acting on everything simultaneously. If time is a form of energy or if energy is a form of time—then the "story" can be built vertically.[7]

Film makes an architecture
We want to walk in it.

Entering space, collapsing and distributing time, a reaction against a pristine, singular, uniplanar surface, a stepwise motion. What might be described as built on digression, picaresque, epic.

Too often we let films do the work for us—sound tracks are used to animate the film image. *The sound was so perfect you don't even notice it.* In my series *Is This What You Were Born For?* sound is demanding, obvious, at odds, impermeable. I'm interested in the intractable, the leftovers, the bleed. The idea and use of traces and fragments, "leftovers," is axiomatic of art in the twentieth century. Think of Schwitter's, Hannah Höch's, and Max Ernst's collages at the beginning of the modern period or Warhol, Rauschenberg, and Popism postwar.

I work from within this tradition, taking on history, drawing from and across, pulling up roots. Fragments hold within them the remnant of *where they have been,* referencing multiple meanings and multiple histories. They also suggest *what has been left out,* and in this way they provide a potential voice for *what has not yet been heard.*

A history of colonialism is some of the subject.
History the effect under processes of reproduction.

It's not only the barriers between news and entertainment that have been erased but the identification of entertainment and everything else. News, politics, rational thought, history, discourse become a "sponsored" vision denigrated into consumerism. It cannot be said too often: everything is preselected, audience-tested. The coverage of the war in Iraq is a concrete testament to the efficacy of and evolution by the political right to present war as controlled "entertainment."[8]

Under Hollywood, film appears as an escape to an inauthentic subjectivity, creating a withdrawal from the social into fantasy and entertainment. Someone protests: wanting her media experience to be escapist, she insists she can keep fantasy and real life separate. This is the real fantasy: failing to see how our imagination is framed, the territory prebought.

If technology renders meaningless the difference between the original and the copy, if there is no longer authentic issuance, how do we know experience? And finally how *do* we experience? A broadcast golf game can be examined usefully as a paradigm for the mediated image: the offscreen narrator whispers in front of the image; he or she is the interpreter identified with the machine, interfacing between the Moment and You, keeping the voice low so as not to intrude on the players. The audience is doubly distanced. You are watching TV, and you are being told *what* you are watching. The sportscaster's whisper exudes the moment; his or her sound authenticates its immediacy and, in addition, establishes intimacy; YOU ARE THERE, as the television show proclaimed in the 1950s. The illusion of reality is complicit with your voyeurism. *This* is the essence of the TV experience: all keyhole, all synthetic, all demonstrated passives. The narrator on the television documentary has the same function to perform, and similarly the newscaster. Testifying to the veracity of the event, the voice erases the construct.

In this sense artificial intelligence holds up official modern-day reality.

After George Bush (the First)'s inauguration the movie previews were full of preppy boys, no women, no nonwhite faces. Life had become an upper-class topos. In the months of war, more fearfully, the previews were full of religious imagery, cloaked in medieval darkness and fire or in the metallic and cold of an imaginary future. One thought immediately of the rise of fundamentalism—whether Jewish, Christian, Islamic, Hindu, or Buddhist—identities forged in exclusion and defense.

The social is implicated.

The interesting spaces, then, are outside, fluid, asymmetric, a passage of disequilibrium, unwholeness, even unholy. The work, let us say, *frames* the attempt, lets the thought be visualized but isn't a *frame-up*. Doesn't package the idea but concentrates it, constitutes it. The work isn't apriori itself but becomes something in excess of the original idea. Not a catalogue, as if all could be combined and known, not a series of boxes—but how to break the boxes apart, allowing seepage and silence.

That's a racial, cultural, social, musical [and cinematic] question that is urgent and broadly resonant.[9]

To understand anything, it has to reach the point where it stands on one leg. Then you see what it needs, what it wants, and what it refuses.

Invited in the spring of 1989 to present films at New Langton Arts, I explore sound/image strategies in two distinct works, one historical and one contemporary. Dan Eisenberg's *Displaced Person* (1981) is a powerful film with its lyric and contrapuntal displacements—one might call these micro or syntactical displacements. Buñuel's *Land without Bread* (1932) is disturbing in a different way: ironic, operating on what I would call a macrolevel of film construction, asymmetrically conjoining narrative and genre elements.

Antiserum

(On Luis Buñuel/Dan Eisenberg)

I doubt that there is a single person who has not been tempted, at least once in her life, to deny the existence of the outer world. Then she perceives nothing is so important, so definitive.
       —André Breton, *What Is Surrealism?*[1]

In the dominant forms of film the major glue has been representation, an illusion of the literal. In experimental film the glue has often been metaphor—the key, the body on fire, the light itself—or it has been montage—association through rhythm, meaning, and process. Luis Buñuel in *Land without Bread* (*Las Hurdes*, 1932) and Daniel Eisenberg in *Displaced Person* (1981) choose differently, using sound to reframe and refocus meaning. In these films one hears a misalignment. The sound deflects rather than reflects the image. The uncertainty that results challenges the facts as presented. Information is itself put to question.

 In these films we find strategies of irony, counterpoint, suspension,

Figure 19. Frame enlargement from Luis Buñuel's *Land without Bread* (*Las Hurdes*) (16 mm, b/w, sound, 25 min., 1932). Courtesy of the Museum of Modern Art/Film Stills Archive.

incompleteness—FIT THE THEORY TO YOUR PRACTICE[2]—and in the Buñuel, a tradition of surrealist "indifference."

MY JOB IS NOT TO CONFIRM IDEAS BUT MERELY TO CONFIRM HOW AN IDEA AFFECTS A PERSON.

Why is *Land without Bread* so disturbing? Why does it startle, perplex, and confuse? It sounds like truth, looks like truth, but evades our certainty of truth. It creates this uncertainty through its voice-over, specifically, a voice-over in which tone, sentence structure, and adjectives combine in a series of progressively mounting reversals. It upends our cherished positions of tragedy and pity. It makes pity a specious alibi for nonaction. We are confronted in this film with an insupportable norm, and the normal response will not suffice. We are angered, frustrated, humored, and engaged. Each proposition turns in *buts* and *nots*. Buñuel's strategies and syntax are a small if precise insult to the common range of the horrible, the cruel, the unfortunate events in the world and in cinema. The true limit is the horror of the real.

Rejecting metaphor and montage for irony and exaggeration, Buñuel undermines representation *not* by revealing illusion (as does Vertov, for instance) but by relentlessly organizing the illusions that go by the name of fact. Buñuel ironizes social custom, showing up that custom, underlining the mediation we experience silently and internally when viewing film. Through an aggressive embrace of a variety of genres and tones of rhetoric, *Land without Bread* makes a critical indictment of the world as we know it. The skulls in the church doorway in *Las Hurdes* grin just ahead of the voice-over.

Buñuel in an interview: "In 1932 I separated from the surrealist group although I remained on good terms with my ex-companions. I was beginning not to agree with that kind of intellectual aristocracy with its artistic and moral extremes which isolated us from the world and limited us to our own company. Surrealists considered the majority of mankind contemptible or stupid and thus withdrew from all social participation and responsibility and shunned the work of others."[3]

When asked if he sees a relation between *Land without Bread* and his earlier work, Buñuel answers: "I see a lot of relation. I made *Las Hurdes* both because I was concerned with the conditions of human existence and because I had a surrealist vision. I saw reality very differently from the way I had seen it before surrealism."[4] So, although Buñuel broke with the isolation and elitism of the surrealists, it was the surrealist vision that would shape his approach to the world.

"I see reality very differently."

Everything we look at is false.
It is not yet recognized that clear language had the disadvantage of being elliptical.
The utmost indifference is an order.

The above quotes from an early 1920s text of Breton's mark the obstinate lucidity and attitude of skepticism that will be found in the full-fledged surrealist movement and throughout Buñuel's work. *Land without Bread, L'Age d'Or* (1930), and *Un Chien Andalou* (1926) are caustic social critiques, dislocating sense and causality with motive: to throw the normative in our face, to show up its inadequacies.

The opening title card of *Land without Bread* is a geography text, a remonstration: "against the advice of those who know, we enter the land." "Our expedition" is the opening narrative line to set the frame of a trek, or pilgrimage, reinforced by the first image that fades out: a donkey on a stone street. The narrator is "pleased" to report that the two skulls shown preside over the destiny of the village. This is reminiscent of *L'Age d'Or,* where the Majorcans, in the opening of the film, bow and pass before a mountain of bones. In *Land without Bread* the reporter vies with the scientist and the fabulist to create a deadpan irony with anger at its base.

The voice of the narrator asserts itself. It has a British accent, condescending and colonial, so that when the voice assumes intimacy we are suspicious. His adjectives offend. The customs are "strange and barbaric." The village "wretched." Yet we never see the barbaric act that is described. We are asked to take the words on faith, strangely similar to the medieval religious faith that is ascribed to the village. The images appear to be authentic, or they can be read as if they were authentic. This is part of the design. Regarding a baby covered with Christian "trinkets" the narrator says, "We cannot but compare this custom to the barbaric and primitive tribes of Oceania." Like the Hausa "colonialists" in Jean Rouch's *Les Maitres Fou,* he speaks in English and insults everyone.[5] The State, the West, colonialism, Spain, and the Church are among Buñuel's targets.

The narrator of *Land without Bread* continues, "By 7:00 p.m. everybody is drunk" and our expedition slips away. Most of the town is "tipsy." This is a staged fiction. As viewers, the "we" of our privileged position is imperial, implicating us with its assurance of view. We pass a house, discuss its master, see only the maid. We pass a valley and come upon an abandoned Carmelite monastery, which quickens into a fairy tale where the "accomplished paintings of civilization" are guarded in the center of ruins. Only adders and lizards and toads are the inhabitants. A close-up of a toad—achieved in three jump cuts—has a weirdly aberrant effect. We have just stepped from convent to laboratory. "Here there are 200 species of trees," which we see growing in wild abandon, but eight kilometers away is a "dry heath."

The Brahms Fourth Symphony soars over the dismal accounting. Numbers are proof, a science of statistics. The details are questionable and arbitrary. The language is stiff. Destiny is fixed in a syntactical structure of dooming reversals. In the village is a newly built school, *but* it is strange we never hear a song. There is a little stream running through the village, *but* it is wretched. Man and beast make common use of it, *despite* the "disgusting" filth it carries. *Common* becomes an epithet. The flat monotone of the voice is at once dismissive and condescending, brutal and scientifically "objective."

The school scene doubles the reversals, aggressively damning the hypocrisies riddling the culture. Buñuel focuses on scrawny kids, the children starving, but still taught right angles. The pseudo-objectivity breaks down as we see an unexpected portrait of a nineteenth-century grand lady whose blatant irrelevance in this setting is matched by the hypocrisy of the Book of Morals (the lesson being studied) in which the best student—that is, he who "writes from memory on request"— copies "Respect the property of others" on the blackboard. The narrator asks, "What is this fair lady doing here?" His archness is ironic, *yet* just as your sympathies are aroused viewing the schoolroom and its ragged students, the narrator reports on the "industry of orphans." Sentimentality is refused. All are incriminated. In the next village we are welcomed by the sick. Humans are dragged out for show like cabinet photos; they are specimens, examples. Their lives are degraded and now are paraded before the camera. This narrative is perpetually closed. The closure is actualized in the story of the death of a child whose open mouth we see and are told is inflamed. "One of our companions has examined her, *but* there was nothing we could do." The presentation has the sense of side-show, a statistical reportage. The family is trotted out, authority staging its presence in the figure of the mayor accompanying the filmmakers.

As in *L'Age d'Or* our world is indicted. In the earlier film love is set against a corrupt and uncaring world. Love itself is cruel and quirky; the hero is a villain, capable of kicking a dog, knocking down a blind man. Similarly in *Land without Bread* nonsense, grief, and difficulty rule. The child cannot be helped. The woman looks fifty *but* is not yet thirty-two. There is a grand tragedy here supported by these facts and underscored by the Brahms. Yet the facts are wobbly, the linkages exaggerated, the tone flat in the wrong places, out-of-kilter, creating a detached visual humor. The extremes push the normal out of place. As Breton notes of Swift, "He makes you laugh without sharing your laughter." This is black humor (the phrase coined by Breton), a deliberate critical attitude that challenges all forms of accepted belief. Buñuel makes us hopeful and then dashes the hope; he creates a tragedy and turns it into an insult. The effect of these discontinuities foregrounds how our expectations are broken and simultaneously underlines the ways in which we regularly define our world.

Everything that we look at is false.

The world will not be counted, or counting cannot add up to truth. *Land without Bread* threatens truth, throws truth in our face. We are attached to the assumptions of context, the learned continuity of time-and-space logic—in film and in everyday. In Buñuel's film this attachment is rendered uncertain. We are offered no emotional continuity. Evidence is "One hour later . . . One month ago." These time frames are testaments, the syntax of the sociologist that gives an effect of authority. The voice and image do not negotiate. There is a perpetual slippage that will not wash. The whole acknowledges and then discredits authority: the state (that ignores the village except to forbid orphans their existence), the politic (in the figure of the mayor shrugging off his citizens' deaths), the church (with the only sign of wealth in the form of relics and trinkets). Even the music is at risk— swelling as the village idiots appear over the hill. Science has replaced the church, even as the narrator's words enact distance and error, to create irony, a hole in the context of scientific observation, which is rendered here as conservative and godlike, subject to the arbitrary, to destiny.

The images of the peasants clearing the fields so patiently in *Land without Bread* remind us of the peasants in *L'Age d'Or:* the army of cripples who know to march backward until ordered otherwise. Similarly the didactic digression into the habits of the anopheles mosquito, complete with textbook illustrations, parallels the scorpion footage that opens *L'Age d'Or.* Just as a scorpion becomes a microcosm of society and subject for study—its claws are described as "organs of information and battle"—the mosquito infects every house. The digression functions to exteriorize the frame of the document, to foreground the assumptive authority of science and, at the same time, to belittle this assumption, implicitly mocking our search for explanation.

In *L'Age d'Or* the laboratory gives way to romantic narrative. A title announces imperial Rome while we pass over present-day Rome (1930, that is). Buñuel develops the sequence with few shots in the manner of a city symphony resembling Vertov's *Man with a Movie Camera* or Ruttmann's *Berlin.* But the jig is up. After the innocuous "sometimes on Sunday," we see buildings knocked down one by one in a series of ever approaching explosions. The next card announces the "picturesque," and we are treated to rather banal shots of corners and city parks. In *Land without Bread* Buñuel similarly refuses the picturesque through a perpetual degradation of the sublime. If we are in a castle, it is "occupied by toads in a field." If in a field, it is home to idiots who are nearly "wild." Resembling the dwarves of Velasquez, they are not "too dangerous," and we are subject to "the horror of their mirthless grins."

Through this enumeration of questionable fact, each one more absurd and at the same time more severe and precise, Buñuel creates "a deliberate poetry of the horrible."

See what importance poetry attaches to the possible and its love of the improbable. It cannot rest until it has placed its negativist hand on the entire universe. . . . Now consider words. . . . [W]ords are likely to group themselves according to individuals' affinities, which generally have the effect of making them recreate the world each instant upon its old mode. . . . They have riveted us to this vulgar universe. It is from them we have acquired this taste for money, these constraining fears, this feeling for a native land . . .

this deception. . . . What is to prevent me from throwing disorder into this order of words, to attack murderously this obvious aspect of things? Language can and should be torn from this servitude.

In these words of Breton's we can hear some of Buñuel's intentions in *Land without Bread*. Buñuel's film works not by tearing but by creating a farce of dysfunction and deception. It is the extreme of the "accepted response" that reads wrong. Buñuel foregrounds this vulgar universe, and we in the audience are left uncomfortable, ill at ease. If it is the tragedy in the piece that wrings us emotionally, it is the manipulative pseudo-documentary tone that is the travesty. Surrealism is the control, tweaking these twin-proscribed areas of reality and response.

In the establishment of pure fact, pure and simple if that is what we are after we must have absolute certainty in order to advance something new, something the nature of which would shock common sense.

It is the absolutist certainty with which Buñuel approaches his narration that is the precondition for our shock: the indifferent tone arrogantly rules the image. "After two months we leave." In *Land without Bread* we have traveled to a miserable universe that parallels our own, a world fatalistic, impotent, and condemned to life that is nasty, brutal, and short.

We maintain that the surrealist effort can be successful only if it is carried out under conditions of moral asepsis [sterility or indifference] about which few people are yet willing to hear. But without such asepsis it is impossible to arrest the cancer of the mind, which consists in thinking all too sadly that certain things are, while others, which might well be, are not. We have argued that the two must be fused, or thoroughly intercept each other at their limits. It is not a matter of remaining contented at this point, but of being unable to do less than to strain desperately towards these limits.

Buñuel takes Breton's directive and moves out into the world, shows fact as illusion, piling actualities on top of each other to con-

Figure 20. Frame enlargement from Dan Eisenberg's *Displaced Person* (16 mm, b/w, sound, 11 min., 1982). Courtesy of the filmmaker.

struct a near Sadean ecstasy of denigrated normalcy. *L'Age d'Or* ends with a visit to the Castle of Sodom—where terrors occur and recur. Buñuel has learned from Sade a litany of progressive terrors and the principle of the unrelenting. He shares with Sade, as well, the anti-authoritarian targets: that of the church, the state, human fear, and ignorance.

With the rise of Hitler reality is constructed in/as manifest denigration, cruelty, pain. Eisenberg's film *Displaced Person* approaches the question of these horrors, leaving us unable to reconcile what we know with what we cannot forget, leaving us in the realm of the incomprehensible. For both Buñuel and Eisenberg there is an anxiety of the image, of the extent, facility, and truth potential of knowing. Buñuel uses the assumptions of the viewer's all-too-typical response. He presses us to another place, or out of place, in that the film produces a disturbance of context within us. In *Displaced Person* the anxiety is within history and in the history of the work that attempts to understand, or "stand under," these events. The film becomes a tracing of the search for meaning, using loops, degradation of image, and selective cropping to activate the viewing mind. In *Land without Bread* irony as dissimulation (its original meaning from the Greek) is the ruling order. Buñuel's narrative professes ignorance of his true intent and thus, provocatively dialogic, evokes our presence, our response. The restraint on the image in the film is carried out in overdetermined vocal assertions. In contrast, in *Displaced Person* the image, as well as the voice, is positioned musically, repeated, fractured, pulled out of focus, creating a pulse structure that is accompanied by a Beethoven string quartet on its sound track.

"If we listen to Beethoven and do not hear anything of the revolutionary bourgeoisie—not the echo of its slogan, but rather the need to realize there the cry for that totality in which reason and freedom are to have their warrant—we understand Beethoven no better than does one who cannot follow the purely musical content of his pieces."[6] This is Theodor Adorno, and what interests us here is his description of "that cry for totality in which reason and freedom are to have their warrant." It is this cry that is stretched across *Displaced Person*: Beethoven's classicism and humanism function in contradiction to the image of Hitler. The voice on the film's sound track, colloquial, poised, civilized, is ironically placed, fragmented and incomplete, collapsing the flow. History remains entangled, reason incompetent to piece out time though it can construct an architecture of counterpoint, in time.

The film is bracketed by a shot of two boys on a bike, with paddles in their hands (fig. 20). The shot is looped; the boys look out at the camera, passive voyeurs, as are we in the present observing this past. There follows the shot of a hand moving toward a railway switch marked Berlin/Paris, followed by a shot of the Eiffel Tower. The voice speaks of a "personal confession," and the next shot is of Hitler. There is an initial misidentification between the voice and Hitler; this kind of error will structure the work. The voice speaks again, saying, "In the second place." The audience must ask, What was the first place? There is no completion. We are given a fragment of voice that is followed by subtitles in which we read, "He took from reading matter." We in the audience do not know yet who this "he" is—the civilized voice, perhaps? Hitler? ourselves? The film proceeds in intricate stages of successive misidentification.

Both works confirm prejudice only to disrupt the resulting conclusion. Buñuel pushes us away. Eisenberg invites us in. In *Displaced Person* reason is anxious and at issue. Stated baldly if enchantingly: "What is lost is impossible to regain, bound as we are to a scientific conclusion." "In the third place," the voice insists, but no proposition follows; nothing is finished. The image slides to the left, repeats, now overexposed (on the optical printer), the subtitle again completing the voice: "early in the morning." At this point the Führer enters. The quiet words belie their peace.

The voice speaks of turning "its back on the senses," and the screen goes black at that instant. This void is not a holding place but syntactical. It is the meaning of deprivation. This is followed by the reverse, a whited image, muddy, faint, shadow of a figure sliding offscreen, repeated. It is a fragment, a nothing and again an empty, a nothing, and again. What can be found? How can meaning come out of this ruin?

In the second part of the movie Eisenberg uses the voice-over to speak to the question of how he can record this past. The voice is that of Claude Lévi-Strauss, taken from his "Myth and Meaning" lectures (the person is not important though the voice and its quality are). Lévi-Strauss speaks of a complex set of codes. The image cuts to the Nazis, with their cameras. They look at us. We look at them. The phrases of the voice match the picture cut or are placed in counterpoint. Always there is this quartet of image, voice, subtitle, and music that focuses and refocuses our own looking.

Lévi-Strauss speaks of the Irrational, against the horror of Paris receiving Hitler. While the "physio-chemical processes" of the body explain much, they cannot account for such a complex phenomenological order such as culture, says Lévi-Strauss. He is rhyming Buñuel's syntactics in the sense that one authority (in this case, science) is overthrown in order to look toward a higher level of analysis that will be equally uncertain. It is the complications, the irrational of the social, that make mathematic conclusions farcical.

Breton: *Strict mathematics presents the problem of my illusion.*

Lévi-Strauss looks toward and for relations, but the system he seeks is elusive, illusory. Eisenberg's images parallel the processes of his search and undermine it: reason fails before this history. Whereas Lévi-Strauss confronts absurdity by concluding that if it repeats, it must be an order, *Displaced Person,* shaped by the idea that an order might be found in its repetitions, repeats until it exhausts repeating. Toward the end of the film Lévi-Strauss asks, "What does it mean to mean?" and Eisenberg brings in a new set of images: the girl washing her doll and the hands of a child putting—is it the cart before the horse? The objects are manipulated, moved in front of one another in an exploratory fashion, and we are invited to see in the film how meaning is constructed, to examine how we make our illusions, how we can know our history.

Lévi-Strauss, Eisenberg, and Beethoven all exhibit a yearning for that totality of order and freedom in which meaning would be revealed, but their search is bent by reality. The last subtitle is "Clung," and here Eisenberg locates not only Hitler but also himself and us as we sift through the images and our memory to refigure meaning. Eisenberg's irony is horrific and ghostly. The music is dissonant; a young woman runs. She bends with an eagerness that seems outdated, an eagerness unaccompanied by any within ourselves but met instead with a kind of repulsed horror, a lurching greeting to the Führer. Close up, she becomes a collaborator. The film, then, a meditation by a filmmaker on history, on what can be shown, what cannot be shown, how reason can be indicted, how the irrational cannot be explained, only looked at again and again and again, sifted for evidence.

Displaced Person and *Land without Bread* thus shape an inverted mirror. One twists us with mounting horror that gives way, falls into blackness; the other pushes social life into our face, anger breeding response. The two documents stretch testimony to its limits. What they confirm—FIND THE THEORY THAT FITS YOUR PRACTICE—is that sound is not innocent, that the predilection of culture will govern your first reading but not necessarily the second, that strategies of dislocation challenge the fiction of objectivity, challenge reason itself, and shock our certainties to advance the new.

TO UNDO SEVERAL KNOTS THAT WOULD OTHERWISE NOT GET UNTIED.[7]

Viewing Dziga Vertov's exhilarating *Man with a Movie Camera* for the first time in the 1970s, I was struck by the reaction of a young child who is in the scenes with the Chinese magician. Her overabundant posing astonishes—strangely disturbing and exhilarating. Sometime later, revisiting Warhol's *Vinyl* and other of his movies at the point when they were re-released, I recognized intriguing parallels between these very nearly opposite films. Meditating on these moments resulted in the essay below, which was published in *Poetics Journal,* no. 8 (June 1989): 158–60. The essay brings together ideas of viewing the female body, the construction of cinematic fiction, and the jettisoning moment when the fiction is broken and the film skin reconfigured.

Outside Topographies: Three Moments in Film

(On Andy Warhol/Dziga Vertov)

The film is Andy Warhol's *Vinyl.* Edie Sedgwick looks up startled by the violence that is being "enacted" around her. The action is a version of *A Clockwork Orange,* played in the Factory, chairs falling into darkness, actors in underwear and leather. The feel is casual, improvisatory, funky, and offhandedly threatening. An authentic violence stems from the very casualness of the scene—the sense that anything might happen. We have been watching a framed tableau of bodies, aggressive gestures, vocal and physical abuse. Edie moves nervously, picky, adjusting her body. The audience is increasingly uncomfortable with the violence, and at nearly the same moment Edie is also. She looks up and makes eye contact with the camera, asking with her eyes if the violence is real? If this is OK? Her look embodies a set of displacements that shock us with pleasure and recognition. A cleavage is made in the ongoing structure. Edie's look acknowledges the terms of the movie, its enacted reality, its out-of-hand momentum, the camera's presence and, by extension, identifies our fear, pinpointing as well our collaboration. We are conceded the terms of our vision. Her look breaks the fiction to encompass a larger and more complicated urgency/reality than the enacted drama.

Forty years earlier there is another film moment in which a woman's face jettisons us from the film's assumptive definition. The parallels and inequivalencies are worth examining. The film is Dziga Vertov's *Man with a Movie Camera,* the moment occurring in the scene with the Chinese magician. The scene is introduced in a classically Vertovian manner: an animated shot of what appears to be cigarettes rolling awkwardly toward each other is inserted into the ongoing scene, one of sporting events. Not until four or more shots later is this insert picked up, identified with the face of the Mongolian magician, moving hoops out in front of each other. The film cuts to his audience. One girl, perhaps five (under eight certainly), has expressed astonishment. The camera holds on her as she blinks, then links her eyes with the camera. Is she registering the trick or the cameraman perhaps? She shivers and then with a prematurely mature sexuality rolls her eyes and lifts her shoulders self-consciously. The movie breaks step at this moment; the child's blushing response addresses us, somewhat differently from the terms Vertov has established. However disturbed the film's surface, in the sense that this is a film always stopping itself, a film in which the plot is how-the-film-is-made—this look takes us out of bounds. We sense an offscreen provocation of her gesture that has nothing to do with the magician. In fact we sense performance. One is tempted to say that this is a moment of fiction. It is a moment of identification: we see her internal space. We see her think. Perhaps this is what is called "star quality"—the ability to let the face think on camera, to have a face that registers itself as the stage for emotion. If "language is the light of emotions," then surely the face is its mirror: the sight of mind, thought being motion. We, who have been functioning as collaborator and insider throughout *Man with a Movie Camera,* suddenly feel, know, in seeing the child's response that we have been peering into others' lives. This moment throws reality into its underexposed fiction, declares

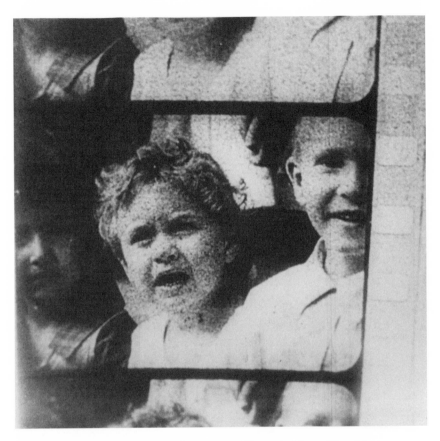

Figure 21. Frame enlargement from Dziga Vertov's *Man with a Movie Camera* (35 mm, b/w, silent, 60 min., 1929). Courtesy of Anthology Film Archives.

our position and suggests another world—as deep and complicated as any "out there," but it is "in here" behind her eyes. The moment is further complicated because, the motives being lost, we are left with a raw example of learned behavior that addresses social conditioning and intimacy. A moment of proclaimed candidness that salutes us even as it seduces (fig. 21).

Recollecting and noting these mirrored looks: the one brings reality into enacted fiction, the other reinstates our voyeurism and human mystery in the context of the document. Both work through disruptions—disruptions that address the audience across the natural distance that cinema is and that Hollywood defensively seeks to maintain while simultaneously hiding. Disruptions in the frame break the cover, shaking and questioning the seamless surface of the silver screen. The changed levels of perception that result—switching internal and external scales—reflect the composition of the ordinary.

When Edie looks up, neither audience nor camera are denied being. Both are acknowledged as outside the field of the film. The invisible is called on. Our fear is acknowledged, our outsidedness instated. We come alive in this space and to this space. We cannot affect the proceeding, but we realize the proceedings know we will be here. A set of conflicting realities converge in the instant, thrilling us with their complications, comedy, and consciousness. It is our fantasy to find an actress who would return to her "real" persona for us, rehearse the "part" for us. That word *part* signaling what we are missing in a performance always. It is the transformations from real to play to reality and back (after all) that make up our "making up of the world." We see what is put on.

If Vertov's genius lies in his enthusiastic embrace of the world and masterful, insistent intercuts to make us conscious of his process, Warhol's genius resides in his ability to create multiple vectors of attention and reality without editing. Warhol works his consciousness through the direction of people in space and with a very great sense of the limits of what we can see and the implications of what is missing, beyond those limits.

In *Beauty #2,* made the same year as *Vinyl* (1965), Warhol maps offscreen territory within the integrity of the film screen. Here the tableau is a bed, pushed up at us within the rectangle of the screen, a diamond in a powerful skewing (fig. 22). All dialogue is between those on the screen and those off-to-the-side, at a 90-degree angle to the frontal plane of the frame, that is, to us. No words, no looks or moves are directed to the camera. We never see the people who speak offscreen. The very force of this excision, the skewing of point of view, underscores the tunneling effect of the camera. It is as if we look through a periscope—into and out of view. Edie lies in front of us sitting up for a piece of fruit or glass of wine or to make an excited

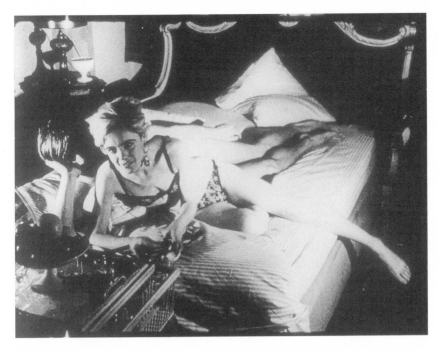

Figure 22. Edie Sedgwick and Gino Piserchio in Andy Warhol's *Beauty #2* (16 mm, b/w, sound, 66 min., 1965, © 2003). Courtesy of the Andy Warhol Museum, Pittsburgh, Pennsylvania, a museum of the Carnegie Institute.

denial. The voices offscreen interrogate her mercilessly. They parody the TV news interview. Edie poses, precisely answers. There is additionally onscreen a male companion who undresses, puts his feet on the pillows, plays with Edie's bra strap distractingly while she talks. The whole scene, indeed, is defined and explored territories: that of the screen, the bed, and the body (fig. 22).

The companion might be a longtime acquaintance or, as is more likely, has simply been invited in for this movie as attractive prop/ provocateur. In some way Gino is there to humiliate Edie or at least transgress her space. He enacts us, which becomes explicit in the moment when his false starts at love play culminate with Edie returning the embrace. The sexuality here feels real in the tension within the shot, and within the theater. There is a sense of anxious and excited anticipation. Which is broken by the voice offscreen suddenly noticing, as if, as he claims, he is looking up from a book. The stage of intimacy is broken. The public space of the film is reestablished with the offscreen query.

Warhol operates here by implication and excision. The world outside his frame is treated as character, is in fact an authentic force directing the action.[1] What manifests in Hollywood as invisible causality is here declared part of the action and director of it as well. With Warhol the outside clamors, pushes onto the film space, defying the invisibility of the screen's fiction. Thus the contradictions of time and space that movies are is accorded place. Territory is redefined and whether by exclusion (Warhol) or inclusion (Vertov) the result is to facilitate/infiltrate marvels of desire to turn reality, and our image of it, inside out. To return a sense of the unexpected to the world and thus to acknowledge what lies beyond our vision. Not subsuming the outside—forcing it to lose its identity—but acknowledging it as presence and difference.

Dennis Kaufmann, a.k.a. Dziga Vertov, became a hero to me when I saw his work *Man with a Movie Camera* (1928) in the mid-1970s. The generous camerawork of his brother, Mikhail Kaufmann, and the crystalline structure of the whole dazzled. There was intelligence and dynamism in the work, which made me want to see more. The more I saw, the more convinced I became of the logic and possibilities for extension of Vertov's discoveries into the present. Beginning as a documentarian myself, I shared some of his sense of the power of and attraction to the *everyday*. There was a retrospective of his work in the mid-1980s organized by Annette Michelson at the Papp Theatre on Lafayette Street in New York, when they still showed movies regularly in the small theater where seats had been designed by Austrian filmmaker Peter Kubelka. I saw all the work then and eagerly read his diaries when they came out. A bit earlier, Eisenstein's book of memories, written on his deathbed, had been published, and as these two were contemporaries, rivals in their theories of montage and their vision for cinema, it was an opportunity to discuss their respective stances from the other end of the century. This essay was first published in *Poetics Journal*, no. 7 (Sep. 1987): 71–78.

The Exhibit and the Circulation

(On Dziga Vertov/Sergei Eisenstein)

Under pressure of events, the material is formed. Under pressure of the material, the body is shaped. The shapes that result translate into allegiances and belief to become a record of the pressures of time.

"You have to know how to peddle your wares," Yutkevich says, reproachfully.

Can one die from hunger that's not physical but the hunger to create?

The educational must not be opposed to the poetic.

What conditions will guarantee success?

Not predigested, but not difficult to take in either. Most important: every-thing your own. A fresh idea, fresh construction, fresh language, and not the depersonalized illustration of slogans.

Flight is impossible without a point of leverage.

We demand the opportunity to test the antidote.[1]

Dziga Vertov's *Kino-Eye* is a history—of cinema, of experiment, of the defeat of formalism in Russia from the late 1920s through the 1950s, and a heroic evaluation of film and its transformative po-tential.

Time has slowed distribution of Vertov's ideas but not his clarity. The book offers us the optimism of awakening consciousness. It is persistent in its "effort to reveal the thinking of the 'living person'" (156).

The book itself is a constructivist text. This edition of "extracts" is divided into three sections: articles and public addresses, notebooks and diaries, creative projects and proposals. The material within each section is varied, the total a veritable mosaic of manifestos, a history of his movement (the Kinoks), with technical specifications, produc-tion procedures, defense, laments, ideas for films, forced apologies. There is repetition, sometimes linked topics, fragments from a shoot-ing log, love notes, anecdotes, a voice of intimacy interpolated with the voice of a scientist, the voice of experiment throughout.

The book recounts a history, shapes an autobiography. In its prose and vocabulary it reminds us of Viktor Shklovsky's *Third Factory*. It reflects its past, documents its present, and casts itself into the future in an active and still meaningful way. Vertov offers us an alternative to the theatrical narrative, to the cinema of his time and ours. He presents us with energy, fact and rhythm (as opposed to act and plot), a belief in the scientific process and a transformative vision.

We affirm the future of cinema art by denying its present. (Vertov, 7)

Vertov shapes a unique equation—a quantum leap—out of the Lumières and Méliès. From the one, quotidian observations of the world, its factories and everyday life, made by the objective scientist; and from the other, the play of cinema magic created through the technical proficiencies of the camera apparatus and editing process. Similar developments in the area of plotless image unified by rhythm are seen in the contemporary work of Fernand Léger (*Ballet mécanique*) and Charles de Keukeliere (*Combat de boxe, Impatience*). But neither emphasizes a documentary bias nor attains (or even attempts) the expansive theory and critical thought that underlie Vertov's work. D. W. Griffith's discoveries are relevant, but they are in service to the fictive; Eisenstein's are as well. Vertov seeks a more radical alternative.

WE *invite you:—to flee—the sweet embraces of the romance, the poison of the psychological novel, the clutches of the theatre of adultery; to turn your back on music,—to flee—out into the open, into four dimensions (three + time), in search of our own material, our meter and rhythm.* (Vertov, 7)

I'll condense what I've said: we have no film-objects. We have the cohabitation of film-illustrations with theatre, literature, with music, with whomever and whatever, whenever, at any price. (36)

Alongside the unified film-factory of grimaces (the union of every type of theatrical film work, from Sabinsky to Eisenstein) we must form a FILM-FACTORY OF FACTS. (49)

In the years to come, the scenario as a product of literary composition will completely disappear. (35)

Vertov's agenda exists within the background of the postwar and postrevolutionary period in Russia. His is a dialogue with other filmmakers, other artists and writers of his time. Together, many lived in the House of the Arts, worked in the film factories, published in *Lef* and *Novy Lef.* In 1926 Shklovsky writes: "Facts are being experienced esthetically. A work of art no longer needs a plot. What used to be working material for the artist has become the work of art."[2] For both writer and filmmaker, in the heat of the 1920s, born of war and revolution: facts are the mortar, factory the image, and science the threshold of invention.

WE *are in search of the film scale.* (Vertov, 9)

"Art and Everyday Life" interests us less than the topic, say, of "Everyday Life and the Organization of Everyday Life." (47)

Montage means organizing film fragments (shots) into a film object. It means "writing" something cinematic with the recorded shots. It does not mean selecting the fragments for "scenes" (the theatrical bias) or for titles (the literary bias). (88)

In fact, film is . . . the product, a "higher mathematics" of facts. Each item or each factor is a separate little document. The documents have been joined with one another. (84)

Vertov speaks of intervals, phrase, composition. He asks for form, not formulas ("rules do not remain immutable"). He seeks a tectonics, or architecture, of editing.

His early works, including *Kino-pravda* (Film truth), are newsreels of facts. He called them film diaries, and these works evidence Vertov's first experiments in linking discontinuous events through rhythm. In *Kinoglaz* he employs a braking effect: (literally) stopping the motion so that the bread and meat on the table return to their antecedents, through reverse photography making flour into sheaves of wheat in the field, returning the cow to the slaughterhouse, reassembling the cow. This film, along with *The Eleventh Year* (1928), is preparatory for *Man with a Movie Camera,* in which the hero is the camera, the plot the processes of filmmaking.

What used to be working material for the artist has become the work of art.

The entire film an exemplary revealing of the device: the movie begins, the audience arrives, the projector is threaded up, the curtains unfold, the movie-in-the-movie begins, to stop repeatedly, display its seams, deploy the film processes.

If one of film's goals was to acquaint people with the grammar of cinematic means, then to hide that grammar would have been strange. (Vertov, 155)

If an artificial apple and a real one are filmed so you can't tell them apart, that shows not skill but the lack of it.
A real apple must be filmed so that any imitation would be impossible. (198)

A laboratory is essential. We must provide models. Shake up people's minds. Break their habits. Stir them out of lethargy, open the way to innovation. (213)

. . . not merely a documentary "keeping of the minutes," but a revolutionary lighthouse set against the background of world film production's theatrical clichés. (104)

It is impossible to read this book, or see the films, without experiencing the active invention—exhilarating and precise—that Vertov champions and achieves. His is a prose of emphasis. Words are repeated, inverted. Sentences have surprising conclusions. His tone shifts from manifesto to anecdote, from anecdote to manifesto. There are lineups of parallel and imperative clauses, juxtapositions, many paragraphs, often composed of a single sentence.

. . . running from us, past us, toward us, in a circle or a straight line, or ellipse to the right and left, with plus and minus signs; movements bend, straighten, divide, break apart, multiply, shooting noiselessly through space.
Cinema is . . . the art of inventing movements. (9)

By the early 1930s it is clear that Vertov has underestimated the reactionary forces of his time. Some of the critiques that will be leveled at him are seeded in his early manifestos.

The "psychological" prevents man from being as precise as a stopwatch; it interferes with his desire for kinship with the machine. (7)

For his inability to control his movements, WE temporarily exclude man as a subject for film. (7)

And later, during production of *The Eleventh Year:* "I hesitate to talk of 'love' when speaking of my feelings toward this plant. And yet I really feel as though I want to embrace and caress these gigantic smokestacks and black gas tanks" (169). From a post–Manhattan Project, or more current, post-Bhopal setting, these are troublesome comments, naive at best, an excess born in the optimism of a successful revolution and the experience of civil war. By 1930, in the sound film *Enthusiasm,* we sense (despite its title) a backing off from his uncritical position: the factories of light, which represented optimism and progress in *Man with a Movie Camera,* here become heavy, dark infernos, the military music an elongated beating of the drum, a prophecy of the clamped-down future.

We move the group of immobilities. (107)

But what were the attitudes of some of our critics?
Either professorial—everything which is not "sharp" or "flat," in a word, everything which does not "doremifasolize" was unconditionally labeled "cacophony." Or we had to deal with the deaf critic—only the visual part of the film was critically examined, while the sound content was ignored. (114)

Under pressure from Stalin and the centralization for film production in both the East and the West, responding to the economic depression and the entry of sound, there is a normalization of procedure. The experiment is disarmed.

The project was canned . . . and the system of agreements. (195)

In practice the management's actions contradicted their decisions. (208)

[The work] proceeds underground, sometimes casting a dozen words onto the surface. . . . The flow of thoughts continues even if one of the interconnecting wires is broken. (118)

The diaries and journals that form the second section of the book are filled with Vertov's struggle to raise poetry against the debilitating facts of censorship and forced inactivity. There's a new intimacy, poignant and pugnacious, in his detailing of person and domestic events.

I'm always doing something, but never what's required. . . . Give up smoking. Eat less. Get up earlier. Do not what you want, but what needs to be done. You must want what is needed. . . . I should stop writing right now because I'm not writing what I'm thinking at all. I'll stop. (173, 175)

A face of film is submerged for nearly thirty years to reemerge with the American and European avant-garde of the late 1960s—to whom Vertov's call for a nonacted cinema, for rhythm as the linkage point, for a mobile unit and lightweight camera, for a recycling of images, for the possibilities of satirizing conventional genres, and for an open and material basis of construction appeared, and appear, resoundingly relevant.

It's essential to triple our energy. (104)

We have nothing against rifles, but we are not against high caliber weapons either. (192)

Yet the terms of the film public, if changed, remain monolithic. Narrative is the mainstream. With the exception of some of the cognizant (and politically based) films of the late 1960s, most documentaries aim for the look of fiction, or fiction absorbs and neutralizes the document. *When the Mountains Tremble* (1985), for instance, is a document aiming to be drama, complete with narrator whose background remains opaque, identity subsumed into mythic persona; or *El Norte*, from the same year, which creates a fiction of documentary fact. *Silkwood* is similar, or for that matter, any number of films that show us how America likes to take its facts—that is, filtered through the fictive romanticist "grimace."

Yet facts are what we need to talk directly to the audience. The aim is for an unesoteric art, and equally, one uncompromised. Vertov succeeds in meeting these demands. It is part of his appeal. Despite the limited distribution of his work, his is a populist art and at the same time a radically modernist one. His films are systematized improvisations, exemplary constructs, a tectonics composed of the everyday.

❖

In counterpoint, Eisenstein and his recently published *Immoral Memories*. It is fiercely ironic to think that the worker realism of Vertov is shunted aside for the historical fictions of Eisenstein under Stalin. But this is a simplification. We recognize that these books are not comparable in scale: *Film Form* and *Film Sense* would be more adequate to address a detailed analysis of respective film theories (which I have not set out to do). What interests me in comparing the two books is that they are both constructivist biographies that form a dialogue: raising mutual and conflicting definitions of the value of fact, of realism, illusion, psychology, drama, metric structure, and media confluence.

The contraries to Vertov, in terms of person and preference, are obvious immediately. In comparison to Eisenstein, a cosmopolitan and sophisticate, Vertov is a redneck and populist. Eisenstein survives by bending, though perhaps, as he himself notes, "unsuccessfully." Eisenstein is fluent in four languages, and his references range from Freud and James Joyce to Frank Harris (*My Life and Loves*). The work resonates with urbanity, with walks through the bookstalls of Paris, nocturnal Hamburg, and Hollywood.

Moreover, I now observe yet another phenomenon. In these writings one more contradiction has been resolved. They're as much reading as they are writing! In the beginning a page, a chapter or sometimes even a phrase, often I don't know where the continuation will lead me. . . . Let the material

be drawn from the depths of my personal reserves, let the factual evidence
be dug out of my personal experience, and here is a whole sphere of the
unexpected and unforeseen with much that is completely new: the juxtaposi-
tion of material, conclusions drawn from these juxtapositions, fresh aspects
and "revelations" stemming from these conclusions.[3]

This is a prose foregrounding process, experiencing itself, literary observations mixed with anecdotes, memoir with theory.

I lived in an epoch without parallel. But it is not of the epoch that I wish to
write. (Eisenstein, 4)

Compare Shklovsky in *Third Factory,* who wants to be in his time yet constantly slips out to critique it. Eisenstein writes from his sense of person, claiming that this is "beyond the historical background, beyond man in his epoch, beyond history reflected in consciousness" (Eisenstein, 7)

It is, then, history reflected in experience. The experience that of a man of the world, a man who leaves theater for the world of film, who becomes famous and now recounts his success. His own life is a drama: the chapter heads read like titles from Griffith's Biograph films—"The Boy from Riga," "The Dismantling of a Tyrant." Each chapter replays this shape: a past event or memory material is recounted, around which Eisenstein weaves a set of lyric, ironic, parallel, and often braking sentences that lead to an observation on film, a defense of method, and then into other critical texts, referring to D. H. Lawrence, Proust, and Shakespeare, among others.

His is a defense of the psychological, of its eminence in defining form. Eisenstein identifies his struggle with his father with the struggle of Ivan IV, "like a lullaby of rebellious deeds—not only in the social themes of my life, but in the area of film form" (28).

What is most interesting for me is how this whole host of interrelationships
with Papa's authority, in analysis atavistic, merges in me inevitably with
evolutionary ideas, as, indeed, does my approach to any question.

> *That is why I am drawn to my own conception of the zone of the prelogical, of that subconscious which includes, but is not enslaved by, sex.*
>
> *That is why the subconscious itself is depicted, above all, as the reflections of earlier and undifferentiated stages of social being.*
>
> *. . . That is why the propagation of the dramatic, and therefore one of its basic themes—that of vengeance—is not exhausted.* (28, 30)

This is a constructivism redefined, serving Eisenstein's lifelong allegiance to drama. He seems to be identifying drama with the urgencies of the subconscious, with sources outside social history. There's an insistence on the personal here and on private values. Written in the last years of his life, from a hospital bed, Eisenstein's speech is unguarded. He titles the next chapter "Cruelty," speaks of unhealthy desires and his first introduction to the texts of Sacher-Masoch and Krafft-Ebing. Later, learning how to dance and how to draw become lessons in rhythm and ethics.

> *[T]he fox trot was a "free dance," held together only by a strict rhythm, on the framework of which one could embroider any freely improvised movement.*
>
> *That's what suited me! Here once more I found that captivating free running line, subordinated only to the inner law of rhythm through the free run of the hand.* (46–47)

This is more like the energetic Eisenstein of the 1920s, the period of *Strike, October,* and *Potemkin.* There, the bristling of shapes and optimistic pullings at the seams of convention. Here, he concludes with regret: "How full of license were our productions in those years" (47). Juxtaposed with the elegiac tone are lyric passages and, at some points, almost Dada-like prose poems.

> Watches. Watches. Watches.
> Pocket watches with chains.
> With pendants.
> With seals.

Cigar cases. Cigar cases.

. . .

And sticks. Sticks. Sticks.

Straw hats.

This was summer. In July. (The third or fifth of the month.) On the corner of Nevsky and Sadovaya. (53)

The list of nouns, the repetition, the use of new lines, the unexpected abutments, the uneasy or ambiguous precision ("The third or fifth of the month") are succinct analogies to film montage. There is free association: a chapter about beds, another about books and roads, another ending with "I have seen quite a few people in my time" (78), followed by a lengthy paragraph of famous names.

This is "a completely shameless narcissism. . . . This is a paradise" (50).

This is a self-conscious consciousness. The book is somewhat of an advertisement, the style montage, the tone melodramatic. The prose is masterful, segueing divergent material, interpolating digressions, jumping off into theory with wit and facility. There are wonderful photographs and reproductions, as well, particularly Eisenstein's Cubo-Futurist costume designs from 1921 and 1922. Nonetheless, the book has something of the pulp biography about it. There are "few shocking details and tidbits" (1). It is immoral, Eisenstein explains in the first chapter, because it will not teach. It is "beyond didactics, beyond edification" (7). Compare Vertov's: "The educational must not be opposed to the poetic." These writings are for pleasure, and a sense of leisure, luxuriance, and person is present.

Certainly, underlying his self-justifications are years of curtailment and, as well, the sense that Eisenstein, knowing he is to die, is no longer constrained to meet the demands of his government. So—this is his pleasure: intriguing, exhibitionist, narcissistic, encyclopedic. An exhibit that haunts us for what was not completed, particularly when he speaks of a "montage of *intellectual attractions*" (207) or when one thinks of his plans to film *Capital* and *Ulysses*.

Yet even as Eisenstein's and Vertov's books draw out our sympathies, against the wall of censorship and for a practice of juxtaposition and invention, their differences strike us. Eisenstein is in the tradition of the international modern artist: Warhol, Picasso, Laurie Anderson. Some compromise is made; Eisenstein speaks of "bending," and it is clear that his later work does not compare in energy and filmic inventiveness to his early films. Vertov is frustrated sooner and more completely. In the last twenty years of his life his film production is fragmentary. We have only his heroic prose. Yet it is Vertov who speaks to us directly, whose work holds out to the present, lengthens its influence:

> . . . *not so much the exhibition itself, but rather a "circulation of the blood."* (Vertov, 46)

Science may no longer be a savior; surely it is no longer a one-sided god. Perhaps the cinema of the present is not such a one-sided devil, either, but rather the "prelogic" of our progress. If film can be read as the psyche of the nation, it's clear we have a bleak picture of even the most advanced technical know-how. *Alien* translates as a metaphor for the failure of the conglomerate; *Blade Runner* is a high-tech experiment run amok; *AI* ends via magical (optical) ascent into-the-future, out of the human picture. These are the atavistic responses. Yet what is needed ("We must want what is needed") is energy that leaves the human in the picture. Confronted daily with the "theatrical cliché," with the most trivial media slogans, with bits of advertisement jingles and characters from soaps, we need articulation, not more exhibits. "Only consciousness can fight the sway of magic," says Vertov (66), and only consciousness can fight the technological nonconscious, the face of the old as even the shape of the deadening new.

> *The worst truth is still the truth.* (Vertov, 210)

> *Do not judge by bare results. A particular defeat can be more valuable than a cheap success.* (268)

Appreciate those who invent, not those who acquire. (268)

You must provide a unique combination of the cells of the cinematic body, a way of grouping them that will resurrect the lifeless shots. (269)

Sooner or later this path shall be opened. (233)

INTERROGATIONS

Figure 23. Magician. Frame enlargement from *Mayhem*.

Among the locales in the United States where experimental film flourishes is the Boston/Cambridge/Somerville axis, churning in some large part through the tremendous dedication and energies of Saul Levine, filmmaker/teacher/programmer, and in the mid-1980s, curator of the short-lived magazine *XDREAM*. The first issue featured essays on my films by fellow filmmakers Marjorie Keller and Anne Robertson, and the following interview with poet, critic, and coeditor of *L=A=N=G=U=A=G=E* magazine, Charles Bernstein. This is the first interview that goes into detail about my process and intentions involved in making films. Equally familiar with my writing and cinema, Charles was well situated to interrogate me and hypothesize their interrelation. The interview was recorded in New York City, in spring 1985, and published in *XDREAM* 1, no. 1 (1986).

Time Corners Interview

(With Charles Bernstein)

ABIGAIL CHILD: Let's talk about editing. In *Ornamentals* I was cutting things together based on color, painterly values, textures. But one of the things that I was interested in was difference—I was interested in how far I could go to have things not match up but have them still fit together. So it became a corner of a building, corners of linkages rather than that surface that Brakhage focuses on. So I started by matching not texture exactly but contrasting color and shape: a circle to a circle, in a totally different space. It became this vortex, which we have talked about before. That's a concern of mine, the way space is experienced. As a teenager I had this sense that things could link in space on multidimensions, and I would think about that in terms of relationships, whether it was people relationships or abstract-idea relationships, that they could link in all three dimensions plus of course time and that's become a focus in my work. That's true of *Ornamentals*. It's true of *Prefaces*. In these and later works I'm attempting to compose elements that are out of step, create a time corner, a bending, instead of an adjacency. I'm trying to break the adjacencies.

CHARLES BERNSTEIN: I was just thinking it was not telling a story, perhaps, but conveying a different kind of progression and accumulation of materials, that has led you to really adopt, in a way, a *bricolage*, a number of different editing principles (and I do think it's *Prefaces* that marks the break) without relying on a single one. Your films have developed an ability to use different kinds of editing techniques rather than reifying a particular principle of editing. In terms of contemporary filmmaking that is very interesting and very unusual—and it seems to relate to work being done with narrative in some recent writing.

AC: It's definitely connected.

CB: But before we get into that, I want to go back a little bit and ask you to speak about the way you edited your films, keeping to some kind of chronological order. Then I want to know more about what you meant by getting away from the adjacencies and the juxtapositions in *Prefaces*. So go back to your first film. What was the conception in editing it?

AC: Well, that might be *Some Exterior Presence*. I had four elements sourced from a documentary on radical nuns that I had edited. It was the last commercial directorial job I did. The women were terrific, and the film was "adequate" within a formula of a half-hour TV documentary: do it in three weeks from start to airdate. Wanting to be more authentic to these women and their spirit, I took some of the work print, and I looked through it; and I was interested, as an editor, in the possibilities that the film could go forward, it could go backward, it could be flipped, and it could be upside down. I originally had seven sequences that I cut up—I was interested in how I could disjoint the movement in these possibilities of permutations. So it was mathematical in a way. I was reading physics at the time and was intrigued by Feynman diagrams, which had submicroscopic motion, the processes of exchange, annihilation, and birth. And it ended up with four sequences that I liked the way they moved, that I then intercut and one of the things I did was set up a score that I diverted from—I mean that I don't pledge myself to one way of being.

CB: What is the basic pattern here that you're talking about, the structural pattern, the score . . . ?

AC: The score was four elements—A, B, C, D—and all the possible permutations and the lineup of them was from original through four generations. There were three generations for each scene: I had the original, though that was in fact a work print, already second generation; and a print made from that, that would go through a printer; and then the printer material. So I had second, third, and fourth generation material, and I had these rhymes, these permutations I was choosing—I could transgress. Where I would look at it and get bored and think it could be changed to be more precise to my desire . . .

CB: You immediately found what some people might consider the formal beauty of the order you were creating didn't interest you, that bored you so you . . .

AC: No, no, that interested me, but I felt like it could be . . . that it could have its exceptions as well.

CB: —could be subverted—

AC: —yes, subverted. There's a desire, a predilection on my part, to break rules to accommodate the proliferation of new ideas, reflect or include thought in transition, and I want to give credence to improvisation of these ideas and the time—

CB: Subversion is a theme that you're interested in, especially as it emerges in the later films.

AC: I agree with that. How could I say yes to this beginning decision and not include these other things? Then it became a structural idea, yes, I can subvert. I can digress and I'm going to purposely, as in *Covert Action*, construct something built on digressions.

CB: Right, this gets us back . . . this is what I meant when I was suggesting crudely picaresque narrative structures. I think that's what I mean by subversion, and what you're saying about *Covert Action*, construct something built on digression. Subversion being that which is under the version, underneath the surface, and that underneath is always repressed, isn't allowed to show through when principled or structural or visionary compositional method is used. It seems to me that the work, over time, has consistently tried to find ways for these things to seep up through and not only come to the surface but to break through it, interrupt. . . . You begin to use intertitles and so on, all these archaic elements, surfacing in the later films. It is almost a rococo, which I think is a reaction against the pristinity of sticking to a singular, uniplanar surface. When you were doing this first film, you were already talking about being uncomfortable with the very principles of editing that seem to have been given to you. At the time of this first film, what other filmmakers excited you? Or were you unhappy with everything and thinking, I'm gonna do something different? Were you trying to emulate something?

AC: Let's see . . . I saw Brakhage at eighteen and appreciated it but was going somewhere else, and it wasn't until years later in New York, when I saw some of Frampton's works and he just opened up the possibilities of what could be. I wasn't trying to emulate him. I was responding to my documentary experience, when you would be grabbing for film, you would reach and get it in reverse. It was a material response. It was constructivist—

CB: What year is this film?

AC: I finished it in 1977, started it in 1976. I had discovered I really liked the feel of film, I liked to put it together, I liked to see its structure. In that period documentary editors would say, "The best cut is the one you can't see," and right away that was not where I was. I always loved to feel every cut and to see every cut and to know it was there. And I also found I was interested in what was happening after the shot was over, where everybody else would cut out and say this is the end of the scene. I was always interested in the bleed part, in the part that was going to be excised. It was often then when people would suddenly think the camera was off and they could be themselves, and I was interested in those kinds of changes. So in the editing, was I doing something new? I was on new ground for myself, and I was trying to do something in response to particular experiences in my life and this piece of footage.

CB: What film work had you done up until this point? You were saying you worked commercially.

AC: I had done documentaries on my own.

CB: How long had you been doing documentaries?

AC: For about four years.

CB: And did you imagine when you started on this documentary work in the early 1970s that this would be a vocation for you?

AC: I knew it would be my life. Film would be.

CB: But you thought documentaries were more kind of . . .

AC: No, I just started in documentaries. I can't say that I thought for sure that I was going to be a documentary filmmaker. I just knew film would be my avocation.

CB: Well, what did film mean to you?

AC: Multiplicity. I was editing my first film and I was in the editing room and I said to myself this is what I want to do for the rest of my life because film is rhythm, words, painting, ethnography—which is, I think, reappearing in the work in the way I'm looking at gesture. It was that I had found, let's say, a prism that would allow me to be in a contained thing and make these works.

CB: What kind of films really excited you at the point that you started first to work with film? Was it ethnographic, as well as Hollywood films?

AC: Ethnographic as well as Hollywood as well as documentary. The works I hadn't seen were the experimental. I was a product of suburban America, and I had only seen what suburban America had seen. It took years before I started to see these other works. It was a real opening for me, other possibilities. There came a point when I realized I was using another person or situation to talk about my own concerns (in terms of the documentary subject), and I just wanted to be clearer, more personal, more straightforward on to what I . . . and also not having to deal with the whole question of public genre. The public forum, the way it was "supposed" to be for a documentary to go on TV. It was just inadequate to my needs at that point. My personal experiences were pushing me towards a political realization—about the shapes of film, and what was excluded, and how it got made and distributed. A position whose implications were more radical than that of the leftist documentarians, which was the milieu I was involved with in New York.

CB: Had you seen, at that point, films from before World War II, say, films from Europe?

AC: Not too many, no. *Blood of a Beast* by Franju I remember liking especially.

CB: And how about American independent films?

AC: I had seen some of the American independent films—mostly the documentaries. *Don't Look Back,* the Wiseman series. Then in 1975 I went to Hampshire to study the optical printer, and there were lots of films being shown there every hour, every day. Landow was there, Peter Hutton was there, Robert Breer was there. Frampton wasn't, but his films were shown, also Brakhage's. Who else? The next year I saw a bunch of Marie Mencken films and that was inspiring. And Andy Warhol . . .

CB: And you made this film within the context of seeing these other films moving out of the context of—

AC: Of documentary, yes. I was aware at the time of something wonderful about using documentary footage, that it was rich in a nonprivate experience. It was rich in the world outside the film-maker's diary. It had that potentiality of people on the street, of that kind of liveliness. When I finally saw Vertov, part of what I love about Vertov is this kind of encompassing world that gets in there. Your subject's enlarged immediately.

CB: So the next film that you did was what?

AC: It was *Peripeteia I.* I was in the Oregon woods, and I had seven one-hundred-foot rolls of film, and I was alone. There was no electricity. And I gave myself permission to shoot anything, opening to a lot of digression, in other words, *not* saying I'm going to do this one thing and do it, but in fact doing a number of things. As a result, I think it holds a certain kind of innocence and digression in the final film.

CB: How did you edit that film?

AC: I looked for the end of a sequence, where it would go to the next one. A continuum that stops in the middle and takes off to the end so it has two halves, but very simple. It was really a camera film more than an editing film. *Peripeteia II* too, even more. It has never been edited. I just have a work print, and that was going back to the same place, and giving it a structure, taking two elements, one stable, the other mobile as the focus. . . . I was looking at ways to structure work. But it wasn't until *Ornamentals* that I began to look for the difference *between shots*. For every time I could turn a corner. Also, *Ornamentals* was based on material that I felt had so much emotional expressive hold that I wanted to subvert that. I didn't want you to make up stories about each of the images. I wanted to place it in a context, where each image was single and would leave, would go away, like thought in the process of thinking, or maybe the thing that happens where you go to bed at night and all the images that you didn't have time to process during the day come back. They're disconnected, but there's this flow. I think images should go together with more than one connection, however, that they . . . have to have at least two connections to stand there, to stay in the work.

CB: After *Pacific Far East Line* you did—

AC: *Pacific Far East Line:* then *Ornamentals* in the same year, and it was almost as if they were two opposites. I was doing *Pacific Far East Line* shot out of my window; I was limited in shooting. I couldn't be on the street, yet I was going out on the street shooting [for *Ornamentals*], going through old footage and there it was: two different structures. *PFEL* is very straightforward, elements coming in of similar subject material, whereas *Ornamentals* is all fragments, from all different places instead of one place. I thought about making that film [*Ornamentals*] for a year and a half. I wanted to do a film on the color spectrum. And I also had this sense of an expanding field. Whereas, in a way, *Pacific Far East Line* is more like a field painting. It's almost equal throughout, there's a slight build, but it is basically equal. *Ornamentals* builds differently. And I saw that as a real distinction.

CB: Explain that more. What does development mean to you? Do you think that some of your films, like *Pacific Far East Line,* did not have development in that way? That they began and they ended at the same place?

AC: Well, time goes through it, so it's always different, but I think it collapses time. It creates a static but shaky, writhing really, architecture. Something like Smithson's entropy: another level of mapping action and reaction. Looking at a box or dirt, or in this case a horizon, two horizons in fact, and making that the world. It makes you aware of time in the sense that the extent of the film could be, well, the sense that it could be three years or it could be ten minutes. I think of it as twelve-tone cutting because I was reading a lot about and listening to twelve-tone music. But then again, my tendency to disrupt my own rules led to certain kinds of dramatic openings, dramatic middles, and ends. I was aware of those shapes.

CB: You have a continuous rhythmic movement in *PFEL,* almost a musical rhythmic unity of perception. Even though it takes place in time, it's really spatial; it's like entering into a building. I mean to say that it has development temporally, but it doesn't have development in terms of plot, in terms of metaphor, metaphor meaning to move from one place to another.

AC: You can't say *Ornamentals* has development of any plot either, but it does have by the way it's constructed; it becomes, I think, analogous to the brain's way of moving, which does build. It constructs on top of something so that things jump off at different places in space. Additionally I was trying to destroy plot in *Ornamentals.* I feel like the human figure and certain kinds of loaded situations or intensities throw up narrative immediately. I'm interested in that, a sort of minimal narrative.

CB: Obviously words like *narrative* and *plot* are loaded in one way and *plot* especially misleading. *Narrative* in its more neutral sense simply means the methods by which you move from one point to another, from one item to another.

AC: Yes. Passage.

CB: Recounting. But counting is part of it.

AC: But it also means difference. At the two points of passage, I mean. It doesn't mean an equilibrium to a passage to an equilibrium that's the same. It's an equilibrium that is *disequilibrium.* . . . I mean it does suggest that change, I think.

CB: Well, some kind of progression, you mean, differential. Still, it seems to me in some of the earlier films you're suggesting that progression isn't really what they're about at all but that they're—it's more an overall compositional realization.

AC: That is true. The progression then is spread throughout to make a construction, an architecture, is how I think about it. But it does, I think, change the effect of how a film reads if my intent is to build something like an overall composition or a more process-oriented work. The film reads differently. The energies display themselves differently.

CB: Well, let me bring up something that you said before that interested me. . . . When you were editing documentary films you were told that the best edit was one you can't see, something like that. But you were interested in having them seen as edits. Now to some degree, even within an unconventional style of filmmaking, if the structure of the editing is done in a highly delineated or highly "poeticized" way, you certainly see the edits taking place, but they seem so clearly to be compositional and rhythmic elements that they don't disappear but become aestheticized. Yet there might be another sort of editing in which the edits were really disruptive and didn't seem aesthetic, didn't seem programmatic, didn't contribute in an obvious way to plot development—that seemed to be generally ragged, or to just show as being not edits, only, but *stitches*. It seems to me that when we get on the other side of *Pacific Far East Line* in your work, your more recent work, you seem interested in these genuinely more disruptive kinds of things, and you're actually creating a music with the disruption. I think of eighteenth-century literary narrative techniques, such as those in *Tristram Shandy,* or, you know, little narrative descriptions of what's gonna happen next, which don't necessarily follow up on anything, material that's primarily about the way in which progress in the story is taking place. Gesture is obviously another thing, and your use of sound. I mean there's all kinds of new things that enter in after *Pacific Far East Line.* With the focus on the gesture, the human body, or the human figure I should say, becomes more central to the films. And the sound track becomes an autonomous element that seems very important to the strategy of the editing, that the sound in your film could stand on its own. It doesn't simply fill out the images. So often sound tracks are used to animate the film's image. Think of Philip Glass's music pouring over the National Geographic landscape of *Koyaanisqatsi.* It's as if the visual images are porous, and the sound is like oxygen being seeped up by the porous film images. Whereas your sound and image are impermeable to each other just as certain segments of the film seem impermeable to the rest of the film. They're not absorbed into the overall composition of the film. You seem interested in including intractable material.

AC: In *Prefaces* I wanted to make chords. I didn't want the sound to complete the image. I wanted it to be an additional note that would change the sound of the image. And yes. My interest in gesture is an interest in the human body and how it means. I suppose gestures are of interest because they are also intractable. They don't speak, gestures don't vocalize, so that one can read them variously.

CB: The subject matter is intractable, so that the gestures elude being matched up.

AC: But full of meaning, so that they're full of this resonance that is indecipherable in its finality, but you could be accurate about it.

CB: What got you interested in wanting to do sound and wanting to employ some of these more, for lack of better words, narrative and figurative elements?

AC: If one of the things I was exploring was compositional strategies, another thing that seemed to me apparent was abstraction and image, image building, concrete images, object images, and human bodies. In *Ornamentals* the surfacing of images out of the abstraction was of interest to me. This becomes close to language—that films can denote, be both abstract and realist, with a high degree of complication and field for combination. It seemed logical for me to move in that direction. In my next film, *Prefaces,* the image has surfaced much more. Sound, in film, seems to me an open area that hasn't been fully explored. I mean—here I can be with something that hasn't been dealt with, looking at this larger grammar of what's possible in film. So that was a challenge to me.

CB: What kind of sound films interested you, once you thought you might make sound films, or immediately before that?

AC: There were a few films that I had seen by then that were of great interest. Kubelka's films, *Our Trip to Africa* particularly. And another film that was very impressive was *Critical Mass* by Frampton. Do you know those?

CB: I haven't seen *Critical Mass.*

AC: A terrific film—he has two students arguing—"Where were you . . . well, where were you?"—and he films it with the sync track and makes all these cuts and loops so it becomes this magnificent design. But also very expressive with the human relationships fore-grounded. To me it was one of the most beautiful, sound, perfect little films.

CB: Whose work with film sound interests you?

AC: Godard definitely. In some of his latest work he lets the voice slip, and a man's voice replaces a woman's voice; and he's playing really, many, many subversions. Also Bresson, his *Lancelot du Lac,* for instance, where we hear the horses coming for two minutes before they appear.

CB: One of my favorite films actually.

AC: And currently there are a number of people who have done interesting work in sound—this list is provisional whom I'm thinking of right now—Henry [Hills] of course, Charles Wright, Betzey Brom-berg. Leslie Thornton, Manuel DeLanda, Alan Berliner, to name some. And there's . . . I just saw these Polish films, one of them is a continu-ous yell that was shot with the light changing and then reworked across the tone of the yell. Almost an Alvin Lucier composition with a single tone. I think there's a number of people working today, who are working with sound, not just filling out the picture but working in the way that they're trying to actually make something that plays against or adds or, what I keep calling chordal, *changes* the picture.

CB: Is there some audiotape work—as opposed to instrumental music—that interests you?

AC: There probably is a lot being done that I'm not familiar with. I was just in this show in Holland, for instance, that included a hun-dred women's tapes of which I only knew a few. It included work by Hannah Weiner, and Diane Ward's "Cuba" tape among others. And of course there's music tapes, some of the early Stevie Wonder collages and rap collages definitely, yes. Musicians have been using tapes for a long time. That's happening with John Zorn's compositions, and, of course, that's also in Cage, in Stockhausen. I think everybody, they get the tape recorder and the first thing they do is make a tape collage.

CB: Talking about sound seems a good segue into your work as a writer. Not only have you written and published a good deal of poetry, but you also read an enormous amount of poetry. Could you talk about the relationship, if any, between poetry and your film work?

AC: Sometimes I think it doesn't have anything to do with it, but it seems to be more to do with it now, perhaps, than it did. . . .

CB: Well, I'm going to venture a comment on this but because it's, well, it's almost easier for somebody else to comment on a relationship that you're so inside of it's hard to see. And it has to do with my own interest in writing and how I understand film in terms of that. I think writing is from the point of view of the *physical* production much less onerous than filmmaking and film editing. Using pen and paper, it's very easy and quick to edit. So there's an incredible amount of research and investigation you can do if you're involved in a fairly complex revision-oriented writing style, research into the kinds of associations and relations between syllables and word, between sentences and stanzas or paragraphs, between intruded and internally generated material. You get really tuned up to the possibilities of putting things together. The fusion that takes place—working with—and at—writing, you begin to understand the power that editing has to disguise itself and how hard it is to make the editing apparent. Because it's so easy for the editing to close up the gaps. Many poets at this time are involved in a number of quite different and interesting approaches to how to put divergent materials together, how to deal with digression, how to deal with narration. So it's a parallel area that has much information, literally, for a filmmaker. I think writers, of course, can find a lot out from film. Many writers I know are almost obsessed with film.

AC: Yes, film materializes what we know about cognition and memory. It materializes these things, which I think does change how we see. Perhaps editing is more onerous in film than in writing, but the result in film is more exaggerated, enlarged I might say, and certainly at the beginning of the century less *elided*, a very concrete non-segue from image to image, a cinematic positioning of impossibilities. For Joyce, Stein, Proust, film cuts must have been very exciting concretizations of the movement of thought. But what is also interesting to me is music and very specifically from the turn of the century on—Satie, for example, and Antheil's *Ballet mécanique* or Ive's music using marching tunes and folk hymns, and Varèse, Cage, Stravinsky, Kagel, Berio. I think of them, putting materials together, incorporating tape with music, and considering noise as music as well. And also, the sense of tape in the latter half of this century as producing a kind of library. If there's a library of filmed images in all the movies made, there's also this library of sound that tape allows you to access that begins to approach the library of reading, the library of books, the printed word. These things are coming in, and like reading, film and music create a kind of pool of information to incorporate and process. I was thinking one of the advantages if my films go to videotape is that you can replay it, reread it. Video as a kind of improvisational optical printer.

CB: Yeah, but do they have different speeds that you can use on most videos? I mean do people ever use those?

AC: They do actually, I think.

CB: I find it very exciting, in seeing films on flatbeds, that you can stop the film and go back and see the thing again. But I'm just thinking even the idea of making the film is very dense, is related to a concept of reading as opposed to a passive viewing . . .

AC: The reading is actually the engagement—to look at this, decipher it.

CB: Right, and look at it in different ways, at different angles, a number of times at different speeds. So it seems to me that's another area in which absorption in what's going on now in writing would direct one even further away from some of the so-called given constraints of filmmaking. Which would seem to me increasingly a limitation of film as I become, oddly to say, less and less able to pull myself out to see the commercial products that are being issued in the last couple of years.

AC: Yes, I'm very surprised how some writers will go, and go again and again, to Hollywood movies, even as they disparage, and sometimes vehemently, narrative in writing or poetry. I love movies. I like seeing Hollywood or independent or foreign features, but if that were my only diet in films, it wouldn't be enough. This tolerance, avidness, for the commercial entertainment seems to me only a measure of how large Hollywood's monopoly has become, in people's consciences and imaginations, and how large in culture it is and how it's your kind of hot dog and you can't do without your hot dog and you don't even see the forces behind your desire and that "blindness" gives these monopolies the freedom to shape and change and distort everybody's minds. I want my work to challenge these assumptions, upset the torque of culture, at least enlarge the field.

CB: In emphasizing the value to having a great degree of differentiation, a maximum amount of differential from one element to another from the sound to the image, from the different images, your films seem to be more thoughtfully related as a totality, more thoughtfully conceived and realized, than films that have a more overt strategy that connects them. The connections have to be worked out by the reader. They seem to be composed one by one, and that creates a much richer, denser field of possible meanings for the reader to find. That is, the recent films are not simply compilations of autonomous things, but rather these things have been fused into a whole through your overall workings with them.

AC: That's true also of the entire series *Is This What You Were Born For?* The structure of the work is that each of the parts has these very different relations of sound to image and quality of image changing, black and white or color, figuration or abstraction, or increasing narrative sense. They are a macroscope of difference. Now that three films of the series are done, they're beginning to speak among themselves, and certain concerns become evident. The project isn't a single line, or even an expanding line, but a series of corners in relation to mind, to how one processes material, how they get investigated, how they get cut apart, how something else comes up. I was thinking my work doesn't develop in a straight line, but if you were on top of a building looking down, you could trace out a direct path of turns, so that each work leads into the next, but you can't see it over your shoulder; you have to see it stepwise. And that the procedure of difference in the individual films relates to the total project.

CB: Do you want to briefly describe *Justine* [this project was retitled *Perils* and completed in 1986], or will that be done elsewhere?

AC: It won't be done elsewhere, but . . . I'd rather not right now because I'm in the middle of shooting it. And, one of the things we were talking about on the way over, which is relevant to being "in the middle" of making a film, is not that one doesn't know what one's doing in a work. You do know what you're doing and you have a sense of what it is to become, but you don't know the particulars; and I would say that if I knew exactly what the work would look like when it was done, I wouldn't need to do it. I'm really struck sometimes at the end of a work, when I've been through the process, how close it is to what I imagined it at the beginning. But to get there is a unique, one-on-one experience. That it isn't just descending into a mass and coming up. They're very particular and very specific decisions.

CB: Well, you might say you find out what you know rather than already knowing what you know.

AC: Or that what you know is greater than what you can think about. That making the work is a kind of optimism towards the world, that the world can be refracted to include its complexities, a realization held there to be seen for the duration of the work. That the work, let's say, *frames* the attempt, lets the thought be visualized but isn't a "frame-up." Doesn't package the idea but concentrates it, constitutes it. That the work isn't apriori itself but becomes something in excess of the original idea. That it has a roominess or room for its excess—and for its silences as well. I think that's the pleasure for the filmmaker and audience. That the work exists in its own right, is something beyond yourself, something alive to the resonance of rousing liveliness in the viewer. This great sense making your brain talk, and moving your brain in places it hasn't been before.

Herein is a double-columned transcription of the verbal sound track from *Prefaces, Part 1* from my film series *Is This What You Were Born For?*—the title from a Goya etching in his *Disasters of War* series. New York, with its speed and multiplicity, challenged me to take visual discoveries into the syncopation of sound. Perhaps predictably, the film is compressed, noisy, and full of repositionings—a collaged poetics where different voices join in a fast-paced, spinning continuum. My source recordings include a walk on the Lower East Side of Manhattan with poet Hannah Weiner (who sees words and, at this point in her life, was seeing words in colors) as well as fragments from Little Richard, Billie Holiday, Stravinsky's *Les Noces,* and the sound track "narration" from a found British educational film shot in Africa in the 1950s.

Prefaces

Now this isn't for me
This isn't for me
ho ho
Turn on the tape
We go through circumstance
that to be do
like a cloud
(specifically)
specific shape
Do you?
I mean that is
time
time
whichever system you were
in at that time. You would get

the one you made
Don't push it
well I mean OK
that is
conversations
I I've gone through the ceiling
You ask me how
I the I
by which I
get my
just be careful
It can carry up to

Meanwhile
You got the money

Figure 24. Woman's head. Frame
enlargements of edited strip from
Abigail Child's *Prefaces* (16 mm, b/w
and color, sound, 10 min., 1981).

across the street
the country is lifting
upon cultivation—
fly
I don't see that. Regard—
her
Whose apostrophe? Tell us.
They would jump
in
I said it—world
Mama erupt
The money is the big problem
remote
faction
feeling
immaculate
army
all the more
We're projecting?
stand
talkin' to me
Blank
while the other is the self
same thing
which is and
everything
New York
books, book
fat botheration
psychic messages
or even anything
which is everybody
O. please
I think you have to change
the form
lichten. flowers. times

and then
a dollar gas
Socialism seems more natural
to and fro—
Look it—
religion
It's the old
distribution
problem
too much
like this then
I feel like you can see that
their tribal background is
and pushing it
local
I'm thinking the light
going by.
Put it on the street
everyday
o no
be do or necessarily
we'll omit it
the light
to which assembly committed
groups together

running round
learn the difference
break it
trying to get me hooked
learn bits
and varnishes
offices
sounds like a hierarchy to me
poverty, academie
Name washes away the

but it's true
flashing on more and growing
Put this on the tape
trying to run me up a creek
seen then on the
sumpin' wrong
the local ghetto hole
Make it clear
or something like that
that stuff is next
you're pushing it
running
Help me!
get away
You row
backwards, go back
almost disastrous
I just go
la musica / bright
c'mon
bright, with a lot of light.
once and
yes, dance, making skips
strings
time
in the moon. thinking
plenty of socks (shuffled)
I'm not silly enough it says
drop out
dime gone
don't
32,000
you're kicking her hard
terrific job
Pulses of light
written in smoke

it was so nasty
clear lit in other ways
nor is it a healthy place
the opposite?
down the hole
not as fast
calling me until I die
put it on the line
just be very careful
and don't tell a story
shifts
the instinct (acquire)
the original
they go in
settle down, seeing that I'm
You say
I like this
it shows
I read you
line
sent through
—no not that
They lost it
listen
ah, blah blah
To see
see it gone . . . blah blah
big word
overruled
need more light.
Put it on the tape
because it is
without confirmation
except
to look at things
all time. I think.

"Today it can be well looked
after.
Some of them even cured of
their disease
but unfortunately, there is no
room for all of
them."

This is tape
a tellin' me a tale. Aah.
See if you can
both of them
I you said
Tell us, you said
nothing's happening
Two people
so, it's a
porcupine (ha)
if and, and another—
either

There is by the way
State political—
equal
depending on
feels
production behind it—
he is gone
too blonde
I can't tell much.
No more. Well it's got
three suits
Don't put it on the tape.
suddenly
silence is golden in theory.
de regard.

you need to insure yourself.
No
not so much
no. I know it
so don't confuse it
and then difference is like
it's ok right now

i just got
Child. Get rid of it.
that most advanced type
didn't do it that way
knock out. o
ludicrously
itches
still with them
time when
many of them are killing the
earth
without even a thought
you're crying about it
oarlocks
aren't anything
the light the light
cloudy
we all know of it
Desire
generated
desire
Note that—
heart
whose elements form
in silence
taken that image
connected
my objection

deine Spring off the glass
I got fighting
bad ass
seem to be
doing it
there's a difference in light
still kill kill
but if I see
particularly
perpetually
consistently
split
color
things
a lot
counter
as I could
pervert
I knew I'd be tempted.
Creme. See dream. O
light
She's out of control.
no need to make
explain.
Negotiating
yourself
hard working
breaks
exaggerate
sort of like the light popping off
    the head
then the sky working in
nobody even
maybe what I mean is
clarify
what I love

at all
even to life
can be conscious
we I we
using pure metal
within your own power
to come,
to interact
light screen
in the thick
another flash.
filling
light like past
when I seen you going
light more light
all right
go go go
that's why it's dying
just ask me how I know
(discourse)
can't complain
it's much better not to.
Don't
get come. tremendous skill.
it's your ability to cope
you do
like *ojo.*
One thing after another
time
times

change so much

that's how it goes
almost
at last

and when
completed night
get along in your life
that it's sapient
like that
the

don't quote
it's a different indication
them that's more
life
there's enough.
Enough

Figure 25. Frame enlargements of
edited sequence from *Prefaces*.

After four years in San Francisco I am back in New York living in a downtown neighborhood with drug busts monthly (the potato chip truck delivers heroin to the local bodega), a tenement apartment with a shooting gallery on the second floor (Steve, the "proprietor," has every Billie Holiday record ever recorded), and friends on occasion are stabbed in the entryways. I am at work on my first film in New York, *Prefaces*, which will begin my sound-film series, produced throughout the 1980s, *Is This What You Were Born For?* I am showing the film at the Cinematheque in San Francisco in August 1982 and compile the following for program notes. My "found" material—indicated with italics—includes a cross-section of my reading at the time: critical writings about their work by poets and writers Viktor Shklovsky, William Carlos Williams, and Mallarmé. Mallarmé's contribution is from his *Preface* to the famous *A Throw of Dice*.

Preface for *Prefaces*

Part 1 of *Is This What You Were Born For?*

To create an oppositional force, the images to move, eyes to ear, I wanted to create a fabric. Everything is displaced. The construction not of "regular sound effects" but of prismatic instants. The images are juxtaposed along lines of difference (as defined by filmic values, shape, scale, direction of movement). The sound cut exists in a durational relation to function rhythmic. Meanings are placed in unfixed relations, tangent, illustrative, vertically, and horizontally, and circularly, splicing-in-at with-around-and-from. You could say the sound plays the part of the page, the way its field excites the eye turning the meanings the word sounds make (polyphonic) or that it is modeled after the mind's divergent attention (jumpy overlaps) or perhaps that the relation of sound to image is prepositional, is a repositioning. *To sever the connections which have become scar tissue.*[1]

But this analysis is *after*. The motives are set in motion from a more tentative dream of a landscape of vortices, constant corners, contrast switching, and the concrete simultaneity of every day. To meet that, exist within and with it. I don't want to erase what I can't summarize.

The invisible orchestra gives way to a sharp note, a human voice sounding vowels (*a, e, o, u*) over the four shots matched in direction of movement, leading into the image of an iron bar being placed in fire. The vowels (opera) become a phrase in Japanese (speech).

There's a continuity of line through motion, a piling up of image and affect in the steady accretion of vortices, stops, starts, sharps. The film builds an evolving and *reversing* play between levels of representation, between combative levels of "kinds" of image/sound relations. There is compression: the work a massive fluidity held to its tension (hypothetically) in bebop rhythms and a surfacing narrative located mostly in holds sentences denotative language. The declarative phrases of the voice-over—*Socialism is more natural. Put that on the tape.*[2]—act as punctuation within the flux.

The paper intervenes every time an image on its own, ceases or retires within the page, accepting the succession of the others.[3]

Don't speak to me of the anti-poetic.[4]

Become an extension of time in effect in its detail to the fraction's attention.

The radical nature of *disorganization* challenges the assumed whole. The second look—the chord, memory, recording, print—subverts linearity, cross-links, intersects, and rewires the breathing body, creating new horizons, new spatial and civic relations.

So—not a catalogue of slots. Rather—a twisted interlocking of time, a "realism" as elastic as thinking is. Time and rhythm riding on massive arms. A schema of relations are wires crossed. *Roundness, full-*

ness, all sorts of attractive detail are abandoned and are replaced with array, disarray, congestion.

A history of colonization is some of the subject.

But what counts in topology is whether one shape can be continuously deformed into another.[5]

History is written under—reprocessed *by* and *through* reproduction. Think what we know of the American West and how much that sources Hollywood. The media distributes *fiction,* and it is taken "for real." The fictional past is reconstructed more sturdily in the process.

In *Prefaces* I wanted to use found images as a resource, a dictionary, to deacculturate our "image bank"—to break the bank image in fact, to redistribute, to structure a pulse-field-pulse through which and with which permutations act exchange. The structure is density, a tessellation. More than any "once" to even see it. The desire—for maneuverability (to meet every day), and sense, the base of position in principle.

The character of the material analyzes the mind.

The second film in the *Is This What You Were Born For?* series, *Mutiny,* incorporates documentary and performance film in a staccato structure. The film was originally planned as a montage of outtakes (those images not used) from a documentary I had directed seven years previously for a Public Broadcasting national television series, *Women Alive!,* on teenage girls in Minneapolis before their senior year in high school. Ultimately, the high school material felt limiting, and the need to get out of suburban alienation, albeit multicultural and class revelatory, proved imperative. I scavenged my early documentaries, including *Game* (1972), about a prostitute and a pimp in downtown Manhattan, and *Savage Streets* (1974), a portrait of South Bronx street gangs, to add to the mosaic that was becoming *Mutiny*. I filmed downtown colleagues: Sally Silvers dancing in a Manhattan office, Polly Bradfield playing violin in Chinatown, Shelley Hirsch singing in Little Italy at the Sullivan Street Fair. Combining the materials, usually with their synchronous sound attached, I wanted to create a dissonant percussive *musique concrète.* The transcription below is of the language that appears in the film. What you do not experience here are the noises and music, machine-made or otherwise, that accompany and punctuate the flux.

Mutiny

That my mind

goes like this
(child)
blow it
signifies
ah—go here
might be, that's what we'll—

at the
the time
time
twice
twenty seconds
this is hard to tell but
but, but ah
c'mon—it's more than

it's inaudible
inconnu

remembering
remember
do you think bobby-socks
are that ugly?
so silly. Hoy.
or other.
e-va
there's something
coming back
oh—or
decisions/decisions
anyway.
I was
re-view
everyday
man—
with
everyday
oooo
violent situation
o don't
whatever you do
why?
I'm the citizen
just—
where you let your mind
it's the position
The pictures aren't linear, and
that
spotlight
I love
high, beyond
mass of

remember, it
the one
remember
automatically—
bongo
you know?
no! but
but I was straight out tight
straight out
straight out
all right

wipe out
oh you mean that goes up
you're
with all your heart.
or any more
what. If
I mean
yeah, félice,
on another
for instance
or occasion
you love it.
either
you're in there or you're not
whereas feelings,
feeling
very emotional
feelings
look at
the man—
this
plates.
all day.
all right

approach
siding
no. we don't have this
connected right
the jerries or something
anything
you do know
community
something serious,
seriously
reason
we are subject to
rats and roaches
all lines
unless it ain't cold
still yes.
To work in a
I, I—
Why is it so?
there was nothing
people flashing
to flashing
blah bla bla
this
blah bla bla
at that point
maybe the earthquake was
coming—
We hustle

get enough?
uh—no
that's how it goes
exactly
that's right
I love it

and it's difficult
shoving the calls at you
saying really no
you gotta
do this
gotta gotta
let go
but when I think back on it
beforehand, before before
what is
that situation
and ah
Frank Sinatra talking
it was kind of ridiculous
switching
what's that one?
dormé
are you?

perhaps, but
but
but
what? no buts. oh
you know like
let's cut out, and
whoa
ever since those
this. *They run up on you*
because if you're not in there,
you know, I felt this incredible
pang. feel good?
it's my love, the peace,
peaceful
a beautiful but maybe
embarrassing
beauty

more
You might as well keep going
great balls of fire
breathless
without a story
you are wise
Ah come on
and they would dance
souped up on new york
let's go outside
something like that
got together both
yes you know.
no
alright. it doesn't go linearly
a deedle dee
what?
sticky.
is appealing
to make it
break
to
I
eye
eyes

beauty
was always
unconscious
for weeks—
just, just
my attention
sleep encapsulated
the satisfaction
situation
projection
communication
if it be any

why I'm liable to get
limit

politically or physically?
realistically
momentum
desire
I mean
so
this is called
moving

In the late 1980s, writer and editor Michael Amnasan interviewed a number of artists for his "Regional Differences" special issue of *Ottotole* 3 (1989). The following is a selection from his interview with me, which I have edited to more closely comment on relations between film and writing. My comments are, in a number of ways, developments of my thoughts from a decade earlier in "Cross-Referencing the Units of Sight and Sound/Film and Language." I add, as well, some contemporaneous comments regarding narrative.

Locales Interview

(With Michael Amnasan)

MICHAEL AMNASAN: Have you ever tried to weigh the two, filmmaking and writing?

ABIGAIL CHILD: Yes. I'm interested in how the process is very similar for me, in terms of gathering material over a period of time and then sitting down to edit it, which is the construction of the work. In more subtle considerations like how they contain sensuous thought, I'll look at the films and I'll look at the writing, and I'll see a certain kind of abrasive or saturated—I'm thinking of saturated color, but there's also saturated vowels. Sometimes I can see or create a kind of architecture in both film and in writing. Sometimes I feel film is more unspoken, more open, more ambiguous. I'm thinking about the difference between the representational quality of the image, the representational scale. That the image in a frame can contain many ideas. Even if it's just a picture of a couple, and a house, and a driveway and flowers, one frame. It's saying so much. If not exactly as Kodak says: "one picture is worth a thousand words" (laugh). Just that a frame, like a photograph, can be a swash of color or a whole icon with a complicated reading. The scale of meaning can change enormously,

Figure 26. Frame enlargement from *8 Million,* a video by Abigail Child, with music by Ikue Mori (b/w and color, sound, 25 min., 1992–93).

frame from frame and frame to frame. Recently I've been looking at process, at how one medium will let me say something that I'm struggling to say in the other.

MA: Have you felt that recently in terms of a specific case?

AC: The new work I've been working on seems to me . . . I'm pacing it differently.[1]

MA: Like the pacing in the process of writing?

AC: Perhaps. In this new work the parts are totally connected, but they're connected in meaning. There are graphic connections, but it is the meaning that supports the adjacencies. It's a thought reading, a reading of what you are looking at, of visual vocabularies, how the image is framed, is shown, and how the next cut could change what has been established. Pen and word allow for these kinds of experiments to happen on a sheet of paper. There's a moment when the work, writing and film, is cut up, laid out on the floor as hard copy or hung up on the bin as film. The physicality enacts the adjacencies. Or the physicality of the act restores the materiality to the meaning, underlines it. I'm not sure exactly, but it seems the physicality of the construct is comparable to learning how to drum. In India presumably you learn to dance as a way to learn to make music. That that kind of physicality, that the distance of striking your body in different places can begin to create different rhythms. That cutting word "lines" and cutting film create their own kind of physical rhythms. The structure of film, the frames separated by sprockets, the *discontinuous* nature of film projection, parallels mental processing. Film becomes, or can become, a structural model for brain connections. The *illusion,* seeing the discontinuous as continuous, is what our eyes do as they send electric charges, those lovely cones and rods, up the dendritic weave to our brain. The mind wants to smooth over the gaps, is charged with that, and of course, our culture encourages that "smoothing" as well. You become aware of the machinations, the apparatus, but it also hides from you.

MA: Do you mean in the sense that some people want to cut something in that would have an impact, but very briefly in a fraction of a second so that the viewer wouldn't be aware of what was having an effect on them?

AC: No no, you see everything. That's a total fiction. You can see a frame. You can see a twenty-fourth of a second. Film simulates more of the elements of reality; the visual mode and our brain so influenced by our eyes, that this becomes quote "real." In film you can open a door in New York and you can be in Ethiopia. It's such a magical kind of space and that's what your mind does when reading as well. Your mind can be in different locales and both writing and film enact those "locales" so completely; both are these *representative* arts which contain the world and come apart. I reflect about putting things together, taking them apart, recombining, and cognition— how you can put one and one together and make something else? That act of construction seems exciting to me, as dialogic *hit.*

Also I have a different relationship to film than an audience would have, not only because I am a filmmaker but also because I get to look at film in ways an audience can't. Maybe vhs is different in that respect, videotape. Film is linear, but you can't see film over and over again like you can open up a book at any place and read. I have a unique relationship to film because I have a machine that will start and stop it so it begins to have a quality of a book, or at least, like video, I can actually go back and spend an hour looking over three scenes, which people couldn't do in a public theater situation, but they can do that in their own homes with videotape.

MA: Would you be comfortable if people spaced out—well you wouldn't really know . . .

AC: I think it would be great if somebody was in New Orleans and they say, "Did you see what she did in that five frames?" going back and forth and back and forth. That's one of my more optimistic visions of the future. As films get transferred to VHS—they diminish, they lose texture, they lose the quality of light coming from behind instead of coming off the screen. You don't have the communal relationship to film, which is a whole other thing, less about film than the performance of film, but VHS could change the way people view work. When records came out, suddenly the music of the world was available to people, and they could study it. You could find somebody in Arkansas who would listen for ten hours to a particular horn riff and learn how to do it and thus start whatever he or she was going to do in music. I think that, for my films, I wouldn't mind if people spaced and said, "Look what she did, look how this happened, look how what we saw feels this way, and this is how it's made." Through a VHS they can study that. I don't know if it's going to happen though because distribution is so controlled.

MA: I feel the need to identify myself as working out of particular conditions and to recognize that I have certain priorities suspended by work. I've got to have a certain amount of narrative that can make that clear.

AC: Narrative moves throughout my work. I think it is hard to remove narrative. Think of Duchamp and his word poems, trying *not* to make sense. It's extremely hard to do. The mind wants to link. I want to *unlink*. *Continuity* in the Hollywood sense has never seemed true to life to me, not to my experiences, not to memory. What seems truer is some kind of jumpy continuity, something that skips, makes leaps, surprising connections. This seems to me the real mirror of "life-likeness." I once spent two nights trying to compose a script and could never get through the door; it would open out into another country, outer space, or revert to my mind trying to imagine following the character. I was stuck on the threshold and this seems the locus of the creative: discontinuous and obsessive.

Modeling: this is mostly the commercial image, what is held out to sell. The image of the model takes hold, distorts, fixes itself as the image (false) of what *should* be. The power of this corralling seduction is revolting. A consumerist democracy transformed into a monolithic obsession fed by a parade of spectacle. I try to misuse the materials, the leftovers, the trash that reflect and infiltrate our lives. That's one strategy: the slogans, the posture broken, recombined, faulty. Not to limit oneself to what we imagine is the *correct* position, but to reposition. So, a nonmodel, a mobility rather, a double-take, a state of interruption in a matrix of interrogation.

In 1984 I complete *Covert Action,* part 5 of *Is This What You Were Born For?* and my first multiple-track sound film in the series. I use the voices of poets Steve Benson and Carla Harryman as a through line in the work, cutting them against the found images, in dialogue with the intertitles. The transcript of the film text includes both the words spoken and the title cards (indicated by small caps in the transcript). You are not hearing the nonvocal sounds: the noise and fragments of musical song that accompany the text in critical and rhythmic counterpoint. The film is the first in the series that directly tackles narrative, in the sense that the bodies, though disjunct, form a digressive line around which speculation and fantasy, rumor and talk, coalesce.

Covert Action

All right, are we ready?
Oh yes you know
I mean
Let's discourage our obsessions
Yeah
Why be so obsessed about these
things?
Yes. We don't want obsessions
What we want is to be halted
     in our
tracks.
Don't you agree?
No. They keep us going. They
     keep us
going.

Ok
climbing the walls. Ah—
THE WHOLE LUMPISH QUESTION
OF B'S PAST
As I fronted this argument
I had but one desire.
Daddy.
Oh no
oh

Well I'm not sure exactly, that
that's what I was asking for
No no

no
Why don't you let me go?

Figure 27. Frame enlargements of couples from *Covert Action.*

HE HAD TO BE ELIMINATED
SHE HAD TO BE BITTEN
OK now
So so
We're talking about
a series of previous.
In fact
actually I

yeah
Does that make any sense?
and this went on for
today
for an hour
Show us
That's the way
Baby

I was saying it
IN THIS SOCIETY, FLESH IS GUMMED
 WITH SENTIMENT
Their bodies were completely
automatically political
moving around a little
We have to find out.
I don't know—
Let's see. I've been thinking
Interact with it
In front of my face?
No
Well yes
No
SCENE FOUR
HISTORICALLY,
He assumes knowledge he
 doesn't even
know
It would be that
I've just got my head in the
 clouds and
I'm thinking
in the way that
that were constantly correcting
 their
bodies
in the hips
Nooooo. I don't like to do that.
If you look at me
I want you to answer this ques-
 tion. You

only wait to—
We were talking about things
 that I don't

One thing led to another

You've wanted
cry and cry and cry
O a.
Let's
Can you imagine?
We're not going. I'm not going—
That's
that's real life
o. oh. o
What was I going to say?
Oh yes
urgent display
of symbiosis about them
ENDING WITH A RUPTURE OF THE

HYPOTHESIS
Yeah, they were completely.
exactly

it occupies time
every time

time
several times
gaps—
Oh boy
A BEAUTY CONTEST AMONG

FRIENDS
ALEX AND JOAN
ALBERT AND BEATRICE

want to talk about
I know. I know
But now I have to pause
He stepped out

going to see a movie
FIVE YEARS LATER
I felt that I was in a kind of
    improbable
body
in this particular photograph
What is she looking for?
SOUTHERN CALIFORNIA 1937
No voices no voices
Then what? Listen. Listen!
I think it was
totally awkward
Yes! It's the rhythm of my life
You're in orbit.
Ah, . . . huh?
I didn't think about it.
So you go on that track and I'll
    go on this
track
Oh oh.
Sworn anarchists
Yeah
I was really trying to communi-
    cate
something to you
You think that
it demands
that you feel
but it definitely feels like
that I'm a fool
This isn't like the point

ALEX AND BEATRICE
FRANÇOIS (YOUNGER) AND
BABS
Now,
if you had to
I liked that actually but there're
certain physical discomforts that
went around it

I see these are the things in your
life
Yes there was a feeling—
Oh and then
moving around that
(what)
sorta like
I mean maybe they were
supposed to be somebody you
knew again but you didn't even
know that person.

very vibrant

I didn't even feel like we could talk
to each other
oh, huh?
Where am I? Wait
Never mind. I'm not going to

I can't break loose.
Mean mistreater
bodily function
Exactly
What are you doing?
that bring you pleasure
But the fantasy was

Ok
ok ok
be good as I can be
Somehow you have to counter-
    act, what
could I say?
An ironic feeding, hyperstasis
The point is
at each point, there was a
    whole series
of events
but you can actually enter this

complication,
and I was dreaming
being in relationship to that
thing
Right?
umm.
But I didn't really mean to be
    telling you
that,
ok?
So, so
No?
I'm talking about this series of
    gestures
very intense and slippery.
Yes
Being so erratic myself. Right
here.
What?
maybe

If man
For myself.

Stand
right here
Every gesture could be
interacting with those kinds of

relationships
I could just sit by
Oh, no
but no no no

Don't
commit yourself
MY GOAL IS TO DISARM MY MOVIE

and it was ready
I'm going to show this audience
what a real lady astronaut looks
like
(wow)
This could—o yes
please

be the the night
whoa baby
In fact
it was like these laws of nature
were wrong

Right and that's the whole
problem.
Oh yeah
I mean, this is a political speech,
but well you know
ok

It's not lyricism and forgetfulness,
but actually a constructive
attitude
towards remembering
It alerts you where
your regular life *is*
[explosion]
Do you want me to say more?
Oh no
That's enough. [laugh]

In December 1988, in my first solo European tour, I had screenings of *Is This What You Were Born For?* at the Arsenal and Kino Einzeit in Berlin. After the Arsenal screening Madeline Leskin, an American who had been involved in the downtown music scene in New York City, interviewed me at length about the work, its social interactions-intentions, my praxis and influences. The interview was published with an introduction in Berlin's *SKOP* magazine later that winter (1989) and, subsequently, in shortened form in *Motion Picture* 2 (fall 1990).

So This Is Called Moving? Interview

(With Madeline Leskin)

MADELINE LESKIN: At the screenings in Berlin you described *Is This What You Were Born For?* as positing the body in the social landscape: the body as alternately talker, worker, and lover. You also referred to the body as "jeopardized." Does its specific function or plurality of functions determine its status? Do the more aggressive (faster) works challenge this threat?

ABIGAIL CHILD: I use that word *jeopardized* because it seems appropriate to the films. There are definitely different degrees of jeopardy; in the films that exist in a more public space, like *Prefaces* or *Mutiny*—it is the landscape that is interfering; here, the body is jeopardized by these omnipresent machines. In *Perils, Covert Action,* and *Mayhem,* which present more intimate spaces, the body of the lover becomes the site of fantasy and potential jeopardy. In *Covert Action* I use home movies, which are "private," yet what occurs is both familiar and awful in the way that the bodies are being jerked around from situation to situation. In examining the connection of sex and violence, *Mayhem* explores a potentially threatening space: the point where we fan-

Figure 28. Frame enlargement of hula dancer
from *Covert Action.*

tasize eroticism. As I worked on the film, I discovered that it wasn't
the violence in noir that was erotic. For me the thrill lay in the anticipation and the suspense. The idea that we don't know what is
around the corner is fearful and incredible, and we are teased and
excited by the unknown.

ML: Do audiences sometimes take the more aggressive films as violent, almost a direct assault on their senses?

AC: Even the fastest of the films, I think, give a comprehensible
feeling and sense of the world, even, if what is being presented is
not conventional. I do get upset if people walk out of the work and
remember only the speed, because that element is very specific, a
musical device, and speed is not just or "merely" violent. In some
ways the density originated out of a "political economy": if you don't
have much money, you have to make everything count. At one point
in the mid-1970s, I thought the most "political" film would be the
shortest—in that it would use the least of the world's resources, it

would be this ecological model, less excessive or flagrant. When I came to New York in 1980, I was living in a room the size of a closet with a shooting gallery in the building and police coming by every week. That compression affected my work. I've had people describe the experience of viewing some of the films as similar to being on the streets of New York.

ML: You use a lot of found footage in your work; *Covert Action* is culled from home movies. *Prefaces* contains material from scientific and medical films, as well as newsreels; even *Mayhem* employs scenes from old romance and science fiction works. The connection between memory and found footage is a question posed historically in *Covert Action,* both as "a constructive attitude towards remembering" and as an "assumption of knowledge (he) doesn't know." What is your relationship to found material?

AC: Found footage is always an archaeology. You only know a piece of it, and you have to ask where did it belong? Who did it belong to? What was it saying? Who was using it? There's this level of partiality and, conversely, multiplicity involved. *Covert Action* was the first in a series that began to look at narrative structures, the way of making up a story and filling in the gaps. But the beginning of narrative *is* speculative fiction. As an indictment of patriarchal authority, *Covert Action* operates in the field of speculation, what we *don't* know. When I saw the raw footage, it seemed to be an account of two brothers who on successive weekends or successive years, I never knew, take out two different women. I could never make that totally clear to the audience. It was like an attempt to order a family history that had a peculiar, hidden secret.

ML: At one point in the film a title card declares: MY AIM WAS TO DISARM MY MOVIE. Did this come in the act of disseminating the footage?

AC: One bit of the material was very powerful to me, both familiar and awful in the way the women performed for the camera. I'd look at this footage at midnight, and sometimes it was horrific to me and sometimes it was sweet. I felt the need to disarm both of those positions in order to make something that would last. The shot of the uprooted tree at the end of the film is the moment where I'm saying enough of this congealment; enough of those embraces, those gestures, those postures to the camera, the "front." It blows the lid off *Covert Action,* what is hidden to the world.

ML: It seemed also to signify pulling up the roots from old behavior patterns, what is fully entrenched in our everyday lives like family histories, blood ties, the ways we pose for the camera . . .

AC: Yes, training. I really think that women have to go against their training. We're trained subtly and overtly all the time.

ML: Found footage also has mythic qualities. We often tend to think of memory in softer, more nostalgic terms.

AC: But it's not about "lyricism and sentimentality"; it's about, as you noted, "remembering constructively." One audience member asked if I thought the film retained its power because it comes from the past, looks "old" and, thus, wasn't "current" to our lives. I disagreed—I don't believe that the footage is lost. It speaks and fairly directly, I think, to our time. It reflects the landscape of our brains shaped by the social, an ethnography of the seen—all puns intended.

ML: It's impossible to regard the footage in *Covert Action* as benign; by playing and reordering the given, you ironically distance yourself from the material.

AC: I'm looking at the material critically, upending, trying to undo sentimentality and nostalgia. Unfortunately, occasionally someone will look at my work and complain that I've torn things apart too much and ask why I didn't leave it wholer, or softer. There's a demand for that in film, perhaps more so than in painting or music. People want to be cajoled.

ML: Rupture as a threat . . .

AC: Exactly. Whereas to me, it's interesting. Rupture seems part of the world. Someone in London was very upset with the aggression of the images, and I suggested that the world is more aggressive than anything I could do on this two-dimensional screen, that I am calling your attention to the world, to the realities and complications in the world. It's important to remember that.

ML: In what ways do your films subvert classical cinematic language?

AC: Movies dominate our fantasy life and our political life. We all respond to media images. You have to fight every minute of your life to reject the images of fashion, behavior, posture, lifestyle. In *Covert Action* (at home) and in *Perils* and *Mayhem* (in the social) I'm examining how these postures of behaviors of romance have seeped into our consciousness. It's not only that I'm using cinematic convention to subvert genre, setting these conventions in alien contexts, unfinishing them. These very conventions have taken over our ideas of romance, are substrate. It's difficult to upend legislated values. They appear "natural," and I invert that, try to go under the natural to say that things are *not natural,* that there are no givens. So when I'm looking at memory, I'm looking at our *corrupt* memory.

ML: One that is somehow dictated by what the culture allows.

AC: Right. We then sentimentalize this corruption. You get completely bolloxed in. We know most of the American West from Hollywood. The same for what we know of World War II. Too often, we let Los Angeles producers write history, which is an outrageous, fantastic idea. That's what I'm trying to look at, to leave you conscious of the simulation, of the construction: by cutting, by interjecting contradiction or an extended accumulation of disparate information, by creating an untotalized surface, unsmooth, unfixed—

In my idealized audience you walk away from seeing these films with some knowledge of how the world constructs your vision. I try to show you behind the curtain and the pleasure of the levels operating in between and round back, above and below it. In *Mayhem* the idea was to seduce and pull the carpet (curtain/frame), to have the pleasure but to be aware of the dynamics and origin of this pleasure. I hoped it would make it impossible to look at noir in the same way. The interest lies in opening up what is seamless; uncovering the hidden.

ML: . . . and guilty pleasures are inherently ambivalent.

AC: In *Covert Action* I use country music in the sound track. I love Loretta Lynn, but the emotional world she describes is dependent and plaintive, ambivalent and tough. Her work is a bundle of contradictions. Now, I don't want to say I can't use this music at all because it is not "correct." I derive a lot of pleasure from this "immorality," but I want to know where my pleasures are being defined. That's true for the image as well.

ML: Where images are concerned though, there is often room for misinterpretation, and reappropriation is confused with mere re-articulation. Has this been a problem?

AC: With *Mayhem* I had some misunderstandings . . . not in regard to appropriation so much as to content. How could I use pornography? Why was I being "masculinist"? Was I being "masculinist"? Things like that. Frankly, I was surprised. I knew I was handling "hot" material, but I was intent on playing with it.

ML: The gaze as pleasurable!

AC: Yes, the glance, the "look." In *Mayhem* I wanted to examine what it is in sexuality that's being turned on by those sorts of situations and images, the enticement of the tough guy or the gangster moll. In some way it's an examination of a taboo. I'm trying to re-assert, examine, play with the taboo of sexual relations, from another perspective, or more exactly, from various perspectives. Located in the ambivalence and contradiction is a real place to work, a place where I can have enjoyment and still maintain a thoughtful analysis.

ML: *Mayhem* meticulously employs the language of noir—the lighting, camera angles, even the latent sadism present in films like *Kiss Me Deadly*—but takes noir to the next reflexive level by drawing the connections between sex and violence.

AC: In noir convention the woman gains power through a criminal act. Usually at the end, there's a revelation where she either kills herself, goes to jail, or kills the hero. I wanted to play with all of those conventions and then disturb it. To let the women remain empowered rather than imprisoned at the end of *Mayhem* is to throw off some of that entrapment. That's another definition of jeopardy for me. Not just exterior aggression but interior entrapment. Some of the found footage I use comes from a French resistance film that had little to do with noir but contained interrogation scenes that corresponded to this feeling of entrapment, of inevitability.

ML: In *Covert Action* the two poets on the sound track argue about obsession, the male voice states that "we don't want obsessions," the woman countering that "obsessions keep us going". Are obsessions another form of entrapment? Or the fact that we try to hide our obsessions?

AC: To pay attention is to be obsessed. A motive for work comes out of our private obsessions, which we play out fully to uncover. In that dialogue I'm looking at the dynamics between men and women and each in relation to romance. The exchange is humorous and not totally true. "We don't want obsessions" is followed by "What we want is to be halted in our tracks." The suggestion being that obsessions prevent us from being people "on track" in the world and that what we want is to be "on track." But if you are on track, you wouldn't be motivated to *continue,* to explore. The image I'm using is ironic, as well, shots of people approaching the camera and unable to come close, held back by what seems to be intense wind pressure, a wind tunnel in Hawaii. They're moving forward but are being constrained by the invisible. It's a perfect metaphor for the way we try to advance in our lives and are constrained by all our errors and half-truths . . .

ML: . . . the stories we tell ourselves in order to live, as Joan Didion might say. How does speech, for the subjective "I," interface with the objective world?

AC: There is a whole section in *Mutiny* featuring high school girls, full of telling gestures, interrupted speech. They are talking about intense emotional experiences, and they are embarrassed to speak in front of the camera. Someone once critiqued the film, saying that I didn't let the girls talk. Frankly, I felt their gestures spoke worlds, if not words, and their speech was foregrounded by the machine between us. All those blurps and bleeps of the camera in *Mutiny.* It's about constraint and repression, or rather it uses the bunched gestures as the vocabulary for a musical composition in film. The question is how to let us speak, be present without falling into romantic personae, or other "assumed" poses.

ML: Is speech illusory in comparison to the image? Or vice versa?

AC: Speech can be very explicit in a way that the image is not. I remember being surprised working on the sound track for *Prefaces* and seeing how the sound, as words that is, "nailed" down meaning, or at least I felt that. That images leave more room for interpretation. Although I've had poets disagree with me on this, citing the level of advertising images that control responses. But we don't seem to have an alphabet of images as clearly defined as words. . . .

ML: There is also a speech of movement. In the public and private spheres under investigation in *Mutiny* and *Prefaces,* the body moves easily or not so easily between expression and repetition, between natural and man-made phenomena.

AC: In *Mutiny* the body is both worker and talker. I use images of women engaged in activity and repetitive acts of movement. The dancer in the busy office is not so much trapped in her dance as she is underlining the mechanism of the workplace. In *Prefaces* it's clearly the body as worker, and it's a body that is very embedded in machinery in a troublesome way. One of the clear images of that condition, that sense of the distorted body, appears in the footage from a British imperialistic film of Africa. Under the image of the natives walking toward the white "gentleman" in safari hat and coat, I put a voiceover that introduces the sense of selection and class: "Unfortunately there wasn't room enough for all of them." I wanted the juxtaposition to convey the ways an imperialistic power selects who will live and who will die. I also use images—mountains of sawdust, machines pouring liquids, surgical procedures—that communicate this sense that the body is being pulverized. But at the end, to counter the technology and force, I use shots of dancers and children skipping, part of a Billie Holiday song. It's a way to present the alternative power of the human body to reject this pulverization, or . . . at least dance with it. *Prefaces* is a fast, vividly colored world—I'm trying to raise with energy and rhythm a certain sense of the human will to persist.

In a formal way the question of *natural* is raised in *Prefaces.* At one point I cut to black leader and use the sound of the sprocket holes going through the projectors; I leave a lot of the splice marks. Everything is toppling over itself. I did not want it to be the artifice of the clean and natural. It was meant to have not only the whole world in it—which means it's partial and compressed—but that it would be the whole world in fragments, dense and inaccurate, pushing and cutting through. I left the rough edges as material manifest of a raw, imperfect world. It's counter to the Hollywood model that is clean, neat, precise, put together, not shattered.

ML: Musician composer John Zorn, in his notes to his piece *Spillane,* describes his music as ideal for people with short attention spans, accustomed to a world jam-packed with fast changing information. Are your films made for impatient sensibilities?

AC: I would say my current movies set an urban pace. They come out of an urban space. One thing I discovered with *Prefaces* is that we blind ourselves in order to survive an urban environment. I want to be fully conscious, which necessarily means to stay alert. It's exhausting, hard and problematic. Yet we are trained to ignore the world; that's what the News and Property does. The question, then, is can I make myself eye-open? In a way that's what my films are for, and that's the reason I ask audiences not to grab at what they see and hear; better to experience the work on the level of, say, a musical composition and remain open for change. The films are definitely for people who can accept the pace and are willing to confront the realities of a supercharged world. The challenge is to be open in an uncontrollable environment. That challenge is one of my concerns when I make the films.

ML: The challenge is also one of striking a balance between the split-second image and the collage of sound.

AC: The sound has this density. When I started doing sound films, I had a sense of chordal structure. Films are linear, but perhaps music could give a different shape, like an orchestration. I can have different elements play against one another as counterpoint. For example, in *Covert Action* I use two voice-overs edited from improvisations between the poets Carla Harryman and Steve Benson; they talk to each other, they talk to the film, and they talk to the viewer. The sound operates in several dimensions, in several contexts simultaneously. It makes textural density and rhythm, which are elements that musicians and poets are aware of.

ML: How important is pacing in sound? Zorn speaks of this "cloud effect," how people are overwhelmed by the individual movements if the speed is too fast. At what point in the editing process do the interludes come?

AC: I think I'm learning about the use of pause and quiet spaces in a piece. In *Perils* my first sound track was all cartoon music, and the sound was too dense overall. I peeled it back and called in Christian Marclay and Charles Noyes, who looked at the piece on video and laid down three tracks against the image. We then picked one and added two additional tracks in sectional pieces, similar to composing for silent cinema. Which seemed appropriate because the film is a homage to silent movies. Mixing the different tracks was a way to break up the wall-to-wall-sound construction I had originally made.

ML: You become a composer in a way.

AC: I think I was always composing, as early as *Prefaces,* influenced by John Cage, his tape collages—I loved his *Variations.* When I was filming the high school scenes in *Mutiny,* I was struck by how noisy everything was. The toilet paper roll in the bathroom even sang a little song when you pulled it! It was a sort of revenge that I could make a music out of this noise.

For *Mayhem,* before I brought in the musicians, I had completed most of the sound track using Latin soap operas as my skeleton and then sound effects. For example, under the shot of a woman running I put the sound of some quails I had recorded in Mexico that sounded like Zorn's sax! It was great because I liked the ironic interaction between the sound and the image. Basically, I'm playing with sound but being specific to construct these textures. I had this revelation after seeing, of all things, *Mad Max 3:* that film sound could be a character, and it could direct the action, the movement of meaning.

ML: How important is the mechanical process of the work?

AC: The hand manipulation and editing of the films hold tremendous interest for me. It's the creative process, a kind of cut and paste, which relates to my writing, as well as for authors like William Burroughs or Kathy Acker. They write and cut up and replace and reorder and move in and add and separate. That's how I make my films. I usually have a strong feeling of what I want and then the process is how to get it on film. Feature filmmakers have to locate their intentions more exactly because they have other people working in the service of the idea. Although Godard, from what I've read, used to say, "Let's film today" and then suddenly change his mind. Or Griffith, who would pull these pieces of paper out of his pocket that would say "Give me a lily" and then six months later be forced to rewrite because it didn't work. That's closer to my process. [laugh] I wonder if the mythical Hitchcock, completely set once the script is done, is real . . . ?

ML: How has your vocabulary changed over the course of *Is This What You Were Born For?*

AC: In terms of editing, the later films have a more differential, more variable, rhythm. *Mercy,* which I'm finishing now, is similar to my first film, *Prefaces,* in its range of variegated material, in the way it regards the body in the social landscape. But its rhythm is very different, more stops and starts with different pacing. And I have structured it with images of men—unlike most of my recent work, which focuses on women. The found footage I'm using is funny and disturbing, in the way the men place themselves, or are placed, in relation to the camera. They are machinelike—and vulnerable. It's a false mimesis.

ML: Has the way you work with performers changed as well?

AC: In *Mutiny* I had the subjects do what they do. I filmed friends of mine, artists, talking or singing or dancing. I also used outtakes from a television documentary I did in the 1970s on prostitutes and pimps. For *Perils* I didn't work with a script. It was more a translation. I took still photos from strongmen movies of the 1930s and had the performers strike poses, moving from point A to B to C back to A then to D. Like dancing. And for the video *Swamp* I'm planning to deal more with performers and, for the first time, writers, as well, for dialogue.

ML: You're also drawing a lot of visual inspiration for set design and framing from illustration and painting.

AC: I look for pictures that work like scripts. For *Mayhem* I used Mexican comic books, detective novels, and Japanese pornography. In particular, I studied the nineteenth-century painter Utamaro, whose paintings almost look like illustrated comic books. Oshima must have used some of his images for the set design for *In the Realm of the*

Senses. And for *Swamp* I'm going to use bright and saturated colors to keep the comic book angle because I think that's basically what soap opera is.

ML: Your early background is in documentary. What was the process of turning to experimental film?

AC: I had begun to be uncomfortable using the documentary to talk *about* things. That that was putting something between me and the world or the subject of my obsessions. And I wasn't completely comfortable with the form. I was doing work for WNBC and PBS, and I met Marcel Ophuls at a film seminar. In discussion he critiqued an idealized "cinema-verité" vision of film and made a strong argument that you, the viewer, and the camera, are always affecting reality. Ophuls strengthened my resolve to search for a form that successfully combined the realistic *and* constructive approach to art. I had gotten a grant to make a film that might have ended me up in Hollywood. But by the time I finished it, I was more involved in the sculptural part of filmmaking, the handmade. So that, and my dissatisfaction with what else was available, pushed me in new directions.

ML: Who were some of your influences among experimental filmmakers?

AC: I have an anthropological bias in my work. Part of my love of Vertov comes from his immensely humane look at the world. I've also learned great amounts from Stan Brakhage and Hollis Frampton, through their liberating ideas about film: that you didn't need plot, that anything can be used, their sense of the visual nature of the medium, of all the areas that hadn't been tried. Frampton was using words, which was especially appealing to me, a modern poetry of images. You could say *sugar,* for example, and film *black,* take things of different kinds, in surprising or unstable relations, and let that direct your process.

ML: Is there currently an experimental film community in the U.S.?

AC: It seems there is a little renaissance at present, a small but very lively community of filmmakers in New York and San Francisco and Boston. The 1980s were not a good time for experimental film in New York, funding wise, but great work was accomplished in that decade, and I think the future will prove it. So many people working off formalist, structuralist discoveries of the 1970s—adding to that a new content, or intensity. I don't know if the funding is changing in the United States, but the atmosphere definitely is.

ML: These may be the final years for 16-mm film. What does that mean for your work?

AC: It will obviously frustrate me to an extent if stock isn't available because I like the hand ability and sculptural quality of film. But I think there will always be a way to do the work. Even video is being developed in a user-friendly mode to film. On another level, if this is the last twenty years, it could be very exciting. It's even more of a reason to make these works.

In the 1980s I imagined a series of films, one section of which would examine sexuality. I had just read Sade's texts (in the then new Grove Press edition) and was excited by the pyramidal structure of the writings. By 1986 I was ready to begin the Sadean section of *Is This What You Were Born For?* I used the film as an opportunity to explore noir lighting and to reshoot noir from a feminist, anarchist position. I had multiple heroines, impossible plots, and organized the "scenario" around the sound tracks from Mexican cable television soap operas, abetted with recordings of my own and, ultimately, a session with four downtown musicians: Shelley Hirsch, Christian Marclay, Charles Noyes, and Zeena Parkins. The work explored the film gaze, then the obsessive subject of theorists, pushing at the boundaries or contradictions of the contemporary discussion. When shown, the film caused much dissension, attention, riots (even). What you have here is a transcript of the verbal text, rather more spare than in my earlier work, without the music, which by this film had become the "lead through," or score.

Mayhem

Why do you ask?
I saw it
No. Not so close   Why did you call the police?
It's ridiculous. I mean   No. ah. O.
to believe someone would have·   Cleveland's this other friend of
committed such a deed?   ours
Yes.   yes.
No   oh. aah oh. No?
Both of them   Cut
It's complicated   Its. its no.

Figure 29. Diane Torr
and Ela Troyano. Frame
enlargements from
Mayhem.

One thing doesn't follow. It's
   not so
logical.
Que dice? ummmm.
it's not tall, it's not soft
ummm . . . yes
Don't they look at you as well?
Que quiere?
What was that?
Love
yeah
no ustedes. Evoca.
in fact, I wanted to keep it   aah
   mysterious
Ella es un persoña importante.   (scream)
Nah.   Yo no quiero nada
Hokaido (ha ha)   no quiero ella
Should I say yes?   no.
I still don't understand   I mean. just obsessed.
yes no yes yes   ah, oh. o.
yes   oh yes yes. oh ah. oooo.
How many? how many? how   Aña.
   many?
more hostages   ah! (scream)
Do you want me to be more   Police! Police!
   violent?
Why?   No. No
hija. adios   ah Just
That's what I forgot to say   Yes
eh? ah nah nah nah eh. No   yes.

Writing and film—how they relate, translate, share methodologies, perceptual acuities—converge in this essay of the late 1980s, where I write "off" still photographs, mostly from my films *Perils* (1986) and *Mayhem* (1987) that figure as two parts to the "Black and White Trilogy" at the center of *Is This What You Were Born For?* The series of seven 16-mm films concerns itself with gender and genre, and in the Trilogy (which includes *Covert Action* [1984]) directly addresses and utilizes narrative syntax and subjects. The "stars" of the films include downtown divas Ela Troyano and Diane Torr, as well as other performers on the scene who could be roped into participating. Writing while examining the "stills" from these movies, in turn, created a detached descriptive state in which, among other things, posture is semantic. The result is a reflection on process, construction, illusion, gender, and spectacle.

A Motive for Mayhem

She's looking out of the picture. The bars across her face hold her in the picture and hold her from us.

The next is a negative. There's a pause in her lifted left shoulder. She's about to say something, and he's listening, but his attention is in the other direction. There's another person in this room. We can't see them.

Now it's later and we're up closer. There's a sense of action in the angle of her head, her sharp chin. Her collar is rolled, which both covers and seduces.

He's twirling something. Behind him are two maids. That's the second thing you notice. Imperial twins against a backdrop of altar. The altar is this stage, the curtain: the space of strangeness. The dots on the curtain and the patterns of the cans (stacked) mime the whirling flags he circles. The maids wear aprons, are icons of discomfort. The magician needs aprons on bodies behind him to underline his possession: these are his maids (not apprentices). The maid on the left is relaxed. She won't go "on" until later. The second bends forward to see what is happening. The two women are the backgrounds to his repeated circling. In the background they are the repeating figure.

Here is another. She is on her knees between chair and umbrella. The field is interior. The body is waiting. She looks up, seductive and luscious. She's arrogant. Her breast is big. It's a perfect volcano. In an encased waist, glitter to point with just a hint of fat pout.

The light makes her dangerous.

The onslaught of someone else. A big back in front of us. A dead body. A big cop cap. These are the business dead. You can tell by the brims of their suits and their posture. One's got his hand in his pocket. The women are screaming.

The light makes them desperate.

Significantly earlier, pictures are taken. It's poses happening. It's a stage, a stage against a wall in the outdoors. We identify with the one being kissed and, as well, with the camera. We are both subject and object. We're the movement between the subject and object. We become the subject, and we can also become the object. We can tell. NO. This picture is about us as subject. But we have not yet been forced to see that the subject might become the object. This is because there are no eyes looking at us.

In the next picture everything changes. The flesh has been used. The brow is tense and along the nose is a wary ennui (a weary abrasion). He is looking out from under. Everything is covered. From under his hat, from out of the shadows, from under his mustache, from out of

Figure 30. Frame enlargements from *Perils. Top:* Elion Sacker; *middle, left to right:* Diane Torr, Elion Sacker, Jim Biederman; *bottom:* Elion Sacker and Sally Silvers.

his collar. His ears are flat. Their color is silvered. The skin is lived. Like a tree, he's been there. His hat could be a priest's hat but you know it is not. It is a worker's hat. The lips are firm. The frame is tight. The person is deep inside himself. He is close up, he is on the surface, but there remain his unassimilated parts.

It's the surface and the unassimilated parts that give us a grasp of the world. They provide the stage for our imagination and what the author can do with absolutely ordinary people.[1]

This is not really comfortable. It does not climax. Everything is off-balance. The wall is tilted; the hair hangs weirdly; the legs are not at ease. One eye looks out; one looks off. Nothing has connection. On second look: though their bodies are entwined, his hand on her leg, her arms around his neck, they are falling off each other in perpetual stasis.

This is just the beginning. The moment says stop but is not going to make it.

I'm moving faster. There's a sense of humor with all this action and nothing happening. There are also holes in the wall. They tell everything.

Here is another. She is reflection. She is texture and seduction, and she's lying under the light. She's the point of focus. And yes, she's unclothed. She's holding a drink, inviting you in. She's holding a drink, and the bit of cloth draped across her loin looks like water, a waterfall. Her breasts hang down. There's all this darkness. She is so actually distant. She just moved in with my action. But really, she is so distant. She's more like the door. She's double-handled. It's a double-handled door. It's a door, which leads you on. There's a light under this door, luring you in, up to the window: her stage. This is the stage of the still life. We try to move away our eyes. But the folds, all the imperfections, the shadows force, focus us back onto the figure. You attend. She waits. You look. She eludes you. You wait.

You pick up the original. This is the hubris of definition. You fall. This maneuver introduces clarity. You foreground the exception and the threshold, deflect the mean, redefine the motive, reread the need for causality. In the largest sense this means we shape our causes; we expect them and then reshape them.

I begin my pictures under the effect of shock. In a picture, it should be possible to discover new things every time you see it. For me, a picture should be like sparks. A modelled form is less striking than one which is not. Modelling prevents shock and limits movement to the visual depth. Without modelling, depth is limitless. Movement can stretch to infinity.[2]

Our age is distinguished by its distortions.
Our visions are fulfillment of our needs.

I had long conceived of a film composed only of reaction shots in which all causality was erased. The isolation and dramatization of emotions through the isolation (camera) and dramatization (editing) of gesture. What would be left would be the resonant voluptuous suggestions of history and the human face.

Some of my love for found materials must in part lie with this sense: of the value of the half-formed, the incomplete. An artist who seeks a classic unit, a formed whole, a balanced vision, or harmonious work is looking for a different landscape. My topography demands negative capability.

As clear as I can see it. Rough and expansive, wet and dry, angles irritation cogs smooth-running fondnesses mixed, not anything, but everything and silence. Held together by the wires of its exhilaration. Raining art out of cross-purpose. Living off tension squirming to earth, re-exposing shock and the mind at its metaphorical limit. The mind itself is a network of channels. The mind is shocked and flooded. There are no borders in the mind.

A back brace of pileups. All our needs are perjured.

This manipulation tries to hide itself, so the spectator sees only the arranged reality. Explosive force is attractive as a means to escape the arrangement. It arranges its escape. It deforms the attraction. This form reordered rereads the audience. The audience knows the language, recognizes its disorder and denotations. Is not really comfortable. What is two is one and one also. What is separate is lost and immanent. There's the tension and impossibility of fact. It's all surplus.

This is how generation works. The edge moves out from the center. The spaces get occupied. The not-previous becomes present, is named, to eat away the boundaries of the art. What type of sentences move through this space? The sentences are true when true spaces move through it. If there is enough of the world in the work, it is a world, and if not, you add more.

To get that envelope of sound. They would hit the spots, and I was interested in where they were mobbing. The exciting drama in the meeting between ambivalent shapes. Sexuality evoked as a line against which the body can move.

Against sad mechanics of distribution and an economics of production held by a nostalgic politics, in obeisance to the observant authority. Misappropriate this moment. Demand its emergence, blunder, unbounded. Will you to it. Exterior anomaly equals organic splice. This is not comfortable.

The meat of any image is the suggestive material that circles the edge of the body running on a tangent to it.[3]

In 1989 I complete *Mercy*, the seventh and last film in the series *Is This What You Were Born For?* (1981–89). I used both found and original images, borrowing acoustic material from earlier sections, specifically Shelley Hirsch's vocal improvisations created for *Mayhem*, much of which had not been used in the final mix. Her vocals find their place as the "lead line" in this film. Additional sound includes fragments from Kagel's *Exotica* and from recordings I made over the years at places as various as the Oakland Planetarium and Mexico City. You are not hearing here the bulk of sound and music, noise as music, that constitutes the textured track.

Mercy

Tse
teVa
No
MERCY   changing faster than people are
sha   hoa!
Each one threatens and neither   whoa!
   throws
Buy buy buy   Ummmm
It's colorless. it's odorless. if
   you could
drink it, it would be
tasteless   aah . .
and then one evening,   No
                                         No
doggana fo   higher. higher
when the psychiatrist looked at   whoa baby
   the
whoa   You're as proud as he is

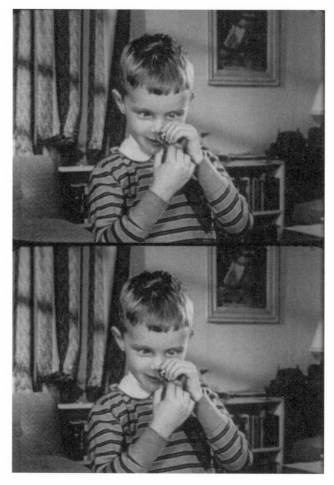

Figure 31. Frame enlargement of boy from Abigail
Child's *Surface Noise* (16 mm, color and b/w, sound,
18 min., 2000).

Was even worth a thousand words	Your son
This is it	How does it feel to see your son
right here and now	become a man?
How does it feel	ah.
to see your son become a man?	acch.

ahhh.	Nein
You won't. no	Nein
No.	Nein
Darest this challenge of change	(whistle)
Yeah. No.	Nein
aaaah	Yes yes yes
GO	Nein
	Oh—
	O. yes

In addition to the interview for *Ottotole* in the late 1980s, Michael Amnasan requested an essay on localities, the theme for that issue. I wrote on New York City, its architectonics, streets, and community: New York as theater, painting, lavish sculpture, street performance, ghetto neighborhood, and urban icon—Metropolis and Gotham. My sense of a social or political context in the work emerges, as well as my sense of "translation" as ideational and structural motor: i.e., borrowing from comics for choreography, from soap opera music for score, from painting for ideas of offscreen space. How architecture in space could become a movement unfolding in time? The necessity and appeal of inequivalence in any translation.

The Furnished Frame and the Social Net

What comes between us is sometimes language and sometimes shyness and sometimes the realities of economics.

I (you) know the colonization of peoples internally.

Evoked margins.

In deed: perversion of vital interests estranged from life, money ruinously at center.

One strategy: block disposition of contingencies. Or alternatively (additionally) take sides with the irrational, the illogical, the inexplicable, the marginal, what is undefined. Or additionally (alternatively) utilize *all* threads, creating jumpy indepenDancies that relate, torque, and bend. An inclusionary interdependency.

Figure 32. Sheila Dabney (right), with sleeping man on Avenue A, in Abigail Child's *B/side* (16 mm, color and b/w, sound, 40 min., 1996).

The word is a relation of definition and limit, constraint and community, bound and sprung.

It's a question of angle.

On a number of levels New York is the most *local* town in which I have lived. The scale is that of the human body, the streets are human sized. It is a city designed for the foot walker, the jaywalker, the cross walker, and the onlooker. It is a city of neighborhoods that define themselves building by building, block by block, street by street: Ludlow, Canal, Orchard, Saint Marks. Without the capsulation and segregation of (need for) cars, which bring worlds with them, within them (protective air supply), New York exists in the flesh. There is no real (lasting) retreat from the streets. Neither the city nor its people have Defense. Its urban disturbances and absences advantaged by speculators and greed surround the poor, invade the rich.

This begins right where her back leaves off

The man's head a raw bundle knocked raw wrong wrapped (coming unwound).[1]

LURK AREAS

The landscape (language) of my identification. The STREET is the habit of focus. The darkness, the shadows demand increased attention. OUR focus is this difference, complete with blind spots and strategies.

blocking the streets sawed-off getting shot and the fleet feet on the roof escape

ALARM

is the mediating mechanism. New York is all alarm, all mobilization.

These realities rewrite the body, rewrite concentration

ATTENTION

FOCUS

Does this help writing? What distortion does it produce? What subjects of interest? What interested subjects? Twist apart, or perch?

The street or urban event demands multiple perspectives, translated vortical structures. The street mandates Kurosawa's imperative—"never to avert one's eyes."[2] Movement of the citizen becomes a choreography in time across neighborhood and class, intersection and obstacle. The result is a multifaceted image, a life-impregnated portrait; mesmerizing, shape-shifting sunlight patches the street. We encourage the conjectural—which appear as occasional, immediate, almost accidental—as well as the dialogic—interrogative and oppositional. The reality of the street makes new alternations inevitable *and* functional.

The fact is proximity, flesh, necessity, intensity, intention. YOU CAN'T ESCAPE. Infect your presence under pressure in the (opposed) mill of homogenous social structures.

> Walk on the wall.
> It's a question of angle.
> Taking more than one side.
> THE BOTTOM LINE:
> WHERE we would fight for meaning

We learn to assume the function of destruction and decomposition as accomplishment.
We find hard evidence that distortion indicates a changing harmonic system.
We believe the city as we know it today is to die.
We are witnessing the acceleration that precedes dissolution.

"Organic consequences of these changes, unperceived at first, now appear: new freedom of human reach and human movement."[3]

fundamental interaction
> ACCESS
> > A COMMUNITY OF AUDIENCE:

Eye's dialogue with DANCE: the separation between sensibility and mobility is artificial. The eye is satisfied (recognizes) the sensual meaning of the parts, the dramatic implications of their motion. This moment-by-moment articulation allows the imagination
> AMPLITUDE
exhilarated by presence. The integral is body. To be PUBLIC to a number of dancing bodies is to become conscious of space and frame, the correspondence and discordance of viewing linear events within a field, the stage as platform, offscreen space as articulated alternation, quick change and the movement in and out of representation, alternating with abstraction and re-presentation. The proscenium of the street enlarges the idea of the "frame."

Local MUSIC proffers structured improvisation and embrace of noise, traditional and invented composition, and the question: what might organize these sounds? Combinatory structures, utilizing phrasing, rhythm, genre, and silence collect bodies and instruments and the omnipresent street to shape a spectacle of sound in the "round"— where visuals and passing bars and cars and planes and alarms play out against any "line." Mix is the performative rhythm.

PAINTING, and where we view it, complicates the exchange. The first state museum develops concurrent to the French Revolution and the development of the guillotine. A paralleling of conceit: mass organization (and mechanization); a grasping to collect and arrange, whether names and bodies or painters and genres; a cutting out of context, a listing, a wrenching "for the public good" under state order.[4] In this sense the museum lies somewhere between department store, tastemaker, treasure trove, and piracy. It is also Archive, and though this does not mitigate the curatorial contextual displacement or the originating collecting mentality behind the "colonized" art object, it enables public display of historical splendors. Attending Manet's retrospective at the Metropolitan Museum: his studies of foreshortening alter the picture plane radically and plangently, pointing toward the historical matrix of painting, forcing the observer to think about the materiality and representative assumptions inherent in portraiture. In this way a selection of paintings that trace the growth of a nineteenth-century artist resonate with ideas and observations that a century later are relevant in regard to cinema: ideas about the frame, about simultaneity of time, graphic pleasure, reflexive positioning, and audience consciousness of the construction of the work of art.

These image (events) reverberate from my personal topography (overlapping histories) to create the matrix (intersecting localities) from which writing and film are generated.

While working on my film *B/side* (1992–96), I kept extensive note-books of process, questions, and ideas. I compiled them into a poetic text for a presentation along with a short film of mine (*Perils*) at a poetry conference, "Assembling Alternatives," curated by Rosanna Huk in the fall of 1996 at the University of New Hampshire. Two years later I was asked to give a paper at Columbia University's "Seminar on Women and Society" and reworked my notes exten-sively, addressing issues of ethnography, ethics, aesthetics, and mo-tive. The paper was accompanied by a screening of the film and elicited lively discussion from the women gathered, some of whom found the topic of homelessness not reflective of "a positive image of Puerto Ricans on the Lower Eastside," while others asked, "Where are the talking heads?"—in both of these cases, requesting syntax and substance to conform to their predilections.

Being a Witness: Notes for *B/side*

"[The witness,] on the intellectual or emotional level, . . . must con-tribute evidence to the trial of our present system of values."[1]

Context

In June of 1991 the police descended into Tompkins Square Park in Lower Manhattan to oust 150 homeless squatters from the park. The park, a creation of the renowned landscape architect Frederick Olm-sted, who designed Central Park, had housed hippies and Ukrainians for years in an uneasy truce aggravated by the increasing poverty and lack of city services across the 1970s and early 1980s. The park had been the scene of police riots in the two years preceding, riots involv-ing punks and suburban teens who had come and camped in the park that summer (1989). That riot ended up being broadcast on television through the medium of artist videos recorded in the heat of the ac-

Figure 33. Couple sleeping. Sheila Dabney and Fred Neumann in *B/side*.

tion. But two years later it was a different scene. The police, in the interim, had refined crowd control and brought in black helicopters that broadcast to us on roofs to "come down." More than two hundred helmeted riot cops descended in an organized mass against bedrolls and the people inside them. The Dominican church on the corner of Avenue B and Eighth Street rang its bells throughout the night in sympathy with the dispossessed.

By morning fifty of the homeless had dispersed, another fifty moved further down the block, and the remaining fifty were across the street, between Avenues B and C, settled into an abandoned lot that had served the previous spring for a Michael J. Fox and James Woods movie set. I live on the block, across the street, and had been videotaping the successive urban displacements of my neighborhood during that year, now waking up to a world where life copied art in perverse and tragic design.

For the first few weeks it was blue tents with children and occupants interacting with downtown photographers. Within a month there were no children, and drugs and alcohol began to predominate. The encampment was quiet by 11 p.m., waking up early to the sun, routinizing cleanup and resources: an American displacement camp less than two miles from Wall Street. Soweto in Manhattan.

The video material that opens *B/side* establishes you in this realm, as spectator, apart from, *outside* the homeless, who live with neither privacy of walls nor windows. This is the beginning of acknowledged separation. The distance and position of these shots suggest a surveillance machine. The public as witness, the public as separate. The distance we will have to unravel, if we hope to approach an other.

Shoshana Felman, in *Testimony: Crises of Witnessing in Literature, Psychoanalysis, and History,* speaks of the appointment to bear witness. This is "paradoxically enough, an appointment to transgress the confines of that isolated stance, to speak for the other and to others."[2]

Autobiography

This is my front yard, graffiti. The morning glories have mounted where previously there was dog shit and human piss. Someone has taken special time to carve out a home in the garden: microCosmos. Belonging to a neighborhood. On the ground are a doll house against a tent, a beer, stuffed bear stabbed in tree trunk, knots of broken rope, twist of bits that relay an entire class of marginalized Americans. Pallets, milk cartons, and bread trays are housing materials.

"Autobiography itself thus turns out to be, paradoxically, an impersonal witness to a history of which it cannot talk but to which it nonetheless bears witness in a theory of translation, which is, at the same time, its new historical creation."[3]

An older woman, dark haired, dressed in rags, haggard, comes on the car where we, all 5 o'clock commuters, sit gratefully. Ragged, loud, and shrill, she sings before she begs. Before she is finished, the transit official comes on to hustle her off. We, who are left, don't look at each other.

Taking sides. It's a question of angle.

Reflection

Someone is thinking/speaking to herself. Analyzing beat of energies, of digression, remembering. Memory and this question: *What is the relation between narrative and history, between art and memory?* Articulate the relation between witnessing/events and speculation/fiction. An attempt to see how issues of biography and history are neither represented nor reflected but are translated, reinscribed, radically rethought. History as a *translation,* through which is created new articulations of perspective. Acknowledge the conceptual and social prisms through which we attempt to apprehend.

DISTANCE intervenes. Borders the process in which the eye joins mind to gather, investigatory. The first "speech" is gestures, at a distance. This without sound.

It is in the fabrics and inventive reconstructions of parts—refrigerator gratings used for porches, cloths as roofs, the fire hydrant as a shower—that we witness the creative adaptability of the human spirit in the homeless encampment.

> *As a relation to events, testimony seems to be composed of bits and pieces of a memory that has been overwhelmed by occurrences that have not settled into understanding or remembrance, acts that cannot be constructed as knowledge nor assimilated into full cognition, events in excess of our frames of reference.*[4]

What the testimony does not offer is a completed statement, a totalizable account of those events. Testimony is, in other words, a discursive practice as opposed to pure fact or pure theory. To testify is to accomplish a speech act rather than to simply formulate a statement. Or in this case, a visual act, a depiction of the real that asks us to be contemporaneous with its various parts, that demands the kind of shifting reality and fragmentary evidence that is experienced by the displaced themselves.

A Crisis of Representation

A crisis of representation happens in several directions when artists turn to social issues. On the one hand, there is the invisibility of the homeless themselves, silent on multiple counts: abandoned to the margins of our so-called civilized conscious; without home, displaced, nomadic; feared and despised by both fellow citizens and city hall. What language meets this silence? What language could do more than news sound bites to bring this plight into social awareness? Broadcast news provides predictable decontextualized information, tugs on heartstrings of public morality, usually seasonal, recurring at Christmas, Thanksgiving, Easter. What the nightly news avoids is analyzing the political, social, and economic forces that have created the situation. The sound bites themselves are theatricalized in the context of "breaking news" to reconstruct an artificial melodrama. The homeless become an iconic portrait that is "naturalized" in the urban situation, a fixture of late Capital. Insoluble, endemic.

Independent film has historically attempted to break up the sentimentality of mainstream melodrama, both in fiction and in the documentary. The evolving of a subversive documentary tradition has attempted to erase the authoritative voice of the narrator, who, more often than not, "leads" the viewer through the subject, preventing a more complex imaginative response. In broadcast television, ideas are summarized, discourse and contradiction are regarded as problematic, and fitting the subject into its "time slot" is a prime goal.[5]

On the other hand, issues of the responsibility of the maker begin to be discussed in 1960s North America. The filmmaker starts to theorize her or his intersection in the conjunction of the personal, the formal, and the sociological. Several artists in the 1970s emphasized the complex position of the maker by reflexively recreating the maker in the work, drawing distinctions from social documentary traditions of objectivity and analysis. Such is the case with Jean-Luc Godard, Trinh T. Minh-ha, and Yvonne Rainer. In the 1980s innovative video activism adopted social realist and agitprop strategies to expose the political dimension of urban and cultural politics.[6]

In *B/side* I choose differently, borrowing from literary theory and poetic construction:

the idea that interruption and disruption actually create intensity and rhythm . . . [7]

He had said early on . . . that one had first to learn to use the I and then lose it. This becomes an attack on the "subjective aim" and assurance of a whole culture—not with a false ground—perhaps with a ground that is simultaneously true and false—where a composition begins again.[8]

> This experience, opposed to all that was ready-made and completed, to all pretense at immutability, sought a dynamic expression; it demanded ever changing, playful, undefined forms. All the symbols of the carnival idiom are filled with this pathos of change and renewal, with the sense of the gay relativity of prevailing truths and authorities. We find here a characteristic logic, the peculiar logic of the "inside out" (a l'envers), of the "turnabout," of a continual shifting from top to bottom, from front to rear, of numerous parodies and travesties, humiliations, profanations, comic crownings and uncrownings.[9]

Searching to find a language to meet the torn reality of the homeless, *B/side* moves to include plural aspects of self and history, self and public, to combine a heteroglossic dialogue, experimenting with social, discursive, and narrative asymmetries. To create an unfinished language, "a living mix of varied and opposing voices."[10]

One might ask if or how this differs from news sound bites? The editing strategies of the avant-garde have on occasion been attacked as sharing the speed and superficiality of our commercial culture. The arguments have ranged from a critique of speed to an alignment of the long take with radical viewing.[11] It becomes clear that context is essential to analyzing the *effect* of a work of art. That the work of art activates a number of levels in the viewer and that a simple dichotomous good/bad, corrupt/pure judgment misses the complex node where perceptions and feelings are activated. The long shot in the classic Hollywood mise-en-scène can be radical (as with the moving camera of an Orson Welles film) or unnoticeable (in any number of dialogue-driven movies of the 1930s and current era). Fast cutting can be meaningless attention-getters or attention-flatteners (as with TV advertisements or in, for example, the flatulent Oliver Stone film *The Doors*). On the other hand, editing can be historical and aesthetically subversive (as in Eisenstein, Gance, or Vertov) or spectacularly and cognitively disassociative (as in Stone's more successful *Natural Born Killers*). One methodology is not the Correct Methodology, and, surely, it will not *stay* so. If the theorist is to make sense, she must include the "outside" into her structures; she must include critique and allow for change and instability. Form is *active* as a specific aspect of "message."

In choosing a heteroglossic vocabulary of styles, visual sources, and perspectives, I am consciously challenging a homogeneous position, the classic one-point Renaissance perspective. Instead, film facilitates an array of perspectives, a motility in which breakage is both trope and material of the real. The essence of the scheme is to make the events and the victims of the event visible, *denaturalizing* homelessness as an inevitable part of the urban.

Film Methodology

To accomplish this aim of *denaturalizing* homelessness, the film places us in multiple positions in regard to its narrative. At one point the audience is the homeless, at another the bystander, and at still another point the perpetrator. The film operates as a *movement* between heterogeneous points of view and as an exploration of these differences. *You,* as audience, are moved between spaces of the witness who sees and hears, to images of the victim's past, between exteriorities and interiorities. In cinema both realms are present, and at the same moment. It might be argued that the document and fiction combine in *all* film representation. Roland Barthes, in discussing the photograph, speaks of "the stubbornness of the referent" and, also, its transformation into an "image."[12] With moving images this sliding between history and fiction, this exchange of referent and representation, undermines or interrogates the possibility of the "authentic" even more radically.

For instance, the Hollywood fictions of the 1930s provide lively tableaux for historical and cultural analysis, while documentaries regularly involve some kind of re-enactment, and in all cases there is the intervention of the camera and more powerfully, perhaps, the hand of the editor. If we examine the early ethnographic documentaries, such as those by Edward Curtis (*In the Land of the War Canoes* [1914]) and Robert Flaherty (*Nanook of the North* [1922]), we find the subjects of these films are asked to recreate traditions that are no

Figure 34. Abigail Child shooting on Avenue C. Production still from
B/side.

longer contemporaneous. Note, as well, the overwhelming *tone* of
these films, which overlay a white nineteenth-century image of the
Sublime onto First American traditions. By late midcentury, film consciousness had grown more sophisticated, and in *The Ax Fight,* by
Timothy Asch and Napoleon Chagnon (1975), a study of the Yano-
mamo peoples of South America, we find a critique and analysis of
the realist traditions of the cinema-verité documentary.[13] First we see
uncut dailies: a camera roll with the voice of the cameraman interpreting the events as the film runs out. The second time we see the
film, there is a discussion of kinship relations of the lead "characters"
and a report of events that happened off-camera, thereby changing
and clarifying the meaning of the events we have just witnessed. The
third time, we see an edited version in standard film style that reveals
to an audience nothing of the complexity of what we now understand. The conclusion is inescapable: cinema is a subjective force in
its interrelation with reality. What is real or authentic in film is a
construction.

B/side draws from and critiques assumptions of both fiction and documentary film genres. It utilizes variant modalities of information sources to suggest a portrait of a neighborhood that could emerge from an interweaving of the public and the private. It suggests a neighborhood might be constructed not from a set of realist conventions such as we see on the six o'clock news, or in documentary "specials," but rather from a tapestry of personal and historical displacement, most poignantly, perhaps, represented in the space of memory.

If *B/side* multiplies its subject/object positions, it also reconstructs sound and continuity in strategic ways. The track is intended to creatively resonate with the street. Silence is used for energy. There are abrupt alternations of sound and voices, noise and music. The structures are recursive and incomplete, like a song heard in passing. Both song and story are seen/heard as fragments, interrupted to disarm causality and closure, interrupted in recognition of the interrupted moment-to-moment nature of reality. Aristotelian unities of space and time are foregone for a more complicated relativity that allows the viewer contemplation of the densities of an urban neighborhood marked by radical construction and change.

> History . . . is not, as it is commonly understood to be, a mode of continuity that defines itself in opposition to the mode of fiction, but a mode of interruption in which the unpredictability and uncontrollability of fiction, acts itself out into reality.[14]

Melodrama and Narrative

Then fiction is the privileged position?

The melodramas of Hollywood film and daytime tv offer banal solutions to complex problems. Their plot-oriented and goal-directed scenarios satisfy the expectant wishes of the audience. We feel their power. Is the power of expectation an autonomic process (we salivate) or a visceral consciousness (we chew)? Now, how to interrupt the motor on which we as audiences have been bred?

I'm bored as a hostage.

Through fables of identity and empathy, scale is humanized; this process exhausts even as it extends humanity.[15]

Peter Brooks speaks in *The Melodramatic Imagination* of the rise of melodrama as a signifying aesthetic to a world after the French Revolution, to a world no longer ruled by given sanctities or ethical fixities. Starting with theater history at the beginning of the nineteenth century and moving through Balzac and Henry James, Brooks takes us to the present and argues that at the heart of the modern lies the melodramatic imagination.[16] He arrives at this conclusion, which seems at first surprising, by linking melodrama to the dream and to psychoanalysis and argues that melodrama "exteriorized a world within" (202). For Brooks melodrama is the secularized form for our era, its growth a response to "the dissipation of the mythic orders that made true tragedy possible" (206). For Brooks melodrama is the form of our modern politics, as well as the daytime dramas on our television screens. One might maintain that melodrama is the basis of narrative cinema altogether.

Both originate in the nineteenth century, and both are built on visual gestures. Both traffic in the demonstration of the latent, or silent, meanings in the world. The terms of melodrama have been absorbed into the vocabulary of cinema's cultural coding: the chase, the shoot-out, excessive and coincidental romance, good and evil, the villain and the hero. One needs only to think of innumerable cowboy movies and, internationally, "spaghetti" westerns, with the archetypical hero of Clint Eastwood, to recognize the force of the melodramatic tropes: villainy as motor, complicated plot twists and amazing coincidences, a succession of unmaskings, good and evil literalized in clothing, carriage, color, and character.

For the independent filmmaker these codes are potentialities: where assumptive narrative responses can be dismantled and reconfigured yet still wield latent emotional power. They are a paradigm of signs that can be reordered productively.

The character wants to leave her part.

Dissection of takes. Invent.

In *B/side* another kind of complicated melodrama plays itself out daily. The "characters" are the homeless themselves, the police are the villains who harass them, and the bystanders are extras who walk on. The conflict is exteriorized in the public nature of the encampment.

By definition the homeless body is an exteriorized body that signifies social disorder, even as the classical tropes of the melodrama (virtue, heroes, maidens) are inverted or thwarted and the cathartic closure of a satisfying solution (virtue rewarded, villainy punished) is frustrated. We are in a realm where histories are lost, secrets remain covert, intentions are falsified, and there is no justice. What is left is the iconic drama of the human figure.

The spectator and the camera are part of the embarrassment. The fragments have their own structure and story time. In conventional melodrama the characters *stand in* for us. Paradoxically, because the characters are not fathomed, have no depth, they are also more real. They offer us a level of abstraction that creates available platforms for our imaginations. We want to go closer and know their dirty secrets. To touch that melodramatic icon is to vibrate with the iconic power of human gesture.

In *B/side* the story is mangled, but the characters have something of the power of the golem. The ephemeral moments from the street imbue them with depth and continuity. Spending time deepens them. It is not conventional. The power is from reiteration, not progression. This is actually deeper. There are no clues to climb onto. We begin with hints and surfaces. In the end you suffer an abyss about New York, about homelessness, about revelation. What cannot make sense.

Vibration of design icon.

This dramatization works from multiple polarization, possibilities, competing systems. All the voices with no seal at both ends.

Fragmentation and Motive

The fragmentation in the film, then, is not simply a modern "decentering" of consciousness, a lack of a central plenitude, but rather a series of provisional centers through which an alternative organization can occur. Plot and action are de-dramatized, the coherence of subjectivity is stripped of its significant status, there is evidence of a variegated materialism: calling attention to distance from the camera, to film stocks (whether color or black and white), to disparate film eras (the found material intercut with the East Village of the early 1990s). Yet we are not in the realm of the pure play of the signifier, not in the realm of pure surface or pure fiction. Reality and fantasy are not separated, and in their interweaving, moveable centers and new definitions of community are temporarily created and imagined.

In this context, the *match cut* becomes unreasonable.[17] The homeless are suspended in the world. Intensify their suspension.

> *Refuse, all of you, to set foot*
> *on the double security of Harmony*
> *Truly refuse symmetry.*
> *Intervene in the conflict*
> *of points that contend*
> *in the most rutty of jousts*[18]

What is there? Layers of refuse, falling below the world market, sadness, the blank, off the map. The lower depths. Industrial waste. Not comparable to something else. What can contain it? What is its emotive strength? That is enough.

Enough

Bring to the surface the viscera of being homeless. A fractured narrative of world peoples living in the first world. You identify with character. You become on the street. You have no ground. In the latest version the landscape takes over: a realization of muscled bodies under sun in overdetermined neglect.

Pull back.

Language is the codification of narrative. Images perform the codification. The audience wants a higher degree of system devices.

We want a story

I am unconvinced. First I see the world, and then the world sees me. The way a mind circles back, wants information. "Our memory repeats to us what we haven't understood. Repetition is addressed to incomprehension."[19]

I want you horrified, despite separation.

The story here is the denied past of unfulfilled wishes. The story is fantasy and seductive for just that reason. The story has the seduction of inevitability. The voyeurism of acculturation.

We all get to watch

The whole thing a pretext at the heart of reason, which is why it's so opaque. That excavates the possibility of a sideways motion. What is it in the broken I'm holding onto?

As if history is accountable

People try to appear in these scenes. They jump in to be seen. An antinaturalization matrix: incompatible absolutely, untimely. You work by subtraction, draw all opposing forces.

Immigration umbrella with no capstan.

Endocolonialism

In describing this project early on, I used the term *endocolonialism*, by which I meant internal colonialism, colonialism at home.[20] Indeed, *endo* comes from *in house* (en dom). What could be more appropriate to describe a hybrid colonialism born of urban migration, situated at the center of Metropolis, two miles from Wall Street? The United States has a history of ignoring its own colonialism and imperialism, to not testify to it. Yet both the twentieth and twenty-first centuries have been marked by wars and covert actions of clear imperialist aims.

To reverse Kadiatu Kanneh's formulation: What I wish to argue is that the preoccupations of the migrant in the city are not so neatly removed from "native" spaces of the (previously) colonized world. "The historical conditions that created both and the discourses that created the identities and the self-consciousness of both remain interlinked."[21] If we view homelessness as an incident of internal colonialism, does it not clarify the place of the dispossessed in a state of economic and cultural oppression? Indeed, the Lower Eastside encampment was composed overwhelmingly of people of Caribbean origin, including Haitian, Dominican, Puerto Rican, and Jamaican. The divergent groups mark out their territories and economic sites. You will see in the film marks of nationhood, notably the Puerto Rican flag floating from windows, painted on walls, marking out garden plots.

Central to the film is the image of the Lower East Side as a space that exists between the highly developed first world, represented by the footage of New York City, and the underdeveloped third world, referenced in the archival footage. The homeless are largely migrants who have been doubly displaced: once from their homelands and again from their homes. The archive footage in *B/side* is used to reference this aspect. Kanneh, again, in writing about the African migrant: "Separated from or returned to a homeland (*remembered or dreamed*), her or his position as translator, interlocutor and interpreter through learned languages and politics makes the migrant the inhabitant of a complicated space, both indigenous and foreign, both of the west and alien to it."[22]

This is what we see and experience in Dinkinsville, the name the inhabitants gave the encampment, referring to Mayor Dinkins, the first black mayor in New York City, who called in the police that June in 1991. The homeless assumed within the city the dangerous position of speaking for and representing a native population within the metropolis. Their plight underlines issues of institutional racism, corruption of housing policies and politics, and the permanence of an urban underclass inside Metropolis.

Homelessness and Women

Within the encampment and as homeless, women have a special relation. They are often subject to violence and fear. In the film, we see repeatedly women hit, shoved, and provoked. They are also at times collaborators in their victimization, one of the aspects hardest to watch. The woman who raises her blouse to the men taunting her is the most lurid example. The man attacks from behind, feeling her ass in a casual and insulting manner, even as she presents herself as object.

Their bodies are public. There are no roofs, no privacy. The women undress behind improvised walls of blankets; toilets are in the overgrowth in the corners of the lots, returning, if you will, to nature and geography. The state is displaced into its prior shape. People sleep under plastic, nap at all hours. The bedroom is the "front yard." Territory and home are redefined.

In the film I create an imaginative intimacy with this world,

Figure 35. Sheila Dabney on Eighth Street. Frame enlargement from *B/side*.

through the character of a fictional homeless woman, Sheila Dabney, whose story is interwoven throughout the documentary stories. The film is structured as a fugue, moving from the inquiring gaze that documents the encampment at a distance, to the fictional space in which characters move through the neighborhood and their memory. Lovemaking is enacted both to foreground and problematize the issues of the body and privacy. Cleansing of the private body becomes a public act. The city's hydrants become the shower. Toward the end of the encampment's history, cleaning of the public spaces, or territory adjacent to individual tents, became obsessive. People swept the dirt, folded clothes, rebuilt roofs of cloth and porches that reference Caribbean structures. Even as the encampments became marred by drugs, alcohol, and violence, the perseverance and organization of its population was sustained.

The destruction, when it came, was announced in advance. The encampment members themselves set fire to their tents in the early hours of the morning before the bulldozers and riot cops were scheduled to enter. The ensuing destruction paralleled earlier destruction of homelands. The displacement in history reiterates important memories of forgotten worlds. Later that morning, it was women who gathered their belongings in garment baskets or shopping carts to wheel away the remnants of home. Women remain tied to the domestic, to sex and children, even without a home; men "fix" junk on the streets, threaten and react with anger. The film shows a neighborhood teeming with life, quotidian summer.

The figure of Sheila Dabney operates as the observer of this world, as well as one who is in it. She participated actively in the film, setting up shots on occasion. Her figure gives us a critical position or entry into the film. She appears as if watching herself, which forces us, perhaps, to view ourselves through her, so that empathy is reconfigured critically, involving as well, a repositioning of identity.

Politics
The film is political, personal, and aesthetic. The zone of the poetic is exercised to become a social critique. A radical fragmentation to enact the breakage of a world.

> *you have no ground*
> *you are sleeping in the gutter*
> *contained whispers*
> *between genres*

This one subjective (inside the door). Energy meeting energy, coming to ripeness and settling in darkness. People fall out of the world.
> *Any Idea of filmmaking must go.*

The blanks in the film become the silence of what is not said, of what cannot be said, of the distance between parts of the film, of slippage.

> *Give up to delirium. Give up distance.*
> *Increase in social conscience and revolutionary*
> *syntax, without abuse.*

What interests you in the unequal portions, irregular fragments, fascination with parts?

> *their silences*
> *their resistances*

Imagination doesn't work through identification but rather through difference, an alertness to change, to outsidedness.

The story runs beside itself, until the moment of its arrival, which neglects you. It creates something unstable and digressive until the original pictures design new names you think in. The increasing horror is of representation, hopelessly fixed in simulacrums of waking; the dangerous fascination is the unrepresentable, outside of representation, or threatening to collapse representation, showing representation's limitations or exploded sense thereof.

Carnal desperation: *we're in bodies* and not some mediocre narrative flyby.

> Below the grid of industrial waste
> Beside the waste of industrial grit

The syntax of film falls against mental illness. Homelessness in the 1980s in the northeast United States could be mapped by looking at social legislation and housing development in the inner cities. Throughout the 1980s, mental hospitals were shut down, with avowedly reformist goals. Nonetheless, there was no systematic development of services for the released. This historic legislation, in combination with urban gentrification that, in Manhattan, targeted the SROS (single room occupancies) of the Upper West Side and the inexpensive tenements of the Lower East, resulted in increased numbers of people living on the city streets, people particularly unprepared to meet the challenges of the explosive inflationary housing market at that time. The mayors, Koch, Dinkins, and Giuliani, each contributed to dehistoricize events by wagging police batons at the homeless.

What was denied or left undiscussed were the pressures, both economic and cultural, that fed into and created the crises.

> *the delirium of the situation:*
> impoverished black men
> under trees, dirt cops—
> returning to a theme

Destruction of homeland parallels destruction of Dinkinsville.
Displacement in history reiterates important memories of forgotten worlds.
I don't watch TV, and I know everything.[23]
Feel gravity of body and that means a sensuous response to details, skin and bodies, bodies and faces. When cut works, experience becomes language, making switches synapse in mind parallels. Not a film *about* something. Let memory be the documentary horror—a more terroristic rather than sentimental motor. Not a/b/a/b/a/b but a/b/e/a/c/d/f, not simple alternation but a torque to attend the disposition of sentient things.

> Twists rubble into black
> selfless in delirium

Language here cannot be descriptive: a sustained hole *without* event chapters. A complete integration between street and narrative—

> out of heel-to-toe relations
> BACK WALL FALLS OUT

More orchestrated, more interlocked—a mosaic

> sunlight echoes additional muscle
> bicycle wheel emerges shadow

A selection of instants, mysterious, ungratified, unfixed in audio and rhythm.

At one point the "dollies" are suspension (are homeless). At end they become the main fabric. The figure ground reverses. The slippage by vehicle becomes a vehicle of slippage. Inverted to signal a new kind of language—perform a lateral slide to find her on bench.

Muscles unlocked
Sound growing
Possible cities
In front of you
Open cities
Night over day
Number skin
Outer space
Not anything resembling paradise

One would like to say
The understory becomes the overstory.
One says
You are there on the street.
A local participant, member of the neighborhood, witness with camera. Not subsuming the other in a totalizing gesture but interrogating perspective. Eschewing language, *B/side* creates a "kaleidoscopic sensorium of the urban body."[24] But still, is the production of art here merely a consumption of this experience? This question lurks inside and outside the film.

In crisis there is no scaffolding of person; only a species, of which you are a member, destroying a species, of which you are a member

You have no ground.
We are all object

Limbs at this distance define you as difference, which is what I recognize (deflected)(twice). This is the break in identity across which difference approaches—inviting, enticing (You)

Seen Unspoken
Defined Unchanged

The act of Them eludes us
The act of Us eludes them.

not apart we are,
but that part we are.

Film is a medium that expands the capacity for witnessing. It potentially creates multiple positionalities and, in doing so, interrogates its own authenticity. The camera invades a world, and, in its representation of that world, inevitably leaves gaps, splices. The process measures distance even as it offers evidence and suggests, at its most generous, new forms of vision and new demands for the audience. The combination of narrative speculation, factual report, and silence in *B/side* creates a historical document that reads as translation, open to new ways of meeting the neighborhood, its interactions, and marginal communities. The film exemplifies cinema's potential to render social issues complexly—as layered flow, hypertexts in time, choreographs of space, multiple positioning—even as new energies and agencies in the midst of great economic imbalance are imagined.

Notes

Poetry in Motion: Make Movies, Not Just Meaning
1. "Poetry and Film: A Symposium with Maya Deren, Arthur Miller, Dylan Thomas, Parker Tyler, Chairman Willard Maas, Organized by Amos Vogel," in *Film Culture Reader,* ed. P. Adams Sitney (New York: Praeger, 1970), 174.

Preface
1. Later named collectively "Language Poets," this loose group of colleagues and friends who gathered in San Francisco in the mid-1970s shared events and spaces with a wide range of local writers. Responding to and coming out of modernist and avant-garde traditions as well as sharing antipathies to the United States' involvement in the war in Vietnam, colonialist endeavors, and covert action, these poets flourished before the economic hose down of Reagan and company. There were talks, plays, poets' theater, study groups and cross-fertilization with film and dance audiences. A heady mix—essential to my future practice.

2. The year was 1978. We met at Small Press Traffic Bookstore in San Francisco with a group that included Steve Benson, Bruce Boone, Don Mark Chan, Kathleen Fraser, Bob Gluck, Denise Kastin (who codirected Small Press Traffic at the time), and Ron Silliman. Ron reminds me in a recent email that "the group went on in the fall just before Jonestown and the assassination of Moscone & Milk" and that Nick Dorsky "came by at least once (tho totally hostile to the idea of theory)." We read Barthes's *Writing Degree Zero,* Sartre's *What Is Literature?,* and selections from Benjamin's *Illuminations* and *Reflections.* Also, Marx's *The German Ideology,* George Lukacs's *History and Class Consciousness,* Althusser's "Ideology and Ideological State Apparatuses," Jameson's *Prison House of Language,* something by Adorno (*Minima Moralia?*), and Brecht's "A Short Organum for the Theater."

3. See Lev Manovitch's *Theory of New Media* (Cambridge, Mass.: MIT Press, 2000) for his analysis of how avant-garde film practices predicate ideas embedded in the digital explosion—how a library of film facts parallels the idea of a data bank: how film's ability to transpose, invert, insert, and move nonlinearly in the editing process etched out decades earlier these same processes in the digital revolution that began to take place at the end of the twentieth century.

4. See Rosemarie Waldrop in "Alarms & Excursions," in *The Politics of Poetic Form: Poetry and Public Policy,* ed. Charles Bernstein (New York: Roof Books, 1988), 45–62, where Waldrop discusses the need for new forms, for breaking "laws," for discontinuity, and for distraction. See esp. 60–62, where she specifically addresses the phenomenon of a population that cannot accept, believe, or act on its contemporaneous scientific discoveries.

5. Roland Barthes, "The Return of the Poetician," in *The Rustle of Language,* trans. Richard Howard (Berkeley: University of California Press, 1989), 172. This quote was brought to my attention in Michael Renov's "Toward a Poetics of Documentary," in *Theorizing Documentary,* ed. Michael Renov (New York: Routledge, 1993), 14.

Before Agreement

This essay was first presented at the Second Annual Gay and Lesbian Experimental Film Festival, September 1988, at Millennium, New York City. Other members of the panel included Su Friedrich, Jerry Tartaglia, and Barbara Hammer. The panel was curated by Jim Hubbard. The essay was published the following year in *Millennium Film Journal* (fall 1989).

1. *Oxford Universal Dictionary* (Oxford: Clarendon Press, 1955), 1648.

2. Ibid.

3. Stanley Cavell, "Photograph and Screen," in *The World Viewed: Reflections on the Ontology of Film* (Cambridge, Mass.: Harvard University Press, 1979), 24.

Rewire/Speak in Disagreement

Published in "Women & Language," ed. Lyn Hejinian and Barrett Watten, special issue, *Poetics Journal,* no. 4 (May 1984). An earlier, incomplete version appeared in *Idiolects* (1983), published by the Collective for Living Cinema, New York. The complete correspondence was anthologized in *Resurgent: New Writing by Women,* ed. Lou Robinson and Camille Norton (Urbana: University of Illinois Press, 1992).

1. This and a number of other quotes, not always indicated for reasons of readability and punctuation, come from the tabloids. This one from the *Enquirer,* March 19, 1984.

2. Claude Lévi-Strauss, "The Future of Painting," in *Conversations with Claude Lévi-Strauss,* Series Cape Editions No. 34, ed. G. Charbonnier, trans. John and Doreen Weightman (London: Cape, 1969), 135–37. A transcription of conversations broadcast by the R. T. F. (Radiodiffusion Télévision Francaise) during October, November, and December 1959.

Melodrama and Montage

Written and revised from a Residency at Kootenay School of Writing, Vancouver, Canada, August 1991.

1. Utamaro, "Book of Pictures," in *Shunga/Erotic Figures in Japanese Art,* presented by Gabriele Mandel (New York: Crescent Books, 1983), 20–49.

2. Peter Brooks, *The Melodramatic Imagination: Balzac, Henry James, Melodrama, and the Mode of Excess* (New Haven, Conn.: Yale University Press, 1976), 18.

3. Liz Kotz, "Pressuring the Surface of Reality," in *Exhausted Autumn,* ed. Richard Hawkins (Los Angeles: LACE, l991).

4. Julia Kristeva, *Powers of Horror: An Essay on Abjection* (New York: Columbia University Press, 1982), 26. Kristeva writes that "we are dealing here with a sublimation without consecration. Forfeited." (26). Her sense of abjection as substitution for the sacral, as a place of silence and unspeakability, rhymes with Brooks's sense of the quality and evolutionary history of melodrama, which he similarly aligns with the feminine and compensatory ("I seek. I lose.").

5. Nicole Brossard, *These Our Mothers Or: The Disintegrating Chapter,* trans. Barbara Godard (1977; repr., Toronto: Coach House Press, 1983). The italics in the first section of the essay are from the 1977 text.

6. Hannah Weiner, *Weeks* (New York: Xexoxial Editions, 1990). The italics in the second section of the essay are from this text.

7. Kathy Acker, "Reading the Body," an interview with Larry McCaffery, *Mondo 2000,* no. 4 (summer 1991); and Georges Bataille, *Visions of Excess: Selected Writings, 1927–1939,* ed. Allan Stoekl, trans. Allan Stoekl with Carl R. Lovitt and Donald M. Leslie Jr. (Minneapolis: University of Minnesota Press, 1985), 92–93.

8. Charles Bernstein, introduction to *Weeks,* by Hannah Weiner (New York: Xexoxial Editions, 1990), not paginated.

9. The photos in the book *Weeks,* over which the text is printed, are by Barbara Rosenthal, a New York photographer and longtime friend of Weiner's.

10. Antonin Artaud, "The Theatre and Cruelty," in *The Theatre and Its Double,* trans. Mary Caroline Richards (New York: Grove Press, 1958), 86.

Sex Talk (With Camille Roy)

Published in *Dear World,* ed. Camille Roy and Nayland Blake (San Francisco: Roy and Blake, 1993). The piece is constructed from a correspondence between Camille Roy and myself. In it I have freely cut up parts of an earlier poem of mine, "Beyond Surplus," that itself collages lines from work by

Andrew Levy and Diane Ward. "Beyond Surplus" was published eventually in *MOB* (Oakland, CA: O Press, 1993).

1. Diane Ward, "Crossing," in *ABACUS,* ed. Peter Garrick (Hartford, Conn.: Potes and Poets Press, 1992), 2.

2. Holly Hughes in live performance at PS 122, New York City, November 1992.

3. Andrew Levy's "Rumi Improvisations," in *Aerial* 5, ed. Rod Smith (Washington, DC: Edge Books, 1989), 117.

4. Camille Roy, personal correspondence, 1991.

5. Carla Harryman and Lyn Hejinian's "The Wide Road," in *Aerial* 5, ed. Rod Smith (Washington, DC: Edge Books, 1989), 44–53.

Sade's Motor

Presented for "Fantasy and Desire," a conference held at the New School for Social Research, curated by Simon Watney, fall 1993. Also on the panel were bell hooks, Catherine Lord, and Felix Gonzalez-Torres.

1. Abigail Child and Kevin Davies, "Full Rolling Boil," in "Collaboration Issue," ed. Tom Beckett, special issue, *ACTS* (1993): 36–42.

2. Bertolt Brecht, "The Radio as an Apparatus of Communication," from *Brecht on Theatre,* trans. John Willet (New York: Hill and Wang, 1977), 53.

3. Gilles Deleuze, *Masochism: Coldness and Cruelty* (New York: Zone Books, 1991), 12. Also see Roland Barthes, *Sade, Fourier, Loyola,* trans. Richard Miller (New York: Hill and Wang, 1976). Originally published in French (Paris: Éditions du Seuil, 1971). Reading Barthes's book in the late 1970s influenced my structuring of *Mayhem* (1987).

4. Deleuze, *Masochism,* 22.

5. Dostoevsky, *The Insulted and Injured* (quoted in Deleuze, *Masochism,* 15). Georges Bataille writes in "The Psychological Structure of Fascism" about the "double character" of authority: "In human terms, the ultimate imperative value presents itself in the form of royal or imperial authority in which cruel tendencies and the need, characteristic of all domination, to realize and idealize order are manifest in the highest degree" (trans. Carl R. Lovitt in *New German Critique* 16 [1979]: 64–87). The essay was reprinted in *The Bataille Reader,* ed. Fred Botting and Scott Wilson (Oxford: Blackwell, 1997); see 131 for quote.

6. Georges Bataille, *Eroticism, Death, and Sensuality,* trans. Mary Dalwood (San Francisco: City Lights Books, 1986). First published as *L'erotisme* (Paris: Les Editions deMinuit, 1957). Also see Bataille's essay "The Use Value of D. A. F. de Sade," in *Visions of Excess, Selected Writings, 1927–1939* (Minneapolis: University of Minnesota Press, 1983).

7. Marquis de Sade, *The 120 Days of Sodom and Other Writings*, trans. Austryn Wainhouse and Richard Seaver (c. 1966; repr. New York: Grove Press, 1980).

8. Robert Hilferty, "Child's Play," *New York Native*, April 14, 1986. He is talking about *Covert Action* (1984) and writes, "[W]e get shards of a story, of *ways* of storytelling, rather than the whole thing. Traditional discourse usually refers to a logic of actions, to principles of cohesion and continuity, and to junctures of rupture through which a 'reader' makes sense of fictions. Here rupture and repetition comprise the structuring principle. The film explodes in your face: it drives on until its final image, a summation of its prehistory, history and future—a tree being uprooted. What could be a more apt metaphor for the contemporary crisis in narrativity and sexuality?"

Active Theory

This piece was originally published in *Raddle Moon*, ed. Susan Clark (Vancouver: New Star Books, 1994). A revised selection was published in *Raddle Moon* 13, a literary journal published by the Kootenay School of Writing in Vancouver, in a section titled "Women/Writing/Theory," which included my "Active Theory" (12–33) and additional writing by Susan Clark, Chris Tysh, Johanna Drucker, Jean Day, and Juliana Spahr (34–65).

1. I planned my response originally as a montage made up of quotes from the first round, with additions, freely addressing and including words, phrases, and sentences by all the women involved. After receiving a second-round letter from Johanna Drucker that was a challenge to us all, I kept my main structure but added a number of additional voices, herein credited below.

2. Witold Gombrowicz, *Diary, Volume 1*, trans. Lillian Vallee, ed. Jan Kott (Evanston, IL: Northwestern University Press, 1988).

3. bell hooks, "Stylish Nihilism: Race, Sex, and Class at the Movies," in *Yearning: Race, Gender, and Cultural Politics* (Boston: South End Press, 1990), 155.

4. Homi K. Bhabha, "The Commitment to Theory," in *The Location of Culture* (London: Routledge, 1994), 22. First published in *Questions of Third Cinema*, ed. J. Pines and P. Willemen (London: British Film Institute, 1989). I quote extensively from this essay, often footnoted in the printed text but not always, because of considerations of readability and rhythm.

5. bell hooks, "Postmodern Blackness," in *Yearning: Race, Gender, and Cultural Politics* (Boston: South End Press, 1990), 25.

6. Nicole Brossard, *Picture Theory*, trans. Barbara Godard (New York: Roof Books, 1991), 77.

7. Dodie Bellamy, "Mrs. America at the Congress of Dreams," *OUT/LOOK*, summer 1991.

8. I have switched the noun here, "FILM" to "TEXT," from a series of sentences that George Landow places over the image of his own chest as he runs toward the audience in his experimental 16-mm film *Remedial Reading Comprehension* (1970): "THIS IS NOT A FILM ABOUT ITS MAKER/THIS IS A FILM ABOUT YOU." With this gesture Landow critiques the romantic personalism of leading experimental filmmaker Stan Brakhage as well as challenging audiences' expectations that the film will do the work for them. I use his words transposed to text with the same ideas in mind: to reposition the expected sense of *person* and particularly *female person* that the reader might cling to, and simultaneously to invite the reader to respond actively.

9. Giles Deleuze, *Dialogues/Giles Deleuze and Claire Parnet,* trans. Hugh Tomlinson and Barbara Habberjam (New York: Columbia University Press, 1987), 49.

10. Brossard, *Picture Theory,* 74.

11. Bhabha, "Commitment to Theory," 19.

12. Ibid., 22.

13. John S. Mill, "On Liberty," in *Utilitarianism, Liberty, Representative Government* (London: Dent & Sons, 1972), 93–94. Quoted in Bhabha, *Location of Culture,* 23. I've changed the pronouns in the text.

14. Bhabha, *Location of Culture,* 24–25.

15. Ibid., 25.

16. Robert Bresson, *Notes on Cinematography,* trans. Jonathan Griffin (New York: Urizen Books, 1977), 51.

17. Holly Hughes in performance. PS 122, New York City, 1992.

18. Bhabha, *Location of Culture,* 31.

19. Laura Mulvey, *Visual and Other Pleasures* (Bloomington: Indiana University Press, 1980).

20. Bhabha, *Location of Culture,* 31.

Active Theory 2: Antiphon

1. Peter Brooks, *The Melodramatic Imagination: Balzac, Henry James, Melodrama, and the Mode of Excess* (1976; repr., New York: Columbia University Press 1985), 256.

Cross-Referencing the Units of Sight and Sound/Film and Language

First published in *Cinemanews,* no. 6 (Nov./Dec. 1977), a publication of Canyon Cinema, then being revived under the editorship and energy of fellow filmmaker Henry Hills. I contribute, coedit, and occasionally guest edit the magazine in its new format for four years. Republished in *L=A=N=G=U=A=G=E Magazine* 3 (1979): not paginated; then gathered in *The L=A=N=G=U=A=G=E*

Book, ed. Charles Bernstein and Bruce Andrews (Carbondale: University of Southern Illinois Press, 1983), 94–96.

1. Another section from *"Rameau's Nephew" by Diderot (Thanx to Dennis Young) by Wilma Schoen* (16 mm, color, sound, 267 min., 1974) has film critic P. Adams Sitney recite a text backward, which is then played forward, sounding altogether distorted and elongated. This strategy is picked up years later by video artist Gary Hill in his tape *Why Do Things Get in a Muddle? (Come On, Petunia)* (1985) and by Hollywood iconoclast David Lynch in the dwarf sequence of *Twin Peaks.* Did they see this early film of Snow's?

Hand Signals Overcome Noise, Distance
Published in *Cinemanews,* no. 2 (1978): 10–11.

1. Ken Jacobs, description of *Tom, Tom, the Piper's Son* (1969), in catalogue no. 7 of the New York Filmmakers' Cooperative (1989), 270.

2. The title comes from a correspondence with dancer/performer Melanie Hedlund as do the final lines of the piece, an edited version of a found poem presented to me by Hedlund.

Lined Up Bulk Senses
This review of Larry Eigner's *Lined Up Bulk Senses* (Providence, RI: Burning Deck, 1979) was first published in slightly different form in *L=A=N=G=U=A=G=E* 4 (1978): not paginated. It was reprinted in *The L=A=N=G=U=A=G=E Book,* ed. Charles Bernstein and Bruce Andrews (Carbondale: University of Southern Illinois Press, 1983), 227–28.

All Three Mixed Please
Published in *Idiolects* 7 (spring 1979): 4–5. The epigraph for this chapter is drawn from *Capital and Other Writings by Karl Marx,* ed. Max Eastman (New York: Modern Library, 1932), 9–10.

1. Robert Wilson, *The Life and Times of Josef Stalin,* performed at the Brooklyn Academy of Music for four nights in December 1975.

2. Radio City Musical Hall, 1981: a three-screen version of *Napoleon* is performed with live musicians in an extravaganza before six thousand people, conducted by Carmine Coppola leading an ill-considered score of his own, interpreting the French Revolution in sounds of Yankee-band patriotism. The original score is by Honneger.

3. I quote here from the cards inserted between the scenes in the silent single-screen version of *Napoleon,* by Abel Gance, screened January 1979 at the Pacific Film Archives in Berkeley, California.

4. Screened February 1979 at 80 Langton Street in a two-part series I cu-

rated of ethnographic films. Other works included *A Joking Relation,* by John Marshall (13 min., b/w, 1962); *The Axe Fight,* by Timothy Asch and Napoleon Chagnon (30 min., color, 1975); and *Kinesics,* by Ray Birdwhistell.

5. *In the Land of the War Canoes* is available from the University of Washington as film and videotape. A book by the same name, *In the Land of the War Canoes, a Film by Edward Curtis,* by Bill Holm and George Quimby (Seattle: University of Washington Press, 1972), contains the most complete reporting of the process of Curtis's shoot and the restoration of the mid-1970s. Magnificent reproductions of photos taken of the moviemaking itself, as well as a first-person account of the process of "scoring" the film to Kwakiutl vocals and music, makes this an indispensable study.

6. Holm and Quimby, *In the Land of the War Canoes.*

7. Ibid. George Hunt—half Kwakiutl, half Tlinkit (his mother was from a neighboring tribe)—served as the main informant for Curtis and as director of action from 1911 to 1914, handling all local arrangements. Hunt was, as well, the main informant for the anthropologists Franz Boas and Adrian Jacobsen (collecting for German museums in early 1882), as well as for anthropologist Sam Barrett of the Milwaukee Public Museum. Thus, Hunt is the single source of most of what we consider basic information on the Kwakiutl tribe. The photos show Hunt with a megaphone, directing the action, with Curtis behind the camera.

8. In 1987 I show current work in San Francisco, combining my deconstruction of silent cinema *Perils* (1986) with two of D. W. Griffith's films available in camera-shot order, from the collection of the Museum of Modern Art. They included *The Transformation of Mike* (1912) and *Musketeers of Pig Alley* (1912). Both were startling in these renditions, foregrounding process and structuring a catalogue of gestures, a set of melodramatic tropes.

9. Louis Zukofsky, *"A"* (Berkeley: University of California Press, 1978), 269.

Deselective Attention

Presented at the Society for Cinema Studies conference, March 2000 in Chicago on a panel entitled, "Technology and Sound." Also on the panel were Melissa Ragona and Tony Grajeda, with Maureen Turim as respondent.

1. R. Murray Schafer, "Radical Radio," in *Sound by Artists,* ed. Dan Lander and Micah Lexier (Toronto: Art Metropole Walter Phillips Gallery, 1990), 214.

2. Guy Klucevsek, "Maim That Tune," in *Arcana,* ed. John Zorn (New York: Granary Books, 2000), 179.

3. Mark Ribot, "Earplugs," in Zorn, *Arcana,* 233.

4. Anthony Coleman, "That Silence Thing," in Zorn, *Arcana,* 138.

5. Noel Burch, "On the Structural Use of Sound," in *Film Sound: Theory and Practice,* ed. Elisabeth Weis and John Belton (New York: Columbia University Press, 1985), 208.

6. Walter Murch, from the introduction to Michael Chion's *Audio-Vision: Sound on Screen,* trans. Claudia Gorbman (New York: Columbia University Press, 1994), xvi–xvii.

7. There has been an international community of contemporary artists working in the field who have explored sound/image relations. This list could have been composed of any number of names, including but not limited to Dan Eisenberg, Leslie Thornton, Mark LePore, Betzey Bromberg, Phil Soloman, Vincent Grenier, Lewis Klahr, Bill Brand, Janice Lipson, Su Friedrich, Heather MacAdams, Lana Linn, Kurt Kren, Peter Gidal, Malcolm Le Grice, Craig Baldwin, Keith Sanborn, Joe Gibbons, Dave Geary, and Shelley Silver.

8. George Lewis, "Teaching Improvised Music," in Zorn, *Arcana,* 91.

9. Schafer, "Radical Radio," 216.

10. For a more detailed narrative of Kubelka's process look at Lucy Fischer's "Enthusiasm: From Kino-Eye to Radio-Eye," in Weis and Belton, *Film Sound,* 247–61.

11. Bob Ostertag, "All the Rage," in Zorn, *Arcana,* 194.

12. Bill Viola, "The Sound of One Line Scanning," in Lander and Lexier, *Sound by Artists,* 52.

13. Edgar Varese, quoted by Myra Melford in "Aural Architecture," in Zorn, *Arcana,* 123.

14. See my essay "Antiserum" for Buñuel's similarly impious approach to sentimentality and pity in *Land without Bread.*

15. Roman Jakobson, *Six Lectures on Sound and Meaning* (Cambridge, MA: MIT Press, 1981), 76.

16. Marysia Lewandowska and Caroline Wilkinson, "Speaking, the Holding of Breath/A Conversation Between Marysia Lewandowska and Caroline Wilkinson," in *Sound by Artists* (Canada: Art Metropole and Walter Phillips Gallery, 1990) 54.

17. Coleman, "That Silence Thing," 138.

18. Schafer, "Radical Radio," 211.

Sound Talk

This chapter has been revised slightly from the published version in *Dialogues,* April 1994.

1. Barrett Watten, at a reading in NYC, Segue Performance Space, November 1991.

2. Jean Baudrillard, *Simulations,* trans. Paul Foss, Paul Patton, and Philip Beitchman (New York: Semiotext(e), 1983). See the opening pages, where Baudrillard writes: "Abstraction today is no longer that of the map, the double, the mirror or the concept. Simulation is no longer that of a territory, a referential being or a substance. It is the generation by models of a real without origin or reality: a hyperreal. The territory no longer precedes the map, nor survives it." (2). For his analysis of the "economy of the sign" in commodity culture see Jean Baudrillard, *For a Critique of the Political Economy of the Sign,* trans. Charles Levin (St. Louis: Telos Press, 1981); and *The Mirror of Production,* trans. Mark Poster (St. Louis: Telos Press, 1975).

3. Jacques Attali, *Noise: The Political Economy of Music* (Minneapolis: University of Minnesota Press, l981), 8.

4. Fredric Jameson, foreword to Attali, *Noise,* xiii.

5. Arnold Schoenberg, *Style and Idea: Selected Writings* (Berkeley: University of California Press, 1975), 217. Schoenberg is referring here to his compositional law, "according to which the comprehensibility of the dissonance is considered as important as the comprehensibility of the consonance. Thus dissonances need not be a spicy addition to dull sounds. They are natural and logical outgrowths of an organism" (91).

6. On November 19, 1971, Burden earned instant notoriety in a performance called *Shoot,* in which a friend, at his request, shot him in the arm.

7. John Zorn, "Memory and Immorality in Musical Composition," *Poetics Journal,* no. 9 (June 1991): 102.

8. Written in the early 1990s, this sentence is referring to the first Gulf War, but the statement holds true for the second Gulf War as well.

9. Zorn, "Memory and Immorality," 105.

Antiserum

"Antiserum" was first delivered at New Langton Arts, San Francisco, May 12, 1989, under the title "How to Read a Film, Part I." It was published as "Truth Serum" in *Cinematograph* 4 (1991).

1. André Breton, *What Is Surrealism?* (1922; repr., New York: Monad Press, 1978). Italicized sentences in this chapter are from the reprint edition.

2. Witold Gombrowicz, *Diary, Volume 1,* trans. Lillian Vallee, ed. Jan Kott (Evanston, IL: Northwestern University Press, 1988). Lines in small caps are from this text.

3. Luis Buñuel, quoted in *Luis Buñuel: An Introduction,* by Ado Kyrou, trans. Adrienne Foulke (New York: Simon and Schuster, 1963). Excerpts from "Interview with Andre Bazin and Jacques Doniol-Valcroze," in *Cahiers du Cinéma* (June 1954): 112.

4. Kyrou, *Luis Buñuel*, 113.

5. Jean Rouch's *Les Maitres Fou* records a ritual performance by citizens of the Ivory Coast who, on Sundays, go into the forest to take on the roles of colonial officers and their men, replaying and repositioning power roles, utilizing an improvised theater to reconfigure (exorcise?) social conditions.

6. Theodore Adorno, introduction to *The Sociology of Music*, trans. E. B. Ashton (New York: Seabury, 1976), 62.

7. Gombrowicz, *Diary, Volume 1*, 26.

Outside Topographies: Three Moments in Film

1. The offscreen directing voice is that of Chuck Wein, Edie's former boyfriend, which adds another layer of complicated energies to the scene. The ex-lover gets to "direct" Edie and her new lover, provoking the action from offscreen, while the invisible director (Warhol) with the camera watches—a set of complicated triangles and interrupted attention. Here the quotidian of lovers and breakups is enacted as theater, this nontheoretically.

The Exhibit and the Circulation

1. All quotes here from Dziga Vertov, *Kino-Eye: The Writings of Dziga Vertov*, ed. Annette Michelson, trans. Kevin O'Brien (Berkeley: University of California Press, 1984), 224, 227, 233, 239, 239, 262, 13. Subsequent citations are referenced parenthetically in the text.

2. Viktor Shklovsky, *Third Factory*, ed. and trans. Richard Sheldon (Ann Arbor, MI: Ardis, 1977).

3. Sergei Eisenstein, *Immoral Memories: An Autobiography*, trans. Herbert Marshall (Boston: Houghton Mifflin, 1983), 2. Subsequent citations are referenced parenthetically in the text.

Prefaces

Transcript of the film *Prefaces* (1981), 16 mm, color and black and white, optical sound, 10 minutes. Available through New York Filmmakers Cooperative, Canyon Cinema San Francisco, and the London Film Coop. In the collection of The Museum of Modern Art, New York, and Massachusetts College of Art, Boston.

Preface for *Prefaces*

Offered here is a slightly revised version of film notes from a show of my work at the San Francisco Cinematheque, 1982.

1. Viktor Shklovsky, *Zoo, or Letters Not about Love*, trans. and ed. Richard Shelden (Ithaca, N.Y.: Cornell University Press, 1971), letter no. 24, 87.

2. Hannah Weiner's voice-over from the film *Prefaces* (1981). Recorded spring 1981.

3. Stéphane Mallarmé, *Collected Poems,* trans. Henry Weinfield (Berkeley: University of California Press, 1994), 121–23.

4. William Carlos Williams, "Studiously Unprepared," in *Sulfur 4,* ed. Clayton Eshleman (Pasadena: California Institute of Technology, 1982), 12–18.

5. *Science News,* July 1982.

Mutiny

Transcript of the film *Mutiny* (1982–83), 16 mm, color and black and white, optical sound, 11 minutes. Available through New York Filmmakers Cooperative, Canyon Cinema San Francisco, and the London Film Coop. In the collection of the Museum of Modern Art, New York, and Massachusetts College of Art, Boston.

Locales Interview

Interview with Michael Amnasan for publication in *Ottotole* 3 (spring 1989). This interview took place in Manhattan, New York, on July 18, 1988. This is an edited version of that interview, with additional material added from contemporaneous notes on narrative.

1. The film I was working on at the time of this interview was *Mercy* (1989), part 7 of *Is This What You Were Born For?*

Covert Action

Transcript of the film *Covert Action* (1984), 16 mm, black and white, optical sound, 10 minutes. Available from Canyon Cinema, San Francisco; and New York Film Cooperatives. In the collection of the Museum of Modern Art, New York; the San Francisco Art Institute, San Francisco, California; The Arsenal Archive, Berlin; and Massachusetts College of Art, Boston.

Mayhem

Transcript of the film *Mayhem* (1987), 16 mm, black and white, optical sound, 20 minutes. Available from Canyon Cinema, San Francisco; New York, Canadian, and London Film Cooperatives; Scratch Cinema (Paris); and Women Make Movies. In the collections of the Museum of Modern Art, New York; the Georges Pompidou Centre, Paris; The Melbourne Museum of Modern Art, Australia; Harvard University Film Archive; and Massachusetts College of Art, Boston.

A Motive for Mayhem

Published in *O: An Anthology,* ed. Leslie Scalapino (Oakland, CA: O Books, 1989). *A Motive for Mayhem* became the title of my book of collected poetry (Hartford, CT: Potes and Poets Press, 1989). The essay was republished in *Motion Picture,* ed. Marjorie Keller (New York: Collective for Living Cinema, 1991); and it was anthologized shortly thereafter in *Resurgent: New Writing by Women,* ed. Lou Robinson and Camille Norton (Bloomington: University of Illinois Press, 1992).

1. Kenneth King's writing in *Dance Magazine,* April 1988.

2. Paul Klee, *The Diaries of Paul Klee, 1898–1918,* ed. Felix Klee (Berkeley: University of California Press, 1964).

3. Manny Farber, *Negative Space: Manny Farber on the Movies* (New York: Stonehill Publishing, 1971).

Mercy

Transcript of the film *Mercy* (1989), 16 mm, color and black and white, optical sound, 10 minutes. Available from Canyon Cooperative, New York; and London Filmmakers Coop; the Museum of Modern Art; and Women Make Movies. In the collection of the Museum of Modern Art; the Melbourne Museum of Modern Art, Australia; and Massachusetts College of Art, Boston.

The Furnished Frame and the Social Net

A somewhat revised version of an article published in *Ottotole* 3 (spring 1989): 237–256. The title derives in part from my reading of Erving Goffman's *Relations in Public: Microstudies of the Public Order* (New York: Harper Colophon, 1972). Goffman uses the term *social net* to describe the customs appropriate to one social setting. He is talking of different behaviors, for example, at work, at home, at church, at play, etc. His ideas of context, behavior, and social space were helpful in viewing the urban social territories of my locality, downtown New York.

1. Here, as in the italic phrases that follow, I am making a direct observation from the street, which at this point in the late 1980s was increasingly filled with homeless persons.

2. Akira Kurosawa, *Something like an Autobiography* (New York: Vintage, 1988), 54.

3. Arnold Schoenberg, "Problems of Harmony," in *Style and Idea: Selected Writings of Arnold Schoenberg* (Berkeley: University of California Press, 1975), 283.

4. Georges Bataille compares guillotine and museum in his essay "Mu-

seum," in "Writings on Laughter, Sacrifice, Nietzsche, Un-Knowing," trans. Annette Michelson, special issue, *October* 36 (spring 1986): 25.

Being a Witness: Notes for *B/side*

This essay is intended as a critical preface to my film *B/side* (1996). I want to thank Wendy Fairey and Melissa Ragona for reading the work in its early stages.

1. Michel Leiris, *L'Age d'homme,* trans. Richard Howard (New York: Grossman 1963), 162. The quote as it reads here is taken from Shoshana Felman and Dori Laub, *Testimony: Crises of Witnessing in Literature, Psychoanalysis, and History* (New York: Routledge, 1992), 145.

2. Felman and Laub, *Testimony,* 3.

3. Ibid., 161.

4. Ibid., 5.

5. Exceptions to time-slot rules are indeed "exceptional." *Shoah,* the 1985 film by Claude Lanzmann, eleven years in the making, combines interviews with SS men, local Poles, and survivors of concentration camps to weave an interrogation of past and present. At more than five hours, it exemplifies cinematic form expanding to meet new content.

6. My thanks to Jeffrey Skoller for discussion of the American context of this history, summarized here from his review of *B/side,* "Home Sweet Home," *Afterimage* (Nov./Dec. 1998): 16.

7. Charles Bernstein's *My Way: Speeches and Poems* (Chicago: University of Chicago Press, 2000).

8. Robin Blaser, "The Practice of Outside," in *The Collected Books of Jack Spicer,* ed Robin Blaser (Los Angeles: Black Sparrow Press, 1975), 271–72.

9. Mikhail Bakhtin, *Rabelais and His World,* trans. Helene Iswolsky (Cambridge, MA: MIT Press, 1968), 10–11.

10. Ibid. "There was no longer the movement of finished forms, vegetable or animal, in a finished and stable world; instead the inner movement of being itself was expressed in the passing of one form into the other, in the ever uncompleted character of being" (32).

11. See Paul Virilio's discussion of speed in *Pure War,* trans. Mark Polizotti (New York: Semiotext(e), 1983); and B. Ruby Rich's various reviews of films in the *Village Voice* of the early 1980s.

12. Roland Barthes, *Camera Lucida: Reflections on Photography,* trans. Richard Howard (New York: Hill and Wang, 1981), (6).

13. See various articles throughout the 1970s and 1980s, including Jeanne Allen, "Self-Reflexivity in Documentary," *Cine-Tracts* 1, no. 2 (1977); James

Blue, "Direct Cinema," *Film Comment* 4, nos. 2/3 (1967); Hart Cohen, "*The Ax Fight:* Mapping Anthropology on Film," *Cine-Tracts* 2, no. 2 (1979); Raymond Williams, "A Lecture on Realism," *Screen* 18, no. 1 (spring 1977): 61–74.

14. Felman and Laub, *Testimony,* 148.

15. My sincere thanks to Monica Raymond, poet and playwright, who generously shared her ideas regarding melodrama and its ambiguities and contradictions in many conversations during postproduction.

16. Peter Brooks, *The Melodramatic Imagination: Balzac, Henry James, Melodrama, and the Mode of Excess* (1976; repr., New York: Columbia University Press, 1985).

17. *Match cut* is a technical term that means the unitary view of the camera is not broken. It is *matched,* in terms of movement, color, and design to create the illusion of unitary sight and time.

18. César Vallejo, from "XXXVI" in *Trilce,* trans. Clayton Eshleman (University of Wesleyan Press, 2000).

19. Paul Valéry, "Commentaire de Charmes," in *Oeuvres,* vol. 1 (Paris: Gallimard, 1957), 1510. Quoted in Felman and Laub, *Testimony,* 276.

20. In *Pure War* Paul Virilio speaks of endocolonialism as a "*war against one's own population*" (95).

21. Kadiatu Kanneh, "History, 'Africa', and Modernity," in *Interventions* 1, no. 1 (Oct. 1998): 30. His original statement reads, "What I wish to argue is that the 'native' spaces of the (previously) colonized world are not so neatly removed from the preoccupations of the migrant in the city" (30).

22. Ibid., 31.

23. This is a quote from Nathaniel Dorsky, who, as editing consultant on *B/side* and colleague, shared his humor, skill, and wisdom in many conversations with me.

24. Skoller, *Afterimage,* 16.

Selected Works by the Author

2004   *The Future is Behind You.* (Digital 16 mm original, b/w, sound, 21 min.).
            By Desire. Video (in progress).
            Cake and Steak. Shown as single-channel and multiple-screen projections. Includes *Where the Girls Are* and *Blonde Fur.* (16 mm original, color, sound, 20 min.).

2003   *The Milky Way.* Projected film installation version of 16 mm *Dark Dark.*

2002   *Subtalk.* Digital video (with Eric Rosenzveig and Benton Bainbridge; color, sound, 4 min.).

2001   *Dark Dark.* Part 2 of *How the World Works.* Film (16 mm, b/w, sound, 16 min.).

2000   *Surface Noise.* Part 1 of *How the World Works.* Film (16 mm, color and b/w, sound, 18 min.).

1999   *Below the New.* Video (high-8 and 16 mm original, b/w and color, sound, 25 min.).

1998   *Her Thirteenth Year.* Script (with Melissa Ragona).

1996   *B/side.* Film (16 mm, color and b/w, sound, 40 min.).

1993   *Through the Looking Lass.* Video (with Lenora Champagne; high–8, color, sound, 12 min.).

1992   *8 Million.* Video, with music by Ikue Mori (super-8 film and high-8 original, b/w and color, sound, 25 min.).

1990   *Swamp.* Video (with Sarah Schulman; high-8, color, 25 min.).

1989   *Mercy.* Part 7 of *Is This What You Were Born For?* Film (16 mm, color, sound, 10 min.).

1988   *Both.* Part 3 of *Is This What You Were Born For?* Film (16 mm, b/w, silent 3.5 min.).

1987   *Mayhem.* Part 6 of *Is This What You Were Born For?* Film (16 mm, b/w, sound, 20 min.).

1986   *Perils.* Part 4 of *Is This What You Were Born For?* Film (16 mm, b/w, sound, 5 min.).

1984   *Covert Action.* Part 5 of *Is This What You Were Born For?* Film (16 mm, b/w, sound, 10 min.).

1983   *Mutiny*. Part 2 of *Is This What You Were Born For?* Film (16 mm, b/w and color, sound, 11 min.).

1981   *Prefaces*. Part 1 of *Is This What You Were Born For?* Film (16 mm, b/w and color, sound, 10 min.).

1979   *Ornamentals*. Film (16 mm, silent, 10 min.).
        Pacific Far East Line. Film (16 mm, silent, 15 min.).

1978   *Peripeteia II*. Film (16 mm, color, silent, 11 min.).
        Daylight Test Section. Film (16 mm, color, silent, 4 min.).

1977   *Peripeteia I*. Film (16 mm, color, silent, 10 min.).
        Some Exterior Presence. Film (16 mm, color, silent, 10 min.).

1975   *Tar Garden*. Film (16 mm, color, sound, 50 min.).

1973   *Mother Movie*. Film (16 mm, color, sound, 5 min.).

1972   *Game*. Film (16 mm, b/w, sound, 40 min.).

1970   *Except the People*. Film (16 mm, color, sound, 20 min.).

Index